Fast and Easy
Oriental Wok Cooking

by
Jacqueline Hériteau

A PLUME BOOK

NEW AMERICAN LIBRARY

NEW YORK AND SCARBOROUGH, ONTARIO

*For the blue planet,
small families, and true lovers*

NAL BOOKS ARE AVAILABLE AT QUANTITY DISCOUNTS
WHEN USED TO PROMOTE PRODUCTS OR SERVICES.
FOR INFORMATION PLEASE WRITE TO PREMIUM MARKETING DIVISION,
NEW AMERICAN LIBRARY, 1633 BROADWAY, NEW YORK, NEW YORK 10019.

PLUME TRADEMARK REG. U.S. PAT. OFF. AND FOREIGN COUNTRIES
REGISTERED TRADEMARK—MARCA REGISTRADA
HECHO EN CHICAGO, U.S.A.

SIGNET, SIGNET CLASSIC, MENTOR, ONYX, PLUME, MERIDIAN
and NAL BOOKS are published in the United States by
NAL PENGUIN INC., 1633 Broadway, New York, New York 10019,
and in Canada by The New American Library of Canada Limited,
81 Mack Avenue, Scarborough, Ontario M1L 1M8

Library of Congress Cataloging-in-Publication Data

Hériteau, Jacqueline.
Fast and easy oriental wok cooking / Jacqueline Hériteau.
p. cm.
Includes index.
ISBN 0-452-25985-1
1. Cookery, Oriental. 2. Wok cookery. I. Title.
TX724.5.A1H46   1988
641.595—dc19   87-23181
CIP

Drawings by Edward Epstein

Design by Julian Hamer

First Printing, February, 1988

1 2 3 4 5 6 7 8 9

PRINTED IN THE UNITED STATES OF AMERICA

SAMPLE A GOURMET'S TOUR
THROUGH ASIAN AND ORIENTAL CUISINE
THE FAST WOK WAY!

Try a Thai Dinner

Lobster Claws with
   Coconut Sauce
Chutney-stuffed Won Tons
Steamed Rice

Garden-ripe Tomatoes
Basket of Exotic Finger Fruits

. . . an Indian Dinner

Shrimp Balls
Lamb Korma
Steamed Rice
Onion Samball

Tomato and Pepper Relish
Mangoes, Strawberries, and
   Kiwi Fruit Slices

. . . or a Chinese Dinner

Won Ton Appetizers
Pork Fried Rice
Sichuan Shrimp

General Tso's Chicken
Vegetarian Delight
Hot-and-Sour Soup

All of these dishes are incredibly easy to prepare . . . quick to cook . . . and so special and delicious to eat!

"I am honored to have my recipes featured in this wonderful collection."

> —Bell Wong, chef and owner of
> six Chinese restaurants in
> Maryland and Virginia

JACQUELINE HÉRITEAU is the author of over 25 books on cooking and gardening and numerous articles for *The New York Times, Better Homes & Gardens, Family Circle,* and *House and Garden.* Her books include *A Feast of Soups, How to Grow and Cook It, The Cook's Almanac,* and *Oriental Cooking the Fast Wok Way.*

Contents

ACKNOWLEDGMENTS

The author wishes to thank Bell Wong for his generosity in contributing twenty recipes popular with the patrons of his restaurants, Hunan East, in Bailey's Crossroads, Burke, and Herndon, Virginia; and China D'Lite, in Laurel, Maryland, and Centerville and Chantily, Virginia.

And to acknowledge and give warm thanks for the contributions made by friends far and near: Elise M. Reinish, my editor at New American Library; Irene Pink; Veronica Johnson; Helen Van Pelt Wilson, who encouraged my first Oriental cookbook, *Oriental Cooking the Fast Wok Way*; my father, Marcel Stephan Hériteau, a French chef of considerable creativity and taste; Doris Rich, wife of foreign correspondent and bureau chief Stanley Rich, who contributed research materials she gathered during a lifetime raising a family in the Far East; Suzanne, Nan, and Perce Hubbard, who helped me search out Oriental markets and carry bags and bales of condiments and foods; Carol Takata, of Kibun Products International, for research materials and test supplies of surimi seafoods, especially the fish cakes; Marcy Bedford, and The Maxim Company, who lent me a magnificent electric wok; Shirley D. Boyce of Himark Enterprises, who gave me a wonderful stainless steel flat-bottomed wok; the Safeway chain, in particular Larry Johnson in the public relations department; Roy Herbert, of Chaimson Brokerage, for research assistance; and finally, my husband Earl Hubbard, my children and the rest of my family, who've eaten all I've cooked over the years and helped me select the recipes.

Introduction

Oriental Cuisine and the Wok

Oriental cuisine offers 1001 quick and easy dining delights: exotic, colorful, unusual food combinations rich in fragrance and texture, sweet tastes mingled with sour, meats and fish combined with flowers, coconut, fruit, spices, nuts, and vegetables. The wok is essential in a majority of my Oriental recipes because it allows this assortment of ingredients to cook quickly, sealing in natural juices and nutrients, and using a minimum of cooking oil. The ultimate reward is a nutritionally sound diet in which vegetables, fish, and lean meats are used in abundance.

I offer here stir-fried, steamed, and deep-fried Oriental wok dishes. Many of the recipes come from the Far East, defined here as China, Japan, and nearby regions where soy sauce is the dominant flavoring. The most common seasonings in soy sauce-flavored recipes are ginger root, green onions, garlic, rice wine, rice vinegar, and, of course, soy sauce.

I am taking the liberty of also including recipes from Thailand, India, Indonesia, Malaysia, and Southeast Asia, although these cuisines are not usually grouped together as "Oriental," because many of their traditional dishes can be successfully cooked in a wok. Curry is an important flavoring in the food of these regions. The curry powder we are familiar with is not a single spice but rather a flavoring composed of as many as twenty-eight spices ground together to form a curry paste or curry powder. The term is also used for a stew or casserole that is flavored with these spices. True curry flavor comes from grinding each spice singly and adding them one at a time to the recipe. The recipes in this book are done in this manner. The main spices to have on hand for the curry recipes in this book are coriander, cumin, turmeric, cardamom, cloves, cinnamon, cayenne, and chili powder. It is also important to have coconut milk on hand since it is an essential ingredient for many of my curries. *A tip:* Canned unsweetened coconut milk is not commonly available, so any time you find it buy half a dozen cans. (See page 34 for a discussion of coconut milk.) But recipes calling for coconut milk will be delicious made with cream instead.

Although soy sauce-flavored and curry-flavored dishes share many of the same ingredients, curry-based recipes use a far greater assortment of spices.

So that you can create complete meals I've included appetizers, soups, salads, side dishes, and desserts, many of which do not require wok cooking themselves but complement wok-cooked dishes. I've developed the main-dish recipes to serve two generously or three lightly; if rice is served as an accompaniment, four can eat heartily. Two light eaters will probably be satisfied to share one entrée, a salad or relish, and a fruit dessert. For a more substantial meal, add ⅔ cup rice per person, or a noodle dish, plus soup, a main-dish salad, and a rich dessert.

The key to wok cooking is to have properly prepared ingredients right at your fingertips. In Chapter 1, I will tell you how to cut the ingredients to the size and shape necessary for the wok's fast cooking. In Chapter 2, I will introduce you to a variety of ingredients essential to Oriental cooking; most are widely available. In Chapters 10 and 12, I'll introduce you to an array of vegetables and fruits, and in Chapter 11, you will learn about garnishes.

You'll find most of the ingredients you need at the supermarket and in your local grocery shops, greengrocers, seafood markets, Oriental markets, and health food stores. Such specialties as ground coriander, rice wine, and hoisin sauce can be found in the spice rack and the Oriental food department of your supermarket. In the produce section are silky-skinned fresh ginger root and an array of fruits and vegetables that invite investigation: winged beans, fresh lychees, water chestnuts, mangoes, papayas, Chinese long beans, cilantro, and more. Oriental specialty shops offer a variety of rices, and several kinds of soy sauces, such as sweet, mushroom, thick, light, Vietnamese, Korean, and Japanese. These ingredients may be new to us, but they've been used in Oriental cooking for thousands of years.

Even the butcher is catering to wok cooking these days. Skinned and boned chicken and turkey breast, boneless pork tenderloin, and beef cubes make preparing wok meals faster than ever. More choices at the fish counter, including the seafood analog surimi, will help you vary your Oriental menus. Tofu and bean curd are also readily available to serve as a meat substitute in any meal.

So gather your ingredients and utensils and learn the simple art of fast and easy Oriental wok cooking!

One

Getting to Know Your Wok

The wok is the all-purpose cooking pot of the Far East. There is no Western utensil like it. It's deep, like a soup pot, so you can boil rice and make soup in it. It's fitted with a lid and an inner rack so you can steam vegetables and fish in it. The wok's rounded sides provide enough red-hot surface for stir-frying foods fast—usually in 3 to 5 minutes—the secret behind the intense color and crisp texture of Orientally prepared delicacies. The wok's depth and curved shape also help deep-fried foods cook adequately without absorbing a great deal of cooking oil. The great value of the wok is that it cooks foods quickly, retaining natural juices, fresh tastes, and crispness.

In the early 1970s, when I first began cooking in a wok, I used one I had found in a Cape Cod gift shop that had been made in Taiwan from an exploded shell. I had to travel to New York City's Chinatown to find a second wok. Today, woks are sold in supermarkets, department stores, houseware stores, and through mail order. They vary greatly in price, but usually come in three basic types.

The *round-bottomed wok and ring* made all of fairly heavy metal is the traditional form. It evolved in China and is used with a small cone-shaped portable stove called a "chattie." The round bottom of the wok fits down inside the chattie where the flames are hottest. The food cooks faster this way and fuel is conserved. The round-bottomed woks come with a metal ring that transforms the flat cooking surfaces of a modern stove into something like a chattie. Heat builds up inside the ring and brings the wok's bottom and sides to the correct temperature for stir-frying. The wok and ring should be placed on the largest burner on the stove, and should be

A traditional wok and chattie

allowed to heat for 1 to 4 minutes, hot enough to cause the oil to smoke seconds after you pour it into the wok.

The modern *flat-bottomed wok* also has two handles, but one of them is long, like the handle on a skillet. This makes it easy to move the wok quickly over high heat with one hand while you add new ingredients and stir with the other hand. I recommend you purchase one made of lightweight stainless steel or aluminum—even when it is full it can be lifted with one hand. When cooking with this type of wok, keep moving the food constantly, or it will burn—the flat bottom and thin, light metal keeps the heat intense. This is a good choice for a second wok.

Although *electric woks* are more expensive and heavier to handle, they have the advantage of maintaining whatever temperatures you select. This is especially helpful for steaming and deep-frying. Become familiar with the temperature settings—if you are accustomed to cooking with the other types of woks, you may need some practice to adapt to an electric wok. After your wok reaches the temperature right for stir-frying, let it heat another minute or two. Choose an electric wok with a nonstick surface, and one that doesn't bead oil (mine is billed as "oil friendly"). It is also helpful to have the salesperson demonstrate for you that the upper sides of the wok really get hot; if they don't, try another model. And do buy steaming and deep-frying equipment to go with it, if it is available.

By the way, if you don't already own a wok, or are wary of investing in one before you experiment with wok cooking, you can try any of my recipes in another type of cookware. Stir-fry in a large heavy skillet over high heat, or steam in any large pot with a steaming rack and a loose lid. If you're making a sauce, you'll find a pan with a nonstick surface especially convenient, but any saucepan will do. You can even cook vegetables in a microwave oven and give them an Oriental flavor (although not quite the same texture) by just using the seasonings called for in a recipe.

Wok Utensils

You will find it easier to cook in your wok if you purchase the correct utensils. A Chinese spatula or a slotted spoon are useful for stirring. A long-handled Chinese sieve picks up a large number of stir-fried ingredients while draining them simultaneously. I also recommend a 3-inch cleaver for cutting chunks of meat, then using the side to lift them off the cutting board. The wok becomes a steamer when it is fitted with a steaming rack. There are metal steamers and round bamboo box steamers—both are useful, but the bamboo have the advantage that they can be piled on each other to steam more than one food at once. If you find you do a lot of deep-frying, purchase a tempura rack designed for this purpose.

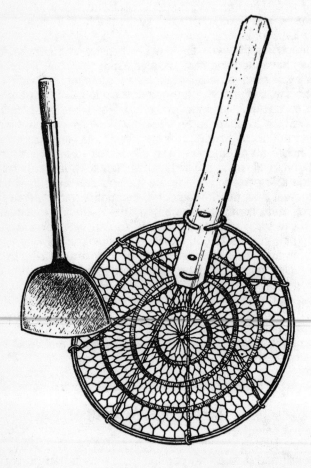

Chinese spatula and Chinese sieve

Wok Care

Seasoning

American-made woks are usually made of aluminum or stainless steel, which won't rust, and so are left untreated.

If the wok you've bought was imported, it may have been treated with a protective coating to prevent rusting before use. The protective coating on foreign-made woks must be removed, and then the metal will need "seasoning" with oil so that food will not stick.

To remove the coating, rub the interior of the wok with a steel wool soap pad. To season the wok, place the wok over medium high heat and, using tongs, rub the interior with a paper towel soaked in vegetable oil. The oil will smoke, so turn on the kitchen fan or open doors and windows. Remove the wok from the heat to the sink and brush clean under hot water with a metal brush. Repeat this process twice.

Cleaning

Your wok must be completely cleaned of any sticky, burned-on food after each use. Otherwise, when you stir-fry the next time, everything will stick to the bottom, just as it does to a burned pot or frying pan. Successful stir-frying depends on a surface that lets food slide around without sticking.

Douse your wok under hot running water as soon as you've emptied it of cooked food. If necessary, soak the wok overnight with dishwasher detergent. If residue remains, use a steel wool soap pad. If yours is a nonstick surface, clean with a plastic pad and follow the manufacturer's instructions. Your wok will probably discolor inside—that's okay. To keep shiny exteriors polished, use a gentle kitchen cleanser.

The only difference in cleaning an electric wok is in the handling of the electric control plug—you *must* unplug it at both ends before you rinse or clean the wok! Follow the manufacturer's instructions carefully.

Basic Cutting Techniques

The size and shape of the various ingredients govern the time required to stir-fry or steam them and their degree of crispness when cooked. It is essential to the success of a recipe to follow the cutting directions. But don't worry, you can handle everything in this book easily and quickly by hand or with a food processor.

Roll-cut diagonals: This cut allows tubular vegetables such as celery and asparagus to cook quickly and retain their crispness. Place the vegetable horizontally in front of you, slant the knife across the vegetable and away from you at a diagonal, then cut through. Roll the vegetable over onto its other side and repeat. The result will be attractive bite-sized triangular pieces.

Roll-cut diagonals

Slicing with the grain

Slices: For meats, these should be thin strips about 2 inches long by 1 inch wide by ¼ to ⅛ inch thick. Cut first into 2-inch-wide strips with the grain, then into smaller strips against the grain.

Shreds: For meats and vegetables, these should be *thin* slivers 1 to 2 inches long.

Cubes should be 1-inch squares; *diced cubes* are ½ to ¼-inch squares.

Chopped foods are cut into coarse bits, and *minced* foods are chopped as finely as possible. To *grate* an ingredient, rub it against the side of a hand or electric grater.

I use the term *smash* to describe whacking a garlic clove on its side with the flat side of a heavy knife. This loosens the skin and makes peeling easy. For *crushed* garlic, use a garlic press. To *puree* is to grind to a fluffy mass, usually in a blender or food processor.

A standard-size food processor, a mini (or cup size) food processor, and/or a blender are ideal equipment for preparing ingredients for Oriental cooking. A food processor will chop onions in less than a minute on *chop*, but don't run it longer, or you'll get a container of mashed onions. Pulsed just a few times, the chopping blade shreds scallions beautifully. The *shred* blade makes elegant cuts of carrots, daikon, turnip, zucchini, summer squash, and other hard vegetables in seconds. *Slice* is useful for cutting firm meats, vegetables for crudités platters, and cucumber for the condiment *raita*. Use *grind* on a blender or *chop* on a standard food processor to puree slices of pork, beef, shrimp, or chicken to a fluffy mass in less than two minutes. To get meat firm enough to slice in a food processor, *freeze* the meat slightly. A mini food processor is ideal for *mincing* ginger, garlic, scallions, parsley, cilantro, and other herbs, and for pulverizing whole spices. A blender can chop and mince, but only in small quantities.

A tip: The recipes here are organized so you should rarely have to rinse or wash your processor or blender when preparing ingredients. Unless there are several ingredients you must process separately, don't bother emptying the processor or blender container, but put it next to the wok and scrape the contents directly into the wok with a spatula when needed.

Cooking in the Wok

I have devised the recipes in this book to be the fastest and easiest methods of preparing dishes which are already known for their ease and quickness. In my recipes, the **preparation time** I suggest is the time it takes *me* to clean, cut, and measure the ingredients listed in each recipe after they are assembled, and to cook any ingredient that goes into the recipe already cooked (e.g., rice). The total **cooking time** of each recipe is the time it takes to complete the dish once all the ingredients are assembled and ready to be combined in the wok.

For example, in the recipe for Chicken Velvet with Snow Peas (page 114), the 20-minute *cooking time* covers deep-frying two batches of dumplings and completing the sauce. (If you deep-fried dumplings for 20 minutes, they would be burned!) In the recipe for Orange Beef (page 130), 8 to 10 minutes is all that's needed to cook the meat, carrots, celery, and the sauce combined, not just one item. For Stir-fried Broccoli and Button Mushrooms (page 196), preparation should take 10 minutes, and cooking 5 minutes, which makes it a 15-minute recipe. The more wok cooking you do, the more efficient your preparation and cooking methods will be.

I have also included in the recipes suggested temperatures at which to set an electric wok. The chart on page 9 will help you translate temperature settings for the electric wok for use with an ordinary wok.

To make your wok cooking fast and easy, remember to:

1. Prepare (clean, cut, measure) all the ingredients before you begin cooking.

2. Place each ingredient or mixture, after it is measured, cut, or mixed, in its own bowl or dish, or on a sheet of wax paper.

3. Place ingredients, including the bottle of oil, near the wok in the order listed in the recipe.

4. Place paper towels, Chinese sieve, slotted spoon, spatula, and tongs, and any other utensils next to the wok.

Then, and only then, begin cooking!

HEATING THE WOK

	Electric wok	*Ordinary wok*
High	400°/deep fry*	day-old cube of bread browns in oil in under 1 minute*
Medium high	375°/stir-fry	smoke arises in 20 seconds when oil is added
Medium	350°	oil swirls, then bubbles when added
Medium low	300°	Oil dimples when added, then bubbles slowly appear
Simmer/steam	over 200°	*uncovered:* sauce barely bubbles *covered:* steam rises above lid
Warm	100–150°	unavailable in nonelectric wok

*To stabilize the temperature, always heat the oil for deep-frying 4 minutes more after it reaches this point before adding the ingredients to be cooked.

Heating the Wok

A properly heated wok is as important as properly prepared ingredients for successful wok cooking. *Stir-fried and deep-fried recipes are not only good and fast, but must be fast to be good.* Each wok heats at its own pace—even electric woks can vary 50 degrees in settings. You must study your wok and use your own judgment as to when it is ready for rapid stir-frying and deep-frying as well as for steaming, simmering, etc. The chart on page 9 gives some approximate guidelines.

And remember this: the more ingredients in your wok, the more slowly they cook. That's why in most stir-frying recipes, we add ingredients one at a time, and push each cooked ingredient up onto the side of the wok before we add the next, so each gets the benefit of the hottest spot in the wok for its cooking period.

Cooking Methods

The key to successful wok cooking, as I said in the Introduction, is to have correctly cut, measured, and mixed ingredients, and to have them all assembled at the wok before you begin cooking. There's no time during the cooking of most stir-frying recipes to stop and read the recipe in detail. This should be done before you even begin to prepare the ingredients. The exception is in steaming recipes, where the pace is a little slower.

After you have measured and cut your ingredients, place each in a small dish or bowl, or on a sheet of wax paper. Once you've completed your preparation, *arrange the ingredients by the wok in the order listed in the recipe, and place your utensils beside them.* You'll then have everything you need handily nearby to make your cooking effortless and FAST.

Stir-frying, sometimes called flash-cooking, is the method I use most often. Heat the wok to the temperature called for in the recipe. As you can see in the chart on page 9, Heating the Wok, when you add the oil to the wok heated to a stir-fry temperature of 375°, a wisp of smoke will rise after about 20 seconds. (*Note:* Never pour oil directly into the center of a heated wok; by moving the wok in a circular motion *swirl* in the oil down the side of the heated wok.) Then add the first ingredient, quickly stirring it over the bottom and lower sides, the hottest spots.

Following the recipe, add the ingredients one at a time in the order in which they are called for. That sequence is given in the paragraph in the recipe which tells how to cook the ingredients. Read it through and line them up in proper order so you can add them quickly. That paragraph will also tell you how long each ingredient is to be stir-fried—usually one or two minutes. You'll soon develop a feeling for the cooking times and will know without checking the recipe at each addition.

Constantly stir the contents of the wok with one hand while adding new ingredients with the other. As each ingredient finishes cooking, push it up onto the side of the wok, leaving the hot center of the wok available to cook the next ingredient. The food you've pushed up the sides is still cooking, because the wok is hot even up the sides. When the dish is completed, place the contents of the wok onto a serving dish. Expect stir-fried food to be a bit under-done as it comes from the wok—it keeps cooking in its own heat, and will be perfect by the time you are ready to eat it.

When adding cornstarch to thicken a sauce, stir up the cornstarch in liquid before adding it to the wok. Push all ingredients to the side and pour the liquid down against the side of the wok, as you poured in the oil. Stir constantly as the sauce thickens and clears, about a minute or two. If the sauce thickens then thins out again, you've stirred too much or overheated the sauce. Mix up a new batch of cornstarch and liquid and try again.

To deep-fry, fill the wok with vegetable oil to a depth of 1½ to 2 inches and heat to 400° (that's the point at which a day-old cube of bread browns in just under a minute). Then continue to heat the oil another four minutes to stabilize the temperature. Food will be soggy if the oil isn't heated thoroughly before you begin and its temperature maintained throughout the deep-frying process. Add your first ingredients, but only as many pieces as can float freely on the surface. Have handy a sieve, a slotted spoon, or tongs with which to lift the fried pieces onto a paper towel to drain when they're done, usually in 2–4 minutes.

If the recipe calls for a sauce, keep the already cooked ingredients warm in a preheated oven while you clean the wok, reheat it, and prepare the sauce. If the oil in which you fried left the wok clean, don't even wipe it out—you'll be adding more oil for the next step of the recipe anyway. If the wok has a sticky residue of food on the bottom, pour hot tap water onto it and scrub with a long-handled brush, then wipe it dry with a paper towel and reheat.

If your recipe calls for a second use of the wok after deep-frying, make sure you have a receptacle for excess hot oil nearby. (I use a four-cup measure in which I allow the oil to cool; then I pour it through a paper-lined strainer into a jar. Oil may be reused as long as it stays fairly clear and close to its original color. Store it covered in the refrigerator.)

To use the wok as a steamer, fill it with water to about one inch below the level of the steaming rack. Remove the rack and place the cut-up vegetables, meat, or fish on it. Cover and heat the wok to simmer (about 200°), or until steam starts to escape from under the cover. Return the rack to the wok, cover, wait for the steam to escape, and begin to time the dish.

The wok can also serve as a *preserving kettle.* The recipe for Chutney with Peaches, Mango, and Ginger (page 218) is a good example, but you can use the wok for any recipe for preserving—just be sure to stir continuously. The wok will cook preserves quite quickly, so be careful your mixture doesn't burn.

It is also easy to make *soups* in the wok. My suggestions for soups appear in Chapter 4.

Doubling a Recipe

To increase a recipe that serves two to serve four, or in general to double a recipe, double the main ingredients (meat, fish, vegetables) and increase the liquids and seasonings by a third (you can add more later if desired). Increase the cooking time by 50 percent, testing for doneness as you go.

When stir-frying for a large group, cook each major ingredient to crispy-tender alone in the wok, then move that ingredient to a large heated pan to keep warm while you cook the other ingredients one at a time. When all the ingredients have been stir-fried, combine them in the wok for a final heating. Chop Suey Chimney Hill, Party Recipe (page 120), which serves sixteen, uses this method. (Notice that in Chop Suey Chimney Hill for six, page 135, all the ingredients are stir-fried together.)

When you become comfortable with wok cooking, you'll be able to prepare and serve more than one wok dish at a dinner party. On pages 13–14 I give some tips for how to manage this, and suggestions for menus.

Using Your Wok Outdoors

You can stir-fry successfully outdoors in a flat-bottomed wok or a wok and ring on a Japanese hibachi or a charcoal or electric grill. Choose a sheltered location so the heat of the coals can be concentrated and not affected by winds. Place the wok on a mound of glowing charcoal with several sticks of kindling set directly under the wok. You can use this same method over an open fire, too.

Planning an Oriental Menu

Contrast and variety are the secrets of unforgettable Oriental meals. Look over many recipes when planning your menu, and select for contrasts in taste, texture, and color. Serve a mild-tasting dish such as Vegetarian Delight (page 206) with a spicy or sweet and sour dish such as Crispy Shrimp with Pineapple Sauce (page 155) or Lamb in Honey Sauce, Peking Style (page 141). Or serve a juicy, succulent dish such as Orange Beef (page 130) or Sichuan Shrimp (page 153) with a crunchy dish such as Chicken Stir-fried with Walnuts (page 109).

It is perfectly acceptable today to combine cuisines and serve a curry-based dish from India with a soy sauce-flavored dish from a Chinese province. Twenty years ago, when I wrote *Oriental Cooking the Fast Wok Way*, we were all purists in our ideas about mixing foods from different regions, not to mention foods with contrasting tastes and textures. Today, we are more experimental in our tastes, and I often serve an Indian curry with a side dish of chutney as the sweet-and-sour entrée in a Chinese meal.

Whether you plan to serve a Chinese-, Japanese-, Indian-, or Thai-style meal, or a combined menu of foods from many regions, you'll find a complete selection of recipes in this book that can be cooked in your wok. The salads, sauces, garnishes, and desserts, while not wok dishes, are included as accompaniments to the entrées and appetizers. Rice and noodle dishes are a unique part of any meal—and can you think of an Oriental meal without them? In addition, I offer you recipes for unusual soups and egg and tofu dishes.

Preparing for a Wok Dinner Party

Plan to have all the ingredients cut and measured well before the party. Using a large tray or platter, arrange the cut, measured ingredients for each entrée in groups according to their cooking sequence: first, the entrées that can be kept warm; last, the entrées that are at their best crisp from the wok. The dishes to be kept warm can be held in the oven along with the rice.

If steaming is involved as well as stir-frying, plan to steam on the steamer rack over a large pot. That way, you'll keep the wok free for other uses. Keep paper towels handy to wipe out the wok after steaming or deep-frying.

In planning timing, allow for the fact that the wok will have to be washed between stir-fried entrées. (If the wok is electric, remember to disconnect it at both ends before washing.)

Most curries are excellent reheated. They are a good choice for a big party since they can be made the morning of or the day before the party. See the recommendations on page 12 for increasing recipes. Chicken and Shrimp, Indian Style, is a good candidate to serve to a crowd. Undercook the dish slightly when it is to be held and reheated. Cook the accompanying rice when the guests arrive.

Favorite Dinner Party Menus

For 6

Vegetables with Peanut Sauce
Orange Beef
Philippine Nasi Goreng
Sichuan Shrimp
Two Sprout Salad
Steamed rice (optional)
Fruit Platter with Yogurt Topping

For 20

Vegetables with Peanut Sauce (double recipe)
Surimi with Teriyaki Sauce
Surimi in Malaysian Curry
Potatoes with Spices, India (double recipe)
Chop Suey Chimney Hill, Party Recipe
Platter of exotic fruits

Before You Begin . . .

As you become comfortable with your wok, you'll develop short-cuts that suit your own cooking style and equipment. Here are some of mine:

- Check your equipment. Your sieve, slotted spoon, or tongs should be nearby when there's food to be lifted from the oil in the wok. You'll need a Chinese spatula for stir-frying. Use a plastic spatula on a no-stick wok.
- Keep paper towels handy.

- Keep knives nearby and sharp!
- Does your wok handle heat up? Then keep a potholder handy.
- Learn to measure by eye. Learn what 1 tablespoon of oil in the bottom of the wok looks like, then 2, 3, and 4 tablespoons.
- Keep a tape measure in the kitchen and train yourself to recognize a ½-inch slice of ginger, a ¼-inch shred of pepper, and other frequently asked-for sizes. The size of the ingredient governs the cooking time, so it's important to have your slices be as close as possible to the suggested size, but it can be approximate—except when measuring chili powder and red pepper flakes! You can learn how much salt is ¼ teaspoon by measuring it out once or twice in your hand—but I am less cavalier with spices!
- Buy skinned and boned chicken and boneless beef and pork precut for Oriental recipes. Most supermarkets carry all of these.

Two

The New Oriental Larder

Cloud ears . . . ginger root . . . tamarind . . . star anise . . . bean thread . . . lemon grass. . . . Every mystery of Oriental dining promises new flavors, new fragrances, new joys. But how do you choose when you are confronted, for example, with at least five varieties of soy sauce: Japanese shoyu; Chinese light and Chinese épais (thick); mushroom; and Thai sweet?

Here are three mini dictionaries, or shopping guides, of the basic ingredients—herbs, spices, condiments, oils, vinegars, and sauces—you should have on hand, or buy once in a while to experiment with, if you are going to make Oriental wok cooking part of your repertoire. I've separated my suggestions into lists: one for Oriental staples, those key ingredients that are particular to Oriental cuisine, one for the seasonings you'll need to make soy sauce-flavored dishes, and one for seasonings for curry-flavored dishes. There is an overlap of seasonings used in soy sauce-flavored and curry-flavored cooking, so if you don't find the item you are looking for in one list, try the other. I've also suggested substitutes for most of the ingredients listed, in case you can't find the primary ingredient called for locally. For mini dictionaries of exotic vegetables and fruits, see Chapter 10 and Chapter 12 and for garnishes, Chapter 11.

You'll find many of the basic ingredients discussed here in your local supermarket, and the more specialized items in Oriental markets or specialty food stores. Most cities and many towns in the United States now have greengrocers and markets carrying Oriental specialties—Chinese, Thai, Japanese, Indian, Indonesian, and others. These suppliers tend to locate where there already are established Oriental restaurants. You can find them by looking in the yellow pages of your local telephone directory under the heading Oriental Supplies, Retail. Or ask the owners and managers of area

Oriental restaurants about the closest sources for Oriental specialties. If you can't find them locally, many ingredients can be ordered from the mail-order sources given in the appendix at the end of the book.

Following the three mini dictionaries are three lists of the items you most often need to complete these recipes. Consult The Well-Stocked Larder, The Well-Stocked Freezer, and The Readiness Bowl to be sure you have the most common ingredients in Oriental cooking available to you at a moment's notice.

Oriental Staples

Baby corn: Cooked miniature or baby corn, used in stir-fries, is available canned in supermarkets. Drain and rinse well before using.
SUBSTITUTE: Bamboo shoots or bean sprouts.

Bamboo shoots: Sold fresh in specialty shops and Oriental markets. Use as a vegetable to add crunch to stir-fries. Parboil fresh shoots 10 to 15 minutes before using, then cut into slices 1½ inches long by 1/16 inch thick.
SUBSTITUTE: Cooked canned bamboo shoots. Drain and rinse well before using. (Store leftovers in water in the refrigerator.)

Bean curd: A cheeselike product made from soybean milk, bean curd is an important source of protein and can be used instead of meat in stir-fries. Also serve in salads. See Chapter 6 for recipes and further discussion. Bean curd is the Chinese type; the Japanese version is called tofu. They can be used interchangeably. Sold by weight fresh or prepackaged in produce markets, supermarkets, Oriental shops, and health food stores.
SUBSTITUTE: Tofu.

Bean sprouts: Sprouts of soy and mung beans, sold by the pound from water-filled vats in Oriental markets and supermarkets. Use as a crunchy vegetable in stir-fries and raw in salads or as a garnish. Alfalfa sprouts (from the grain) are smaller and spicier. Some people prefer to grow their own.
SUBSTITUTE: Canned bean sprouts, though because they've been blanched they won't be as crisp. Drain and rinse well before using.

Bean thread: Also called cellophane noodles or transparent noodles. These thin noodles are made from mung beans. Thrown into hot oil they explode like popcorn into a crispy tangle that makes a pretty garnish for stir-fries, soups, and salads. Soak in boiling water to use as a noodle in soup or noodle recipes. Tastes like a slippery noodle. Sold in Oriental markets.

SUBSTITUTE: For use as a noodle, any long, thin noodle, particularly vermicelli.

Birds' nests: Sold only in Oriental markets, these are either sheets of the gelatinous material from which swifts in the South Seas build nests, or small whole swift nests. Used in soup.

SUBSTITUTE: No real substitute, but try bean thread for a similar texture.

Black fungus: See TREE FUNGUS.

Cellophane noodles: See BEAN THREAD.

Chicken broth: Use instead of water for most sauces in this book. Make in minutes from chicken broth granules seasoned with Oriental flavorings. Or use my Basic Chicken Broth (page 32) or Fast Chicken Broth (page 33).

Chinese vegetables: See A Guide to Preparing and Serving Exotic New Vegetables, pages 190–194.

Chinese mushrooms, dried: Dried mushrooms sold by weight or prepackaged in Oriental markets and some supermarkets. Used more for texture than for flavor. Soak the mushrooms, gills down, in very hot water 5 to 15 minutes, or until soft. Squeeze dry, cut away the tough stem, slice into shreds, and stir-fry. Many recipes suggest that the soaking liquid be reserved for use in the sauce.

SUBSTITUTE: Tree fungus is a fair substitute for the texture; also fresh mushrooms, preferably exotic types such as shiitake.

Dried Chinese mushrooms

Cloud ears: See TREE FUNGUS.

Corn: See BABY CORN.

Egg roll skins: Pastry wrappers for egg rolls or spring rolls. Sold in produce or frozen food sections of supermarkets and in Oriental markets, where the ones you'll find are often thinner and more delicate. Can be kept frozen for several months. To thaw, unwrap the package and defrost for about 1 hour under a damp cloth. When stuffing the skins, always keep the pile covered with a quite damp cloth—dry skins tend to tear and crack.
SUBSTITUTE: None.

Egg roll skins

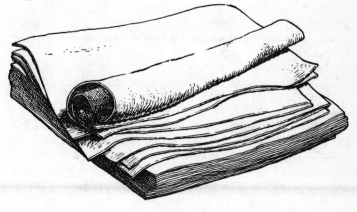

Fungus: See TREE FUNGUS.

Glutinous rice: See OVAL RICE.

Lotus root: Brown tubers about 8 inches long and 2 inches around, found only in Oriental markets. Peel and slice into ¼- and ½-inch rounds, and use in stir-fries for crisp texture. The peeled root discolors, so keep in cold water until ready to use. Store lotus root in the refrigerator.
SUBSTITUTE: Canned lotus root may be found in Oriental markets.

Lychee nuts: Plum-sized fruit frequently offered chilled in syrup as a dessert in Chinese restaurants. Sold canned in Oriental specialty shops. A quick and simple dessert: serve the fruit chilled, halved, dusted with cinnamon.
SUBSTITUTE: Fresh lychees. See LYCHEE NUT (page 248).

Oval rice: Also called short-grain and pearl rice. These oval grains are smaller than those of common long-grain rice, and are sticky after cooking—easy to pick up with chopsticks. The Japanese serve it with main courses; in Thailand and China it is more often used to make sweets. The Chinese generally serve a long-grain type of rice similar to ours, sometimes called Thai rice. Oval rice is available in Oriental markets. See page 77 for cooking instructions.

Pancake wrappers: Frozen pastry wrappers (mu hsu pei) for use in Moo Shu recipes (see mine on page 138). Thaw before using. Sold in Oriental markets.

SUBSTITUTE: Crepes 6 inches in diameter or thin omelets.

Peppers: Both sweet and hot peppers are used in Oriental cooking. Sweet peppers are used as vegetables. Red and yellow sweet peppers are most attractive in curries, but all sweet peppers are interchangeable as far as taste is concerned. For hot peppers, see CHILI PEPPERS, page 21.

Rice sticks: Flat, white, narrow, and pretty noodles. Sold in Oriental food shops. Cook as ordinary noodles.

SUBSTITUTE: Any narrow, flat noodle.

Skins: See EGG ROLL SKINS.

Snow peas: Also, sugar peas, a slightly larger variety. Edible-pod peas eaten whole, with the pod. Used in stir-fries and as a garnish. Sold fresh or frozen in most markets, and very expensive, but ¼ pound is enough for most entrées. If they're wilted when purchased, rinse and store in the refrigerator. Stem and string by pulling the stem in the direction opposite to the way it curls. Easy to grow yourself!

SUBSTITUTE: Italian (flat) green beans, found in the frozen vegetable section of most markets.

Spring roll skins: See EGG ROLL SKINS.

Surimi: A seafood analog which can be used in place of crab, lobster, etc. For a full discussion, see page 145.

Tofu: See BEAN CURD.

Tree ears: See TREE FUNGUS.

Tree fungus: Also called cloud ears, tree ears, or black fungus. A dry gelatinous fungus sold in Oriental markets. Before using, soak 5 to 10 minutes in boiling water until soft, then remove the hard central stem. The size will expand greatly and the texture will be slippery and gelatinous.

SUBSTITUTE: Dried Chinese mushrooms or bean thread.

Vegetable oil: My choice for Oriental cooking is corn oil—the lighter, the better!

SUBSTITUTE: Peanut oil or safflower oil.

Water chestnuts: Available fresh in many supermarkets, these small tubers have a dull black wrinkled skin that when peeled away reveals creamy white flesh that is sweet and crisp in stir-fries. Store in the refrigerator and peel and rinse just before using. Buy only what you need, because they are expensive, and rot quickly. When fresh are not available, use drained canned water chestnuts, which are sold everywhere.

SUBSTITUTE: Cabbage or celery cores, bamboo shoots, bean sprouts.

Won ton skins: Thin pastry wrappers about 3½–4 inches square or round used for making won ton dumplings and dim sum. These are sold wherever egg roll skins are sold, usually in the freezer sections of supermarkets, but the best types are the thinnest, and found in Oriental specialty shops. Follow the instructions under EGG ROLL SKINS.

SUBSTITUTE: Some egg roll skins are thin enough to be used to make won tons, but quarter them before use.

Wrappers: See EGG ROLL SKINS; WON TON SKINS.

Basic Seasonings for Soy Sauce-flavored Recipes

Black bean: Fermented soybeans, with a spicy, peppery taste. Sold in small bottles in supermarkets. Use as a flavoring with fish and in some dipping sauces.

SUBSTITUTE: Hunan paste, see below. This is much hotter.

Chili paste: Used in Sichuan and other spicy Chinese recipes. It is flavored with garlic and very hot, but has a nice aftertaste. Sold in small bottles at Oriental markets. Use sparingly until you're sure you like it.

SUBSTITUTE: Use red pepper flakes, chili powder, or Hunan paste to taste.

Chili peppers: Hot peppers, used in Sichuan and other spicy Chinese dishes, and in hot Indian and Thai curries. Young chili peppers are green, ripe ones turn yellow or red. The varieties of small chili peppers called serrano, jalapeño, and poblano are easiest to find and suitable for use in recipes here. Wear gloves when handling them. Unless a recipe says otherwise, remove the seeds and membranes and use only the flesh. That firepot spice, red pepper flakes, is made from chili peppers.

SUBSTITUTE: Dried peppers, red pepper flakes, or chili paste. Unless you know you love very hot foods, add dried red pepper flakes, which include red pepper seeds, carefully, starting with 1/16 teaspoon. Add more to suit your taste. About ¼ teaspoon red pepper flakes equals one small chili. If you use chili paste: ½ teaspoon chili paste equals a 2-inch seeded minced jalapeño pepper. Or, add cayenne pepper, Hungarian paprika, or chili powder to taste.

Chili powder: A blend of ground hot peppers, cumin, garlic, oregano, cloves, and allspice. Hot! Used in spicy Chinese and Thai dishes and in curries.
SUBSTITUTE: Cayenne or chili paste.

Chinese parsley: See CILANTRO.

Chinese mustard: A hot and sharp but delicious prepared mustard found in supermarkets and almost indispensable to the enjoyment of Chinese appetizers. Often accompanies sweet and sour plum sauce.
SUBSTITUTE: Mustard Dipping Sauce (page 227).

Cilantro: Also called Chinese parsley or coriander. A parsley-like herb with a distinctive, strong flavor used in cooking and, minced, as a garnish on salads, curries, and other Oriental dishes. Plant coriander seeds and grow your own cilantro! See also Basic Seasonings for Curry-flavored Recipes, page 26.
SUBSTITUTE: For color, Italian or curly parsley; for flavor, celery leaves.

Duck sauce: See PLUM SAUCE.

Five spice powder: A combination of five or six ground spices, including cloves, cinnamon, star anise, ginger, and peppercorns, used to flavor bean curd and meat dishes. Available in Oriental markets.
SUBSTITUTE: A combination of these spices, ground.

Fish sauce: Each region where soy sauce-flavored foods are prepared seems to have its own fish sauce. Nuoc mam is Vietnam's version of fish sauce. Thai and Philippine versions, called nam pla and patis, are milder than the Chinese or Vietnamese sauces. All are very salty and fishy. Used in sauces.
SUBSTITUTE: Any fish sauce; oyster sauce. Or, add more soy sauce.

Garlic: Used in most soy sauce-flavored recipes and also in curries. Buy fresh, fat-cloved heads—the larger the clove, the easier to peel. Flatten with a whack of a cleaver or mallet to loosen the peel. Sold everywhere.
SUBSTITUTE: None. Garlic powder is not a substitute for fresh garlic—it's merely an excuse.

Ginger, ginger root: Ginger root is a key ingredient in Chinese, Japanese, Indian, Thai, and other Oriental recipes. Fresh ginger is used in almost every soy sauce-flavored recipe and is almost as common in curry-flavored dishes. Fresh roots are silky-skinned, pale yellow or pink. Available in nearly all greengrocers and supermarkets now, it keeps for weeks sealed in a plastic bag in the refrigerator. It has a number of fragrant relatives worth experimenting with if you run across them, particularly galangal, also known as Siamese ginger, or laos (its Indonesian name).

SUBSTITUTE: Powdered ginger is not an adequate substitute for fresh ginger. Dried ginger root is a better substitute. Pickled ginger shreds are an even better substitute, and very effective as garnish on dim sum.

Ginger, pickled: Shredded ginger root is pickled and sold in small jars in Oriental specialty shops. The brine may be colored red.

SUBSTITUTE: Shreds of peeled fresh ginger root. See GINGER, GINGER ROOT, above.

Golden needles: See TIGER LILY BUDS.

Green onions: Also called scallions, or, in Chinese restaurant menus, spring onions. Sold in most markets by the bunch year-round. To trim for cooking, cut away the fibrous root tip and coarse green leaves where the branching begins to get a shoot 3 to 5 inches long. Peel away the thin outer layer if it looks dead, and the onion is ready to use. A green onion trimmed to 3 to 4 inches and minced makes a rounded tablespoonful. Placed whole in a food processor, after a few pulses green onions shatter into elegant green and white shreds ready to use in cooking, in dipping sauces, or as a garnish.

SUBSTITUTE: Onion. A thin slice of a medium-large onion, minced, makes 1 rounded tablespoonful.

Hoisin sauce: A sweet and spicy sauce used for dipping and in cooking. Sold bottled in supermarkets.

SUBSTITUTE: Sweet bean sauce.

Hunan paste: A hot, oily paste made from black beans, garlic, chili, and sesame oil. Used in Sichuan and other spicy recipes. Sold bottled in Oriental markets.

SUBSTITUTE: Use half as much chili paste, or Thai shrimp paste in bean oil. See SHRIMP PASTE.

Lily buds: See TIGER LILY BUDS.

Mirin: A sweet rice wine used in Japanese cooking. Sold in Oriental markets.

SUBSTITUTE: Chinese rice wine or dry sherry.

Miso: Japanese fermented soybean paste. Sold in Oriental markets. Used in soup.

SUBSTITUTE: No real substitute.

Mushroom soy sauce: A thick, intensely flavored soy sauce used in

stir-frying Chinese meat entrées, such as Hunan Beef (page 128).
SUBSTITUTE: Thick soy sauce, or any soy sauce.

Nuoc mam: Vietnamese fish sauce. See FISH SAUCE. Sold in Oriental markets and through mail order.
SUBSTITUTE: Any fish sauce; oyster sauce.

Oyster sauce: A very salty sauce made from oysters, brine, and soy sauce. Sold in Oriental markets and major supermarkets.
SUBSTITUTE: Fish sauce or extra soy sauce.

Plum sauce: Also called duck sauce. A sweet and sour sauce made from plums, chilies, vinegar, and spices, and often served with duck. Sold in supermarkets.
SUBSTITUTE: Any spicy sweet and sour sauce.

Red pepper flakes: See CHILI PEPPERS.

Rice vinegar: Both light and dark rice vinegars are sold in supermarkets. The recipes in this book call for light, mild rice vinegar, because dark vinegars are too strong for the subtle flavors I look for in most of my recipes.
SUBSTITUTE: For light, mild rice vinegar, use cider vinegar or white wine vinegar. For dark vinegar, use Worcestershire sauce.

Rice cooking wine: A Chinese wine that imparts a light, dry flavor to foods. The best rice wine is from Thailand. Sold in supermarkets.
SUBSTITUTE: Dry sherry, dry white wine, or dry vermouth.

Sake: A Japanese rice wine. Where used in cooking, it adds a characteristic light and dry flavor. Sold in Oriental markets.
SUBSTITUTE: Other rice wines, or dry sherry.

Sesame oil: An aromatic oil pressed from toasted sesame seeds, and deep golden in color. Good sesame oil has a slightly nutty flavor that enhances sauces, salads, and seafoods. Use sparingly, because too much can overpower other tastes. Store in the refrigerator after opening.
SUBSTITUTE: Any nut oil—peanut oil, for instance; other oils are acceptable, but will lack the flavor.

Shrimp, dried: Tiny shrimp that have been dried and have a smoked, hamlike taste. Use in stir-fries and sauces as a flavoring agent.
SUBSTITUTE: Ham, preferably a Smithfield-type ham.

Shrimp paste: A thick paste made of shrimp, oil, spices, and herbs. Thai shrimp paste is hot and spicy. Sold in Oriental markets.
SUBSTITUTE: Fresh shrimp in equal amounts, plus a small pinch of chili or cayenne pepper.

Soy sauce: The dark, salty all-purpose seasoning of the Orient, made from soybeans, yeast, salt, and sugar. Each region has its own soy sauce. In Oriental markets in the United States, the most commonly found types are Chinese regular or light soy sauce;

Japanese shoyu, which is lighter and sharper and a bit sweet; mainland China's épais (French for "thick") soy sauce; and the intense mushroom soy sauce. You can also find a sweet soy sauce imported from Thailand for use with fruit. Then there are a number of American brands of soy sauce and shoyu. For the recipes in this book, unless otherwise stated, I've used a light or regular soy sauce imported from China, Superior brand. For Japanese recipes, I've used shoyu or the mild American brand Kikkoman, which is closer to the Japanese. Mushroom soy sauce and thick soy sauce are used in spicy Sichuan and Hunan recipes.

SUBSTITUTE: Any soy sauce except sweet soy sauce may substitute for another. Add according to taste.

Star anise: A licorice-flavored spice consisting of small brown pods shaped like eight-pointed stars. Sold in Oriental markets.

SUBSTITUTE: Anise or fennel, 1 teaspoon for each pod required in recipe.

Sweet and sour sauce: Also sold as duck sauce or plum sauce, this is a thick orange-red sauce served with many Chinese dishes, particularly those that are deep-fried, such as spring rolls and won ton appetizers. It very often is accompanied by Chinese mustard, a prepared mustard sauce. Sweet and sour sauce is sold everywhere Chinese foods are sold, and in all supermarkets. You can make your own from the recipe on page 227.

SUBSTITUTE: Hoisin sauce or pureed fruit chutney.

Sweet bean sauce: A thick, sweet, spicy sauce made from fermented soybeans and used in Sichuan cooking. Sold in Oriental markets.

SUBSTITUTE: Hoisin sauce.

Tiger lily buds: Also called dried tiger lilies, lily buds, or golden needles. These dried day lily blossoms add a hint of pineapple taste to stir-fries. Available in Oriental markets and through mail order. They're used only in a few recipes and keep forever. Soak 5 or 10 minutes, or until soft, before using. Needles that are stuck together should be cut apart before soaking.

SUBSTITUTE: Half as many shreds of dried or fresh pineapple.

Tiger lily buds (also called golden needles)

Basic Seasonings for Curry-flavored Recipes

Cardamom: A small pod harvested by hand, and therefore fearfully expensive to buy. Whole pods are used as a chewing spice to sweeten breath. Ground powder is used in curries. Buy in small quantities ground from Oriental markets.
SUBSTITUTE: No adequate substitute, but curry powder can be used (see CURRY POWDER).

Cayenne: A very hot, finely ground powder made from several types of hot peppers. Sold everywhere.
SUBSTITUTE: Chili powder, white or black pepper, chili paste.

Chili paste: See Basic Seasonings for Soy Sauce-flavored Recipes, page 21.

Chili peppers: See Basic Seasonings for Soy Sauce-flavored Recipes, page 21.

Chili powder: See Basic Seasonings for Soy Sauce-flavored Recipes, page 22.

Cilantro: Also called Chinese parsley or coriander. See Basic Seasonings for Soy Sauce-flavored Recipes, page 22. Cilantro is an essential flavor in Thai cuisine: in Thai recipes, *substitute* basil, mint, or parsley.

Cinnamon: The bark of the cinnamon tree, available in ground or in stick form in any grocery store. Used in Indian dishes, and in Thai dishes derived from Indian recipes. The recipes in this book call for ground cinnamon.
SUBSTITUTE: Ground stick cinnamon or half as much ground allspice.

Clove: The dried flower bud of a tropical tree. Used ground in some Indian curries, and in garam masala, an Indian spice combination. Found in all markets.
SUBSTITUTE: Five spice powder (see page 22), garam masala, or other combination spices that include cloves. Or ground whole cloves or ground allspice.

Coconut: Used fresh in recipes from India's coastal regions, and an integral part of Thai and Southeast Asian cooking. Dried coconut, sold in spice shops, by Oriental mail-order firms, and in some supermarkets and health food stores, may be used to make condiments for serving with curried dishes or as a garnish.

SUBSTITUTE: No adequate substitute for fresh coconut. Dried sweetened coconut sold in the baked goods departments of supermarkets isn't suitable, but in a pinch may be rinsed off to get rid of the sugar, dried, and used in any cooked recipe: omit sugar called for in the recipe.

Coconut cream: A cream made from the flesh of fresh coconut and used in making Southeast Asian desserts. Sold canned for making piña coladas and other drinks, or make your own from the recipe on page 34.
SUBSTITUTE: As a topping, sweetened heavy cream.

Coconut milk: A milk made from the flesh of fresh coconut and a common ingredient in Thai, Indian, and Southeast Asian cooking. *Sweetened* coconut milk contains sugar and is not recommended. Use *unsweetened* coconut milk in the recipes. Available in cans in Oriental markets and through mail order, or make your own Thick Coconut Milk from the recipe on page 34. Freeze unused milk in cup lots.
SUBSTITUTE: Heavy cream or half-and-half.

Coriander: These seeds are a staple of Indian and Southeast Asian cooking. The recipes in this book generally call for ground coriander, which is readily available or easily ground from the seeds.
SUBSTITUTE: No adequate substitute, but curry powder can be used (see CURRY POWDER).

Cornstarch: Starch made from corn and used as thickener for sauces. Available everywhere.
SUBSTITUTE: Equal amount of tapioca starch, or all-purpose flour mixed in a small amount of cold water.

Cumin: Ground cumin is used frequently together with coriander and cardamom in Indian and Southeast Asian cuisines. Chew cumin seeds as a breath sweetener. Sold in most markets. Seeds may be ground to make your own ground cumin.
SUBSTITUTE: No adequate substitute, but curry powder can be used (see CURRY POWDER).

Curry paste: A paste made of "curry" spices—See CURRY POWDER, and the recipe for Curry Paste, page 35.

Curry powder: "Curry" is not a single spice, but a combination of up to twenty-eight pungent ground spices and herbs, including cardamom, coriander, cumin, and turmeric—the turmeric produces the yellow color—used to flavor Indian and Southeast Asian stews and other spicy dishes. Curry powder is available packaged ready-made, but in Asia, it is usually the custom to buy the various whole spices in small lots, and grind them individually for each recipe just before using. The reason for doing it on the spot is two-fold: each household has its own spice preferences and freshly ground spices have a better flavor. In this book, most of the curry recipes call for separately ground spices. When these spices aren't available, use curry powder, which is sold in all markets; however, because curry powder usually has the bite of ginger to it, you may want to omit some of the fresh ginger in the recipe. Some recipes use a paste made of the curry spices. These are sold in Oriental markets; Thai brands are quite hot. See the recipe for Curry Paste, page 35.

SUBSTITUTE: Any combination of spices noted above.

Fennel: The seeds have a licorice flavor, similar to anise, and are used in Thai and other curry-flavored cuisines. In India, the seeds are roasted and served as an after-dinner mouth freshener. Excellent used as a flavoring with vegetables and seafood creams.

SUBSTITUTE: Anise seeds.

Garam masala: A mixture of several ground "hot" spices used in Indian cooking to flavor meats, fish, and vegetables. The exact spices can vary, but are always those the Indians consider able to bring warmth to the body, such as cardamom, cumin, black pepper, cinnamon, clove, and coriander. Sold in Oriental markets and through mail order, or try my version on page 36.

SUBSTITUTE: Ground allspice combined in equal quantities with ground coriander, cumin, and cardamom.

Ghee: A clarified butter used in Indian cooking as a cooking fat. The term ghee is also used to describe other cooking fats. Not generally available commercially. To make it: melt butter, pour off and retain the oily part, and discard the milky residue.

SUBSTITUTE: Vegetable oil, or melted butter and margarine combined half and half; discard any milky residue.

Ginger, ginger root: See Basic Seasonings for Soy Sauce-flavored Recipes, page 22.

Green onions: Also called scallions. See Basic Seasonings for Soy Sauce-flavored Recipes, page 23.

Lemon grass: Long and wispy, this herb gives Thai dishes their lemony accent. Fresh lemon grass is found only in large Oriental markets. Dried lemon grass and powdered lemon grass are found in smaller Oriental shops, particularly Thai shops. The fresh lemon grass keeps for weeks sealed in plastic in the refrigerator. If it dries out before it is used up, chop it and let it dry thoroughly for use as dried lemon grass. The fresh stalks propagate easily in a glass of water and a sunny window. If fresh lemon grass is not available, use equal quantities of dried lemon grass, but soak before using. To use lemon grass powder, follow the instructions on the container.

SUBSTITUTE: Strained lemon juice, to taste, or grated lemon peel: use half as much as the lemon grass called for in the recipe.

Mustard powder: Both black and yellow mustard seeds are common to Indian cuisine, but for my everyday cooking, I use the mustard powder available in most markets.

SUBSTITUTE: Prepared mustard, preferably Chinese or Japanese.

Red pepper flakes: See CHILI PEPPERS.

Saffron: The stigma of the purple crocus. Along with cardamom, this is the world's most expensive spice because of the labor involved in harvesting. Soak the threads in hot liquid for 10 to 15 minutes before using. Omit this soaking stage in recipes that include a lot of liquid. Sold in most markets, but less expensive in Oriental markets.

SUBSTITUTE: Ground turmeric gives a similar yellow color, but nothing equals saffron's flavor.

Tamarind liquid: Tamarind is a fruit the pulp of which is made into a paste to add tartness and a hint of apricot to Indian dishes. Make the liquid by soaking lumps of dried tamarind, removing the seeds, and processing in a blender or mashing by hand. See recipe on page 36. Dried into chunks, tamarind is sold in Oriental specialty shops and by mail order. Tamarind liquid is available, but it tends to ferment. Tamarind wrapped in plastic keeps in the refrigerator for several months.

SUBSTITUTE: Strained lemon or lime juice: use about a third less than the amount of tamarind liquid called for, and add more to taste.

Tapioca starch: Tapioca is known in the Orient as cassava, a tuber native to South America. Ground, the tuber makes a starch that looks much like cornstarch, and is used in Thai and other curry-flavored cuisines to thicken sauces. Sold in Oriental markets.

SUBSTITUTE: Equal amount of cornstarch or all-purpose flour diluted in a small amount of cold water.

Turmeric: A root ground to make a spicy powder with a taste somewhere between ginger and mustard. Use with care: just a half teaspoon stains yellow anything from curry sauces to kitchen counters. Sold in most markets.

SUBSTITUTE: Saffron for color. No adequate substitute for flavor, but curry powder can be used (see CURRY POWDER).

The Well-Stocked Larder

These are ingredients you will use often in making my recipes—the first group is for soy sauce-flavored recipes, the second is for curry-flavored recipes.

For soy sauce-flavored recipes:

Bamboo shoots, canned
Bean sprouts, canned
Chili paste
Chinese mushrooms, dried
Chinese mustard (prepared)
Corn oil
Cornstarch
Garlic, fresh
Ginger root
Green onions
Hoisin sauce
Hunan paste

Lychee nuts, canned
Oyster sauce
Pineapple chunks, canned, in their own juice
Rice vinegar, light
Rice cooking wine
Sesame oil
Shrimp paste
Soy sauce, light or standard
Sweet and sour sauce
Tree fungus
Water chestnuts, whole, canned

Many of these items are also used in curry-flavored recipes.

For curry-flavored recipes:

Cardamom, ground
Cayenne, ground
Chili powder
Cinnamon, ground
Clove, ground
Coconut milk, canned

Coriander, ground
Cumin, ground or whole
Curry powder
Saffron threads
Tamarind, lump form
Turmeric

NOTE: If you have a spice grinder and wish to buy whole spices and grind as needed, wonderful! However, most recipes call for the ground spice, and they may be the easiest to find canned or bottled on supermarket racks.

The Well-Stocked Freezer

In addition to having a selection of herbs, spices, and sauces in your cupboard, you should have such key ingredients as coconut milk, a varied assortment of leftover cooked meats, and egg roll and won ton skins in your freezer, ready to use. Here are my suggestions for items to have on hand:

- A pound or two of small raw shrimp in their shells, bagged in ¼-pound portions.
- Surimi products: crab legs, and sliced crab salad-style.

- A pound of boneless pork tenderloin chunks, bagged in ¼-pound portions.
- Shredded cooked pork roast and beef leftovers, with drippings, packaged in 1-cup portions.
- Shredded cooked chicken leftovers, with drippings, packaged in 1- and 2-cup portions.
- Chicken and beef broth, frozen in 1-cup containers.
- Egg roll skins.
- Won ton skins.
- Moo shu pancakes.
- Packaged stuffed spring rolls and won tons, shrimp toast, and other appetizers, ready to be deep-fried or steamed.
- Cooked rice, bagged in ⅔-cup lots (1 portion).
- Coconut milk, in 1-cup containers (page 34).
- Piña colada frozen concentrate. A single spoonful enhances commercial bottled sweet and sour sauces, and turns simple fruits into delicious desserts.

The Readiness Bowl

If you plan to stir-fry within a couple of days of marketing, prepare a bowl of pre-cut vegetables to have waiting in the refrigerator. I cover each batch of cut vegetable tightly with plastic wrap; they stay fresh and crisp until I'm ready to use them.

- Cut the outer stalks of celery into very thin 5-inch-long strips.
- Peel garlic cloves.
- Trim green onions.
- Slice the tops and bottoms off purple or Bermuda onions. Cutting from top to bottom, divide each into eight segments, then separate the leaves.
- Seed and shred sweet peppers.
- Rinse fresh snow peas, then remove the strings.
- Shred the tender inner leaves of a cauliflower and the core of a cabbage.
- Cut a head of broccoli into 1-inch florets, then trim, peel, and roll-cut the stem.

Making Your Own Basic Oriental Ingredients

Only God can make fresh ginger and tamarind, but you can produce a few ingredients basic to soy sauce- and curry-flavored recipes in your own kitchen without much fuss. You can make coconut milk, tamarind liquid, an inexpensive, fast, and good chicken broth, and spice mixtures such as curry powder and garam masala. Though some of the recipes given here are useful for only a few of the dishes in the book, they're flavoring agents you'll enjoy improvising with as well.

Basic Chicken Broth

Prep. Time 5 minutes • Makes about 3 quarts
Cooking Time 2 hours

A delicious basic stock for Oriental soups and stews. Save up chicken parts in the freezer to make this.

5 pounds chicken and chicken parts
4 quarts cold water
2 green onions, trimmed to 6 inches and chopped
2 ½-inch-thick pieces fresh ginger, peeled and minced
2 teaspoons soy sauce, or more
1 tablespoon rice wine or dry sherry

In a big stockpot or kettle over high heat, combine the chicken, water, green onions, and ginger. Cover and bring to a rapid boil. Skim the foam, reduce the heat to simmer, cover, and cook for 2 hours.

Allow to cool. Strain through a fine mesh strainer to remove all solids. Add the soy sauce and wine or sherry. Taste, and add more soy sauce if desired. Divide into 1-cup portions, label, and freeze for future use.

Fast Chicken Broth

Prep. Time 3–4 minutes • Makes 1 cup
Cooking Time 1 minute

Instant bouillon granules or cubes will make acceptable broth for use in Oriental recipes if you doctor them a bit, as I do here. But beware of the salt!

1 level teaspoon chicken broth granules
1 cup boiling water
½ teaspoon white vinegar
¼ teaspoon sugar

1 very thin slice fresh ginger, peeled and minced
⅛ teaspoon soy sauce
⅛ teaspoon rice wine or dry sherry

In a small saucepan over high heat, combine all ingredients and simmer 1 minute. Strain through a fine mesh strainer to remove all solids.

Fast Beef Broth

Prep. Time 5 minutes • Makes 1 cup
Cooking Time 1 minute

Instant beef bouillon granules or powder make suitable broth for use in the recipes in this book, but beware of the salt!

1 level teaspoon beef bouillon granules or powder
1 cup boiling water
½ teaspoon cider vinegar
Grinding of pepper
1 small garlic clove, peeled and halved

¼ teaspoon soy sauce
¼ teaspoon rice wine or dry sherry
Pinch of minced cilantro, optional

In a small saucepan over high heat, combine all the ingredients and simmer 1 minute. Strain before using, if desired.

Fresh Coconut Cream

Prepare Thick Coconut Milk (below) to the point where the milk separates. The thick, oily liquid that rises to the top is coconut cream, used to make desserts. You should get about ⅔ to ¾ of a cup of this cream. If you are working with a recipe that calls for a full cup of coconut cream, stretch what you have with heavy or light cream or half-and-half.

Canned coconut milk, available in Oriental markets, is usually thick enough to use as coconut cream in a dessert recipe. However, canned coconut cream sold for making piña coladas has been presweetened and is loaded with sugar; use it in a dessert recipe only if you omit all other sweeteners.

Thick Coconut Milk

Prep. Time 45 minutes • Makes 2–3 cups
Cooking Time 0

Canned coconut milk, available in Oriental markets, is the best choice for main-course Oriental recipes. (Don't use canned coconut *cream*, which is sold for desserts and piña coladas; it is far too sweet.) If you can't easily get canned coconut milk, pressing your own from fresh coconut meat is simple, though a bit time-consuming. One medium-size coconut makes between 2¾ and 3 cups of coconut milk. Freeze any left over in 1–cup portions in Ziplock storage bags. Choose a coconut with lots of liquid inside (shake it to check)—it will make better coconut milk.

1 medium-size fresh coconut   **2–3 cups hot water**

Heat oven to 350°. Use a big nail to drive holes through two of the coconut "eyes." Drain the liquid through the eyes into a measuring cup; strain and reserve the liquid. Place the coconut in the oven for 15 minutes. Remove, and strike with a hammer along the crack lines that developed during the heating to break open. Remove the coconut meat, cut into 2- to 3-inch chunks, and chop to a pulp in a food processor. You may also use a blender, but will have to process in two batches. Measure the coconut meat. Add enough very hot water to the drained coconut liquid to equal the amount of coconut meat. Heat to just below boiling and combine with the chopped coconut. Return to the processor and process until the coconut is pulverized. Strain into a bowl, pressing the last drop of liquid from the pulp with a spoon. Cover and chill until the milk separates into "cream"—the thick oily substance that floats to the top—and "thin milk," the liquid that stays at the bottom. Recombine the "cream" and "milk" to make "thick coconut milk."

AN ADDED BONUS: Freeze the leftover ground coconut meat and add it to curries for healthy fiber and a bit of flavor.

Curry Paste

Prep. Time 3–5 minutes • *Makes about 4½ tablespoons*
Cooking Time 10 minutes

Homemade curry paste keeps a month or so in the refrigerator, and adds character to roasted meats, vegetable sauces, broiled chicken, and stews. Add by the tablespoonful to sauces at the last minute—taste before adding more. (If you like hot foods, double the amount of cayenne.)

1 large yellow onion, peeled
2 large garlic cloves, peeled
1 3-inch piece fresh ginger, peeled
2 tablespoons vegetable oil
1 tablespoon ground coriander
1 teaspoon ground cumin
½ teaspoon ground cardamom
1½ teaspoons ground cloves
½ teaspoon ground cinnamon
½ teaspoon ground nutmeg or mace
1½ teaspoons salt
½ teaspoon ground pepper
¼ teaspoon cayenne
2 tablespoons lemon or lime juice

In a blender or by hand mince together the onion, garlic, and ginger. Heat the wok to simmer (about 200°) and swirl in the oil; then add the onion mixture. Stir-fry until the onions turn a deep golden brown, about 4–5 minutes. Push the mixture up the side of the wok. Raise the heat a little (300°) and add the coriander and cumin. Stir-fry (they will smoke a lot) until the color darkens, about 1 minute. Scrape the onion mixture down into the wok, turn off the heat, and mash everything together. Add the remaining ingredients and mash to a fine paste. Store bottled in the refrigerator.

Garam Masala

Prep. Time 5 minutes • Makes about 5 tablespoons
Cooking Time 0

Garam masala is a combination of various "hot" Indian spices. Some garam masala mixtures omit cardamom, but because I love that spice, I follow those recipes that include it. You'll only be using a teaspoonful of garam masala in my recipes, so the quantity made here will last a long time. This recipe calls for pre-ground spices, but you can make even more fragrant garam masala by grinding your own from the whole spice (use the seed of cardamom, not the whole cardamom). Garam masala is available in Indian specialty shops.

1 tablespoon ground cardamom
2 tablespoons ground cumin
1 tablespoon ground black
  pepper

½ tablespoon ground cinnamon
1 teaspoon ground clove
½ tablespoon ground coriander

Combine, pour into a bottle, and cover tightly. Label clearly and store in a cool, dark place.

Tamarind Liquid

Prep. Time 20 minutes • Makes 1 cup
Cooking Time 0

Tamarind imparts to curries and other Indian dishes a whiff of apricot flavor that is fruity and enticing. It also makes a nice addition to fruit drinks. Dried tamarind comes in a lump and keeps in the refrigerator for months; tear off what you need. The liquid, once prepared, keeps a week or two. You'll use only a few tablespoonfuls in a recipe, so prepare the liquid in small batches, as below.

2-by-2-inch piece dried tamarind   ¾ cup boiling water

Break apart the piece of tamarind, place the pieces in a measuring cup, and cover with boiling water. Allow to soak until softened. If you need it right away, allow only 15 minutes; that is enough for it to get soft enough to break apart under pressure from your fingers. Remove the seeds and discard. Place the tamarind and soaking water in a blender or food processor and process until homogenized. Store in a capped bottle in the refrigerator. Shake well before using.

Three

Appetizers and Dim Sum

The appetizers I offer to you in this chapter can be served as hors d'oeuvres, as a first course, or as one of a sequence of courses during an Oriental banquet. They also make a good side dish to soup or salad for a lunch or a light dinner.

The platters featuring raw vegetables, surimi, and seafoods are served with exotic dipping sauces. The sauces may be made a day or two ahead and refrigerated until ready to serve. The recipes for dipping sauces are in Chapter 11.

Dim sum are traditional finger-foods that are fried crisp or steamed, marinated sweet or sour, served hot or cold. The traditional Chinese way to serve dim sum is as a brunch or lunch with a parade of selections. If you're accustomed to serving appetizers before a meal, you'll find dim sum a perfect complement to any menu.

Many of my steamed dim sum recipes, such as Shrimp (or Chicken, Crab, Whole Shrimp) Steamed in Noodle Cases, use square won ton skin wrappers because these are readily available in supermarkets at the produce counter. The traditional wrappers for dim sum are round and made of thinner pastry, and can be found at Oriental specialty shops. Dim sum items that are steamed without wrappers, such as Crab-stuffed Mushroom Caps and Shrimp Balls, China, are equally delicious.

The recipes for deep-fried dim sum, including Won Ton Appetizers, Spring Rolls, and Shrimp Toast, are the only ones in this book that take much time to prepare—from 30 to 60 minutes. They're included in this collection of fast and easy recipes because they're so special and wonderful to eat! You can buy frozen won tons and spring rolls and fry them up quickly, but I've never tasted any that are as good as these made from scratch.

Menu Suggestions

Appetizers for 4

½ recipe Shrimp Toast
½ recipe Long Beans in Garlic Marinade
Surimi Fish Cakes with Teriyaki Sauce or Surimi Crab Legs with
Dipping Sauce

Appetizers for 4

Whole Shrimp in Noodle Cases
½ recipe Chutney-stuffed Won Tons

Appetizers for 6

½ recipe Chicken Drumettes with Peanut Sauce
½ recipe Seafood and Exotic Fruit Platter

Appetizers for 8

Seafood and Exotic Fruit Platter
Shrimp in Garlic Sauce
Beef Koftas with Curry Dip

Appetizers for 8

Surimi Crab Legs with Dipping Sauce
Beef Koftas with Curry Dip
Lychee-stuffed Won Tons

Appetizer Dinner for 8–10

Tomatoes, Squash, and Peppers, with Curry Dip
Chicken Drumettes with Peanut Sauce
Shrimp in Garlic Sauce
Spring Rolls, Cantonese Style
Chutney-stuffed Won Tons

Appetizers for 10–12

Vegetables with Peanut Sauce
Surimi Crab Legs with Dipping Sauce
Beef Koftas with Curry Dip
Shrimp in Garlic Sauce
Spring Roll Miniatures
Lychee-stuffed Won Tons

Appetizers for 14

Seafood and Exotic Fruit Platter
Tea Eggs
Long Beans in Garlic Marinade
Chicken Drumettes with Peanut Sauce
Shrimp Steamed in Noodle Cases
Ham and Pineapple in Noodle Cases
Won Ton Appetizers

Appetizers for 20

Vegetables with Peanut Sauce
Tomatoes, Squash, and Peppers, with Curry Dip
Crab Legs with Dipping Sauce
Shrimp in Garlic Sauce
Crab-stuffed Mushroom Caps
Chicken Steamed in Noodle Cases
Shrimp Balls, India
Chutney-stuffed Won Tons
Won Ton Appetizers
Spring Roll Miniatures

Surimi Crab Legs with Dipping Sauce

Prep. Time 5 minutes • Serves 6–8
Cooking Time 0

Served with any of the dipping sauces in Chapter 11, surimi crab legs make a quick and easy appetizer. Shelled, cooked fresh crab legs may also be used.

8 ounces thawed surimi crab
   legs, chilled
4 large iceberg lettuce leaves

1 recipe Vietnamese Dipping
   Sauce (page 229)

Cut each leg into three pieces. Arrange the lettuce leaves to cover a round serving plate. Pour the Vietnamese Dipping Sauce into a small bowl or a shallow glass and set it in the center of the leaves. Heap the pieces of crab leg onto the lettuce leaves and serve.

Surimi Fish Cakes with Teriyaki Sauce

Prep. Time 10 minutes • Serves 15
Cooking Time 0

6 packages surimi fish cakes,
   about 16 ounces, thawed
6 large leaves frilly lettuce

1 recipe Teriyaki Sauce
   (page 225)

Slice tubular surimi fish cakes into 2-inch pieces, or cut flat surimi fish cakes into wedges. Arrange the lettuce leaves on a large, round plate or platter. Arrange the fish cakes on the lettuce leaves with the Teriyaki Sauce in a small bowl in the center, and serve chilled.

Quail Eggs with Hoisin Dipping Sauce

*Prep. Time 20 minutes • Serves 6
Cooking Time 10 minutes*

Quail eggs are a specialty in the Orient—a pretty touch to add to a gourmet display—and are becoming available in the United States, so I've included this recipe even though it is not cooked in a wok. The taste is similar to regular eggs, just the look is different.

24 quail eggs　　　　　　　　　**1 recipe Hoisin Dipping Sauce**
6 whole iceberg lettuce leaves　　**(page 229)**

Place the eggs in a small saucepan and cover with cold water. Over medium-high heat, bring the water to a rapid boil, then reduce the heat and simmer 10 minutes. Chill the eggs under cold running water and refrigerate until ready to serve.

Choose small cupped lettuce leaves and arrange on a circular serving dish. Pour the Hoisin Dipping Sauce into a small bowl or shallow glass and set in the center of the leaves. Arrange the eggs in the lettuce cups and serve.

Tea Eggs

Prep. Time 10 minutes • Serves 8
Cooking Time 30 minutes

Simple hard-boiled eggs become a decorative appetizer when they are boiled in tea and spices. Any dark tea is acceptable for the purposes of this recipe.

8 small eggs
3 tablespoons black tea leaves
2 teaspoons salt
½ teaspoon ground ginger
1 teaspoon red pepper

5 cloves star anise
2 teaspoons soy sauce
1 recipe Sesame Sauce (page 216)

Place the eggs in a small pan in cold water to cover. Set over medium heat and bring to a boil. Reduce the heat and simmer 10 minutes. Remove the eggs, reserving the water. Cool the eggs slightly under cold running water. To the water remaining in the small pan, add the tea, salt, ginger, pepper, anise, and soy sauce, and bring to a boil.

Crack the egg shells slightly with a spoon, so the shell is cracked but still intact around the egg. Return the eggs to the pan, and simmer 20 minutes. Chill the eggs under cold running water, shell, quarter, and serve yolk side down so the pretty patterned whites show. Offer Sesame Sauce on the side.

Tomatoes, Squash, and Peppers, with Curry Dip

Prep. Time 5 minutes • Serves 6–8
Cooking Time 0

This is a colorful appetizer plate, especially if you can find the little golden cherry tomatoes, but it's also pretty with red cherry tomatoes. Curry Dip takes about 20 minutes to make, and can be made the day before.

½ small head leaf lettuce
2 small summer squash, quartered lengthwise
1 small zucchini, quartered lengthwise
1 yellow or red sweet pepper, seeded and cut into narrow strips
1 pint yellow or red cherry tomatoes, stemmed
1 small kohlrabi or medium carrot, peeled and cut into sticks
1 recipe Curry Dip (page 226)

Pick off six or eight lettuce leaves and arrange so the rib ends face the center of a large, round serving plate. Place a strip of squash along the rib of each lettuce leaf. Cut the zucchini strips in half and place a piece of zucchini between the pieces of squash so they alternate. Tuck the pepper between the squash and zucchini pieces, skin-side up. Pile the tomatoes in the center of the plate. Tuck the kohlrabi sticks in among the tomatoes so they stand out. Chill until ready to serve. Offer with Curry Dip that has been warmed just enough to soften.

Vegetables with Peanut Sauce

Prep. Time 10–15 minutes • Serves 6–8
Cooking Time 0

This is a very decorative appetizer plate and takes only minutes to put together once the sauce is made. Peanut Sauce takes 10 to 15 minutes to prepare and can be made the day before. If you wish, use different vegetables—broccoli, for instance, or kohlrabi sticks.

½ small head leaf lettuce
2 tiny zucchini, quartered
   lengthwise
1 tiny summer squash, quartered
   lengthwise
½ red or yellow sweet pepper,
   seeded and cut into narrow
   strips

½ small head cauliflower, cut
   into 1-inch-wide florets
10–20 snow peas, strings
   removed
1 recipe Peanut Sauce (page
   224)

Tear off six or eight lettuce leaves and arrange so the stems face the center of a large round serving plate. Place a strip of zucchini along the rib of each lettuce leaf. Cut the squash strips in half and place a piece of squash between the pieces of zucchini so they alternate. Tuck the pepper between the zucchini and squash pieces, skin-side up because it's shinier and prettier. Pile the cauliflower florets, stem-end down, in the center of the plate, building a "flower" tower about 3 inches high. Tuck the snow peas in among the cauliflower florets so they stand out from the flower. Chill until ready to serve. Offer with Peanut Sauce that has been warmed just enough to keep it loose. Wrap and chill any extra vegetable pieces to replenish the platter.

Seafood and Exotic Fruit Platter

Prep. Time 30 minutes • Serves 10–12
Cooking Time 4–6 minutes

An unusual combination of tropical fruits and seafood, sprinkled with Teriyaki Sauce. Any similar fruits may be used as substitutes—oranges for grapefruit, ripe peaches for mango, pears instead of bananas—and any pretty fruit, such as strawberries with the stems on, might be used to decorate the platter.

½ pound raw small shrimp, shelled and deveined
1 can pineapple chunks, drained, juice reserved
1 banana, sliced into ½-inch rounds
1 head frilly green lettuce
1 ripe avocado, peeled and sliced
1 small grapefruit, peeled, seeded, and sectioned
1 carambola, sliced horizontally to make ¼-inch star shapes
2 kiwi fruit, peeled and cut into ½-inch slices

1 papaya or mango, peeled, seeded, and cut into wedges
8 ounces surimi crab legs, thawed, cut in 2-inch pieces
8 ounces surimi lobster claws, thawed, sliced across into 6 pieces each
10 sprigs curly parsley
2 recipes Teriyaki Sauce (page 225)
2 recipes Piña Colada Dressing (page 217)

Steam the shrimp before preparing the rest of the ingredients. Fill the wok with hot water to within 1 inch of the steaming rack, remove the rack, cover the wok, and set to simmer (about 200°). Arrange the shrimp on the rack, and when the steam begins to escape from under the cover, set the rack in place, cover, and steam the shrimp 3 minutes, or until they are pink all over. Chill.

Prepare the fruits. Toss the banana in the reserved pineapple juice, then drain. Arrange the lettuce on a large serving platter, frilly side out. Arrange the fruit, crab, and lobster pieces on the lettuce, along with a ½-cup size glass bowl and a 1-cup size glass bowl. Surround the bowls with parsley hedges. Scatter the chilled shrimp over the platter, and pour the Teriyaki Sauce and Piña Colada Dressing into the glass bowls on the serving platter. Serve well chilled.

Shrimp in Garlic Sauce

Prep. Time 25 minutes • Serves 4–6
Cooking Time 3 minutes

Serve these shrimp on toothpicks stuck into a giant orange or a small grapefruit, or set on thin rounds of unpeeled cucumber. This recipe also makes a savory dinner for two, served with hot buttered rice, a tossed salad, and chilled lychees or mandarin oranges topped with vanilla yogurt.

**24 raw medium shrimp, shelled
and deveined**
1 tablespoon rice or cider vinegar
2 tablespoons vegetable oil
**1 ½-inch slice fresh ginger,
peeled and minced**
**3 green onions, trimmed to 3
inches and minced**

4 large cloves garlic, peeled
**1 tablespoon rice wine or dry
sherry**
1 tablespoon soy sauce
**½ recipe Vietnamese Dipping
Sauce (page 229), optional**

In a small serving bowl, toss shrimp with the vinegar. Heat the wok to medium high (375°); swirl in the oil and then add the shrimp and vinegar mixture and the ginger and onions. Stir-fry, turning the shrimp often, for 1 minute. Crush the garlic over the shrimp with a garlic press, and stir-fry a few seconds. Sprinkle the rice wine and soy sauce over the shrimp and continue turning and stirring until all are opaque and pink. In all, the shrimp should cook about 3 minutes, but might need 30 seconds or 1 minute more if they are quite large. Scrape the shrimp back into the serving bowl, and scrape drippings from the wok over them. Serve at once, with Vietnamese Dipping Sauce on the side if you wish.

Beef Koftas with Curry Dip

Prep. Time 30 minutes • Serves 6–8; makes 30 meatballs
Cooking Time 3–5 minutes

Koftas are Indian meatballs. Fragrant and spicy, with a tangy surprise in the middle, these koftas are always popular at parties. They're easy on the host, too, because they can be made hours before and given a final heating in the wok just before serving.

1 thick slice white bread
¼ cup half-and-half or milk
1 pound ground lean beef
1 egg
2 teaspoons garam masala
(page 36)
¼ teaspoon pepper
½ teaspoon salt
1 teaspoon ground coriander
½ teaspoon ground cumin

30 shreds pickled, preserved, or
candied ginger
3 tablespoons vegetable oil
6 cardamom pods
6 peppercorns
6 whole cloves
Pinch ground cinnamon
6 leaves frilly green lettuce
1 recipe Curry Dip (page 226)

In a food processor, place the bread and half-and-half. Process until combined. Add the beef. Add the egg, slightly beaten with the garam masala, pepper, salt, coriander, and cumin. Process until you have a fluffy mass.

Shape the meat into thirty balls: as you make each one, press a sliver of pickled, preserved, or candied ginger into the center. Heat the wok to medium (350°) and swirl in the oil. Add the cardamom, peppercorns, and cloves and stir-fry until they give off an odor. Stir in the cinnamon, then remove the whole spices and discard them. Stir-fry the meatballs in two batches. Add the meatballs to the hot oil. Stir-fry for 3 to 5 minutes until browned all around. After 3 minutes take one out and break it open: it should be just pink inside. Quickly remove all the meatballs from the oil to paper towel. Turn off the heat. Arrange the lettuce leaves on a serving plate, with the Curry Dip in a small bowl in the center. Heap the meatballs on the lettuce and serve at once.

NOTE: To half-cook the meatballs beforehand and finish them at the last minute, fry them 2 minutes the first time, and 2 minutes more just before serving.

Shiitake Mushrooms

Prep. Time 15 minutes • Serves 6–12
Cooking Time 2 minutes

Shiitake mushrooms are the mushrooms gourmets love to use.
Ordinary fresh mushrooms don't have the same glamour or flavor,
but they're still delicious. Because shiitake mushrooms are so rich, I
allow one per person or at most two—there are about twelve
medium mushrooms in a half pound. Buy only fresh, firm mushrooms.

12 (about ½ pound) medium-size   **1 recipe Sesame Sauce (page**
  fresh shiitake or common   **216) or Teriyaki Sauce**
  mushrooms   **(page 225)**

Wipe the mushrooms clean and remove the stems. Set stem-side
down on the wok steaming rack. Place the rack in the wok, and fill
the wok with 1 cup hot water. Turn the heat to high (400°) and
cover the wok. When steam starts to escape, time for 2 minutes,
then remove the mushrooms to a small, shallow serving dish,
stem-side up. Sprinkle Sesame Sauce or Teriyaki Sauce over the
mushrooms and allow to marinate at room temperature until serving time.

Long Beans in Garlic Marinade

Prep. Time 5 minutes; marinate 20 minutes • Serves 6–8
Cooking Time 6–8 minutes

Long beans, which can grow as long as 24 inches, make tasty finger food for parties when they are steamed and marinated in garlic and soy sauce. Leftovers are excellent in a tossed green salad. Winged beans, Kentucky Wonder beans, or any of the other long edible-shell beans might also be used while still young and tender.

½ pound fresh long or winged beans, strings removed

*Sauce*_____

1 tablespoon rice wine or dry sherry
1 teaspoon rice vinegar or cider vinegar
½ teaspoon sugar

1 tablespoon sesame oil
1 medium clove garlic, peeled and crushed
1 tablespoon soy sauce

If you are using long beans, cut them into 4-inch lengths; if using winged beans, leave whole. Arrange the beans on the steaming rack in the wok. Fill the wok to within 1 inch of the rack with hot water, cover, heat to simmer (about 200°), and steam the beans until crispy-tender, 6 to 8 minutes. While they are steaming, combine the sauce ingredients. Spread the cooked beans while still hot in a shallow serving bowl, and toss with the sauce. Allow to marinate at room temperature long enough to cool before serving.

Shrimp Steamed in Noodle Cases

Prep. Time 40 minutes • Serves 6–8
Cooking Time 20 minutes

These exotic morsels steamed in won ton skins are a hit at every party and are easy to make because the steaming requires no supervision and the dipping sauces can be prepared days ahead. Stuff the won ton skins, store under a damp towel in the refrigerator, and steam just before serving. Or freeze, and steam while still frozen for a minute or two longer than freshly prepared dumplings.

1½-inch piece fresh ginger
1 green onion, trimmed to
   3 inches
¼ pound raw, lean pork loin
   strips, cut in 2-inch pieces.
⅓ pound raw small shrimp,
   shelled and deveined
1 teaspoon cornstarch
1½ tablespoons soy sauce
1 tablespoon rice wine or dry
   sherry

6 canned water chestnuts,
   drained, rinsed, and chopped
30 won ton skins
1 egg, slightly beaten
1 tablespoon pickled ginger
   shreds
1 recipe Sichuan Sauce (page
   231), Vietnamese Dipping
   Sauce (page 229), or Hoisin
   Dipping Sauce (page 229)

In a food processor or blender mince the ginger, then add and coarsely chop the green onion. Add the pork, process until coarsely ground. Add the shrimp and process until the whole is a fluffy mass. Combine the cornstarch, soy sauce, and rice wine and mix into the pork/shrimp mixture. With a spoon, stir the water chestnuts into the mixture.

Open the package of won ton skins but keep the skins under a damp paper towel to keep them from drying out as you proceed with the recipe—uncover only the won ton skin you are going to stuff. Spoon about 1 rounded teaspoon of the mixture into the center of the skin. With your middle finger, brush egg along all four sides of the won ton skin. Bring together opposing corners of the skin and press a shred of ginger into the mixture so it sticks up. Press all four corners together. With your fingers, pinch together the edges of the skin so there will be no gaps for steam to get into. The won ton skin has now become a stuffed noodle case. Set it down on waxed paper or an oiled plate and stuff the remaining skins.

When you are almost ready to serve the noodle cases, transfer the cases to the oiled surface of the steaming rack. Place the rack in the wok, and fill the wok with hot water to 1 inch below the rack. Cover the wok and heat to simmer (about 200°). Steam 20 minutes. Serve at once with Sichuan Sauce, Vietnamese Dipping Sauce, or Hoisin Dipping Sauce on the side.

Variations:

Surimi Crab Steamed in Noodle Cases—Make the stuffing substituting for the pork and shrimp 8 ounces of surimi crab legs, which produces about 1¼ cups of fluffed up processed crab when put through a food processor or minced fine by hand. Serve the dumplings with Sweet and Sour Sauce (page 227) and Chinese prepared mustard.

Chicken Steamed in Noodle Cases—Make the stuffing using 8 ounces of cooked chicken or turkey breast—about 1¼ cups after mincing—instead of pork and shrimp. Serve with Sesame Sauce (page 216) into which you have stirred a small crushed clove of garlic.

Whole Shrimp in Noodle Cases—Toss 30 whole small shrimp, peeled, deveined, with 4 tablespoons of sweet and sour sauce mixed with 1 tablespoon of lemon juice. Seal 1 shrimp into each of 30 won ton skins, along with 1 shred of pickled ginger. Steam 20 minutes, and serve with Chinese prepared mustard and sweet and sour sauce (page 227), plum sauce, or hoisin sauce.

Ham and Pineapple in Noodle Cases—Process or mince by hand ⅓ pound cooked ham, and mix into it ½ cup of drained crushed pineapple mixed with ½ teaspoon of Chinese or Dijon mustard. Stuff 30 won ton skins and steam 20 minutes. Serve without sauce.

Crab-stuffed Mushroom Caps

Prep. Time 20 minutes • Serves 4–6
Cooking Time 20 minutes

This decorative dish is easy to prepare ahead, and then steam just before serving. A good choice for a party.

4 ounces cooked fresh crab or thawed surimi crab
1 small clove garlic, peeled
1 teaspoon rice wine or dry sherry
½ teaspoon ground ginger
1 small egg white, unbeaten
¼ teaspoon salt
18–24 medium-size fresh mushrooms, wiped clean and stemmed
Soy sauce
1 tablespoon grated orange rind

In a food processor or blender, or by hand, chop the crab fine: there should be about a cupful. Crush the garlic clove with a garlic press, and combine with the rice wine and the ground ginger. Mix into the crab. Stir in the egg white, then the salt. Set the mixture aside. Turn the mushroom caps upside down and stuff with mounds of crab mixture. Add a dash of soy sauce and a pinch of grated orange rind to each cap. Arrange on the wok steaming rack. Cover and keep refrigerated until ready to steam.

About 25 minutes before serving time, fill the wok with hot water to within 1 inch of the steaming rack. Cover the wok and heat to simmer (about 200°). Steam the caps 20 minutes. Serve warm.

Chicken Drumettes with Peanut Sauce

Prep. Time 5 minutes; marinate 10 minutes • Serves 8 as appetizer; 4 as main course • Cooking Time 10–15 minutes

Chicken wing halves are sold in supermarkets under various names— one of them is drumette. Small drumsticks may be used instead of drumettes. If you prefer, the chicken may be broiled in your stove on high instead of deep-fried.

24 chicken drumettes
1 tablespoon soy sauce
1 tablespoon rice vinegar
1 teaspoon sugar
1 tablespoon ground cumin

1½ teaspoons turmeric
Vegetable oil
1 recipe Peanut Sauce (see page 224), warm

Sprinkle the drumettes with the soy sauce, vinegar, sugar, cumin, and turmeric and toss well. Set aside to marinate 10 minutes.

Fill the wok to a depth of 1½ to 2 inches with oil. Heat the oil to high (400°), or until a day-old cube of bread browns in just under 1 minute. Heat another 4 minutes to stabilize the temperature. Line a large plate with paper towel and set in the oven at 250°. One by one, slide the chicken pieces into the hot oil, adding only as many as can float freely in the oil. Cook each batch until the pieces are a rich brown, about 3 minutes. With tongs or a slotted spoon, remove cooked pieces to the paper-lined plate and keep warm until all are done. Serve at once with warm Peanut Sauce.

Shrimp Balls, India

Prep. Time 5 minutes • Serves 6–8; makes 24 balls
Cooking Time 20 minutes

Delicious tidbits for a party, or for appetizers with an Indian meal.
Wonderful deep-fried, too.

4 green onions, trimmed to 3
   inches
2 cloves garlic, peeled
1½-inch piece fresh ginger,
   peeled
1 pound raw small shrimp,
   shelled and deveined
1 teaspoon turmeric
1 tablespoon ground coriander
Pinch cayenne
¼ teaspoon salt, or to taste

1 tablespoon grated fresh or
   dried coconut
1 tablespoon unflavored, dry
   bread crumbs
1 tablespoon cornstarch
1 recipe Sichuan Sauce (page
   231), Vietnamese Dipping
   Sauce (page 229), or Hoisin
   Dipping Sauce (page 229)

In a food processor mince the onions, garlic, and ginger together.
Add the shrimp and process until they are a fluffy mass. Add and
process the spices, seasoning, coconut, and bread crumbs. Taste,
and if desired, add more salt. Between your palms, roll the mixture
into 24 balls the size of walnuts. Roll the balls in cornstarch. Cover,
and refrigerate or freeze until ready to cook.

Fill the wok with hot water to 1 inch below the steaming rack.
Cover the wok and heat to simmer (about 200°). Place all the
shrimp balls on the steaming rack, cover the wok, and steam 20
minutes. Serve warm with Sichuan Sauce, Vietnamese Dipping
Sauce, or Hoisin Dipping Sauce.

If deep-frying, follow the recipe for Won Ton Appetizers, page 58.

Shrimp Balls, China

*Prep. Time 25 minutes • Serves 6–8; makes 24 balls
Cooking Time 20 minutes*

These delicious meaty little appetizers have a Chinese accent.

4 green onions, trimmed to 3
  inches
2 cloves garlic, peeled
1½-inch slice fresh ginger,
  peeled
1 pound raw small shrimp,
  shelled and deveined
¼ teaspoon salt
2 tablespoons raw or cooked
  ground pork

1 tablespoon rice wine or dry
  sherry
1 tablespoon soy sauce
1 small egg white, slightly
  beaten
1 tablespoon cornstarch
1 recipe Vietnamese Dipping
  Sauce (page 229)

In a food processor, mince together the onions, garlic, and ginger.
Add the shrimp and process until the contents are a fluffy mass.
Add salt, ground pork, rice wine, soy sauce, and the egg white and
process. With your hands, roll the mixture into 24 balls the size of
walnuts, then roll the balls in cornstarch. Cover and refrigerate until
ready to cook. The balls can be frozen at this point until ready to
use.

Fill the wok with water to 1 inch below the steaming rack. Cover
the wok and heat to simmer (about 200°). Place all the shrimp balls
on the steaming rack and steam for 20 minutes. Serve with
Vietnamese Dipping Sauce.

Won Tons (Basic Recipe)

Prep. Time 30 minutes • Serves 6–8, depending on use
Cooking Time 0

These piquant morsels—thin skins of dough stuffed with pork and shrimp—are deep-fried or steamed to make appetizers, or simmered in broth to make Won Ton Soup, a classic of Chinese cuisine. Raw won tons freeze well: fry frozen won tons a minute longer than fresh in oil at 375°.

¼ pound raw, lean, boneless
   pork loin
¼ pound small raw shrimp,
   shelled and deveined
6 drained canned, or peeled
   fresh water chestnuts, minced
1 ½-inch piece ginger, peeled
   and minced

1 green onion, trimmed to
   3 inches and minced
1 teaspoon cornstarch
1½ tablespoons soy sauce
1 tablespoon rice wine or dry
   sherry
30 won ton skins
1 egg, slightly beaten

In a food processor or blender, process the pork and shrimp together to make a fluffy mass. Turn the mixture into a mixing bowl and add the water chestnuts, ginger, and green onion. Combine the cornstarch, soy sauce, and rice wine and stir into the pork and shrimp mixture.

Open the package of won ton skins, but keep the skins under a damp paper towel to keep them from drying out as you proceed with the recipe—uncovering only the won ton skin you are going to stuff. Spoon about 1 rounded teaspoon of the mixture into the center of the skin and roll as illustrated. Bring the ends together, as shown in the third illustration, then press one end down on the other, firmly enough to seal, as in illustration 4. Set the won ton on your working surface. Dip your middle finger or a pastry brush in the beaten egg, brush the won ton ends lightly with the egg, then press the ends together once more to seal. Continue until all are filled and sealed. Deep-fry according to the instructions for Won Ton Appetizers (page 58) or steam according to instructions for Shrimp Steamed in Noodle Cases (p. 50), or set on an oiled plate, seal in plastic wrap, and freeze until ready to use.

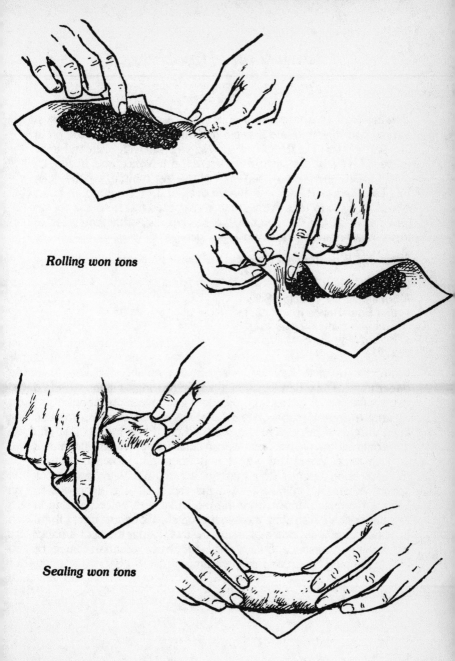

Rolling won tons

Sealing won tons

Won Ton Appetizers

Prep. Time 2–3 minutes • Serves 6–8
Cooking Time 10 minutes

Turning won tons into crispy appetizers takes just a few minutes. Served with mustard and a sweet and sour sauce, they're the hit at any party. If you like things hot, then serve them with Sichuan Sauce (page 231). Won tons can be prepared in advance and frozen, or made hours ahead and deep-fried at the last minute. Or they can be deep-fried, and kept warm in an oven at 250° for up to an hour. About thirty won tons are enough to serve as a first course for an Oriental meal for six. Garnish the serving dish with thin slices of fresh fruit—oranges, carambolas, or lychees.

30 stuffed Won Tons (see page 56)
Vegetable oil
Plum sauce, or 1 recipe Sweet and Sour Sauce (page 227), Sichuan Sauce (page 231), or Hoisin Dipping Sauce (page 229)

Chinese prepared mustard

Warm the oven to 250° and place in it a serving dish lined with paper towel. Have handy a slotted spoon or tongs. Fill the wok to a depth of 1½ to 2 inches with oil. Heat the oil to high (about 400°) or until a day-old cube of bread browns in just under 1 minute. Heat another 4 minutes to stabilize the heat. Place in the oil at one time only as many won tons as can float freely, about fifteen in a 14-inch wok. When the won ton bottoms are browned, 2 to 3 minutes, they upend. Any that don't turn, flip with tongs or a spoon. In another minute or two the tops will be a deep golden brown, ready to remove from the oil. Drain well before placing in the paper-lined dish. Fry the second batch. Continue until all are browned. Serve as soon as possible on fresh paper towel or a paper doily, with plum sauce, Sweet and Sour Sauce, Sichuan Sauce, or Hoisin Dipping Sauce and prepared mustard.

Chutney-stuffed Won Tons

Prep. Time 20–30 minutes • Serves 6–8
Cooking Time 10 minutes

Crispy won tons stuffed with luscious fruit chutney—so good they're sinful! Be sure to serve them with Curry Dip—a delicious combination. This method of sealing the won tons makes them look like little bags.

1¾ cups Chutney with Peaches, Mango, and Ginger (page 218), or other very good fruit chutney that is lumpy and not too wet

30 won ton skins
1 egg, slightly beaten
Vegetable oil
1 recipe Curry Dip (page 226)

Turn the chutney into a sieve to drain excess liquid. Open the package of won ton skins and cover the skins with paper towel that has been wet and wrung out. In your left hand, lay a won ton skin flat. Place a teaspoonful of chutney in the center of the skin. With your finger moisten the inner edges of the skin with egg. With the thumb and forefinger of your right hand, gather and press together the opposite corners of the won ton skin. Transfer the won ton to your right hand. Press the corners together again firmly, then give a half twist. This will gather the skin tightly around the filling. Be gentle—or you'll tear the skin or force the juices remaining in the chutney out through the skin. Before you put the won ton down, press the edges together one more time. Continue until all are stuffed and sealed.

Following the instructions in the recipe for Won Ton Appetizers (page 58), deep-fry the Chutney-stuffed Won Tons for 2 to 3 minutes, or until the skins are a rich golden brown. As you remove each fried won ton from the hot oil, turn it upside down for a moment to drain away excess oil. These taste best when they are eaten lukewarm and cooling. Serve with Curry Dip.

Variations:

Lychee-stuffed Won Tons—Stuff with 1½ cups drained canned lychees instead of chutney. Depending on the size of the lychees, cut into thirds or quarters to get 30 pieces. Deep-fry as directed and serve lukewarm.

Cashew-stuffed Won Tons—Stuff won tons with ½ cup drained chutney combined with 30 cashews. Deep-fry as directed and serve lukewarm.

Spring Rolls, Cantonese Style

Prep. Time 45 minutes • Serves 5–6; makes 10–12
Cooking Time 4–5 minutes

These crisp stuffed pastries, also known as egg rolls, are a popular first course in Chinese restaurants. Freeze after preparation and they should keep fresh for several months. Cook frozen spring rolls 5 to 6 minutes in oil at 375°.

1 cup minced raw shrimp (about ½ pound small shrimp, shelled and deveined)
1 tablespoon vegetable oil
1 cup ground raw pork loin, (about ⅓ pound boneless)
2 teaspoons soy sauce
2 teaspoons rice wine or dry sherry
2 green onions, trimmed to 4 inches and minced
1 stalk celery or 6 drained canned or peeled fresh water chestnuts, minced

⅓ head small cabbage, shredded fine (about 2 cups loosely packed)
1½ teaspoons salt
⅛ teaspoon pepper
2½ teaspoons sugar
10–12 spring roll skins
1 egg, slightly beaten
Vegetable oil
Chinese prepared mustard
Plum sauce or 1 recipe Sweet and Sour Sauce (page 227)

Reserve any liquid from the shrimp and include it when you add the minced shrimp to the wok.

Heat the wok to medium high (375°) and swirl in the oil. Add the pork and stir-fry until it begins to brown, about 3 minutes. Sprinkle with soy sauce and wine. Add the onions and stir-fry 1 minute. Add the celery and stir-fry 1 minute. Add the cabbage and stir-fry until the cabbage turns a brighter green, 2 to 3 minutes. Push everything to one side of the wok and add the shrimp and shrimp liquid if there is any. Stir-fry 2 minutes, mixing everything together after the first minute. Season with salt, pepper, and sugar. Taste and adjust seasonings to suit yourself. Turn off the heat.

Open the package of skins and peel off one skin. Wet a piece of paper towel, wring it dry, and place it over the skins to keep them from drying out as you work. Place the skin wrapper so that a corner is facing you on the counter or cutting board. Measure about 1½ slightly heaping tablespoons of the pork and shrimp mixture and pile in an oblong heap near the corner of the skin, as shown in the illustration. Roll the skin through the third step in the illustration.

With your finger or a pastry brush moistened in the slightly beaten egg, wet the edges of the fourth corner of the skin as shown in step three. Roll and seal as shown. Complete nine to eleven more rolls.

Place a paper-lined serving dish in the oven at 250°. Fill the wok to a depth of 1½ to 2 inches with vegetable oil. Heat the oil to high (400°), or until a day-old cube of bread browns in just under 1 minute. Let the wok heat another 4 minutes to stabilize the heat. With tongs or a slotted spoon, place half the spring rolls in the oil and fry 4 to 5 minutes, or until dark golden brown, turning often. Lift each roll from the oil and drain well before placing on the paper towel-lined plate. Fry the remaining rolls. Change the paper on the plate for a clean doily. Serve the rolls at once with Chinese mustard and plum sauce or Sweet and Sour Sauce.

Rolling spring rolls

Sealing spring rolls

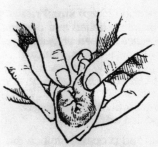

Spring Roll Miniatures

Prep. Time 30 minutes • Serves 6–8; makes 30 pieces
Cooking Time 8–10 minutes

These tiny spring rolls are a delicious dim sum item.

1 recipe stuffing for Won Tons
  (page 56) or Steamed Shrimp
  in Noodle Cases (page 50), or
  ½ recipe stuffing for Spring
  Rolls, Cantonese Style (page
  60)
30 won ton skins

1 egg, slightly beaten
Plum sauce, or 1 recipe Sweet
  and Sour Sauce (page 227)
  or Hoisin Dipping Sauce
  (page 229)
Chinese prepared mustard

Stuff and seal the won ton skins following instructions for filling and sealing Spring Rolls, Cantonese Style (page 60). Refrigerate under a damp, wrung-out paper towel and plastic wrap until ready to cook. Deep-fry following the instructions for Won Ton Appetizers (page 58). Serve immediately, with plum sauce or Sweet and Sour Sauce and Chinese prepared mustard or with Hoisin Dipping Sauce.

Shrimp Toast

Prep. Time 40 minutes • Serves 8–10
Cooking Time 15–20 minutes

These triangles of bread heaped with shrimp and ginger, then deep-fried, are very good! You can fry them at the last minute, or do them hours ahead and reheat in a medium oven. Leftovers freeze nicely: refry for just a moment before serving.

½ pound (1 cup) small raw
  shrimp, shelled and deveined
4 drained canned or peeled fresh
  water chestnuts, minced
1 egg, slightly beaten
1 tablespoon rice wine or dry
  sherry
1½-inch piece fresh ginger,
  peeled and minced

½ teaspoon salt
¼ teaspoon sugar
¼ teaspoon pepper
10 slices toasting white bread,
  slightly stale
Vegetable oil

In a food processor mince the shrimp to a fluffy mass, then turn the shrimp into a bowl and combine with the water chestnuts, egg, rice wine, ginger, salt, sugar, and pepper. Arrange the bread in two piles and remove the crusts. Then cut the bread from corner to corner twice, making 40 triangles. Spread with the shrimp paste. Make sure the paste is really stuck to the edges of the bread so it won't separate. Wrap in plastic wrap and refrigerate or freeze until ready to cook.

Heat a paper towel-lined serving dish at a 250° oven. Fill the wok to a depth of 1½ to 2 inches with oil. Heat the oil to high (400°), or until a day-old cube of bread browns in just under 1 minute. Heat another 4 minutes to stabilize the heat. Lower the pieces of shrimp toast into the oil one at a time, shrimp side down. Add no more than can float freely on the surface of the oil at one time—in a 14-inch wok that's about ten or twelve pieces at a time. When the edges brown, in 2–3 minutes, flip and brown the other side. Remove when browned on the top edges and keep warm until ready to serve.

Rice Chips

Prep. Time 5 minutes • 1 cup rice serves 2–4
Cooking Time 5–10 minutes

This recipe should be called How to Make Debits into Credits. It turns rice that has cooked dry and stuck to the pot into an appetizer. Tasty both with and without a dipping sauce.

Stuck-together cooked rice	Vegetable oil
Pickled ginger shreds	Dipping sauce of your choice
Garlic salt	(e.g., Teriyaki Sauce, page
Paprika	225), optional

Break the rice into lumpy shapes the size of a big potato chip. Press a shred of pickled ginger into the center of each lump, and sprinkle with garlic salt and paprika.

Heat a paper towel-lined serving dish in a 250° oven. Fill the wok to a depth of 1½ to 2 inches with oil. Heat the oil to high (400°), or until a day-old cube of bread browns in just under 1 minute. Heat another 4 minutes to stabilize the heat. Lower the rice chips into the oil one at a time. Add no more than can float freely on the surface of the oil at one time—in a 14-inch wok, that's about ten or twelve pieces. When the edges brown, flip and brown the other side. Remove when browned on the top edges and keep warm until ready to serve. Serve with dipping sauce, if you wish.

Pakoras, India

Prep. Time 20 minutes • Serves 6–8
Cooking Time 10 minutes

These vegetable fritters are a blessing when unexpected guests arrive and you've nothing to offer as an appetizer. Use any vegetables, from sweet potatoes and Bermuda onion rings to spinach and mushrooms.

2⅛ cups buttermilk pancake
  mix or plain pancake mix
1 tablespoon vegetable oil
1 cup milk
1 tablespoon curry powder
1 teaspoon salt
24–30 ½-inch-thick vegetable
  pieces, peeled if necessary

2 tablespoons pancake mix or
  flour
Vegetable oil
Dipping sauce of your choice
  (e.g., Curry Dip, page 226),
  optional

In a large bowl, blend the pancake mix, oil, milk, curry powder, and salt for the batter. In another bowl toss the vegetables in the 2 tablespoons of pancake mix. Place a paper towel-lined serving dish in a 250° oven.

Fill the wok to a depth of 1½ to 2 inches with oil. Heat the oil to high (400°), or until a day-old cube of bread browns in just under 1 minute. Heat another 4 minutes to stabilize the heat. While the oil is heating, add the vegetable pieces to the batter, mix to coat well, and when the oil is heated lower the pieces into the oil one at a time. Add only as many pieces as can float freely, about 10–12. Fry until golden brown on both sides—3 to 4 minutes for thick pieces, 1 or 2 minutes for thin pieces. Remove, drain, and keep warm in the oven until ready to serve.

Clams on the Half Shell, Shanghai

Prep. Time 15 minutes • Serves 4
Cooking Time 10 minutes

Clams and mussels have a tangy flavor done this way—a good appetizer for a party dinner. They render their juice as they open—but if there isn't enough, add chicken broth.

1 ½-inch piece fresh ginger, peeled
½ cup water
2 dozen small hardshell clams (cherrystone), cleaned

1 green onion, trimmed to 3 inches and minced
1 small clove garlic, peeled and minced
1 cup clam cooking liquid
3 tablespoons vegetable oil

Sauce

1 teaspoon rice vinegar or cider vinegar
2 tablespoons rice wine or dry sherry
2 tablespoons oyster sauce
1 tablespoon soy sauce
1 tablespoon thick soy sauce or soy sauce

1 teaspoon sugar
1 tablespoon sesame oil
1 tablespoon cornstarch
4 green onion bundles (page 233), optional
Parsley sprigs

Heat the oven to 400°. In a food processor or blender, or by hand, mince the ginger and measure out 1 teaspoonful. Combine the teaspoonful of ginger with the water and pour it into the bottom of a large flat baking dish. Set the clams on the dish and heat them in the oven until they open, 5 to 8 minutes. Add the onion and garlic to the remaining ginger, and mince. In a small bowl, combine the sauce ingredients. When the clams open, remove them from the oven and twist off and discard the top shell. Set the clams on a warm serving plate near the stove. Measure 1 cup of the clam cooking liquid (juice) into the sauce mixture in the bowl.

Heat the wok to medium low (300°), swirl in the oil, then stir in the ginger mixture, stir once or twice, mix in the clam juice mixture, and cook until it thickens and clears. Spoon the sauce over the clams and garnish with lots of parsley sprigs. Add the green onion bundles if you wish. Serve each guest six clams, one green onion bundle (if you are using them as part of your garnish), and a few sprigs of parsley.

Four

Classic Soups

Soup warms the heart, as well as the hands, and is a welcoming course to offer guests. It's easy on the cook because it can be made ahead. And it is even more fun when you have your guests use Oriental eating utensils.

In the cookbooks written for countries that use soy sauce, the chapter on soups often is last, or toward the end of the book. That's because broths, rather than teas, are the drink with food and are served toward the end of the meal. In colder regions of the East, a thick soup may be served early in the meal and the broths later. For this book, I've adhered to Western tastes by suggesting any of these soups as a first course, but see the menus for Chinese Dinners for 6 and 8 for examples of the Oriental sequence of serving soup.

The soups in this chapter are of both types: zesty, nourishing broths, such as the Japanese specialty, Miso, and thick gruels flavored with Indian spices, coriander, cumin, turmeric. Dried Fruit Soup, Iran, is Middle Eastern and doesn't quite belong, but I couldn't resist including it for its rich fruit flavor and because it complements any curry-seasoned meal. Won Ton Soup is a broth with dumplings and a classic of Chinese restaurants. All are easy to make, with either Basic Chicken Broth or Fast Chicken Broth, which are themselves excellent (see Chapter 2 for recipes).

Menu Suggestions

Chinese Luncheon for 4

Hot and Sour Soup
Rice Stick Noodles with Shrimp
Exotic Finger Fruits

Japanese Luncheon for 4

Miso Soup
Tofu and Vegetables Japanese Style
Steamed rice

Arabian Nights Luncheon for 4

Dried Fruit Soup, Iran
Pita bread
Tomato and Pepper Relish
Miniature Cantaloupe Stuffed with Mango (double recipe)

Indian Luncheon for 6

Dhal Mulegoo Thani, India
Toasted English Muffins
Three Color Salad
Fruit Platter with Yogurt Topping

Chinese Dinner for 2

Hot and Sour Soup
Hunan Bean Curd
Ginger Chicken Wings Marcel
Wilted Green Vegetable Salad (½ recipe)
Crushed Pineapple with Coconut Cream Topping

Chinese Dinner for 4

Won Ton Soup
Pork Fried Rice
Crisp Shrimp with Pineapple Sauce
Stir-fried Broccoli and Button Mushrooms (double recipe)
Chilled canned lychee nuts
Fortune Cookies

Chinese Dinner for 6

Won Ton Appetizers
Pork Fried Rice
Sichuan Shrimp
General Tso's Chicken (double recipe)
Vegetarian Delight
Hot and Sour Soup
Fortune Cookies

Chinese Banquet for 8

Spring Rolls, Cantonese Style (16 pieces)
Pork Fried Rice (double recipe)
Crispy Shrimp in Pineapple Sauce (double recipe)
Kung Pao Chicken (double recipe)
Vegetarian Delight (double recipe)
Steamed rice
Winter Melon Soup (double recipe)
Basket Exotic Finger Fruits
Fortune Cookies

Won Ton Soup

Prep. Time 10 minutes • Serves 6
Cooking Time 10–15 minutes

A clear, piquant chicken broth with pretty little won ton dumplings and bright green spinach leaves. A nice way to begin a Westernized Oriental meal, or serve it between courses at a banquet. The won tons can be your own, made from scratch, either fresh or frozen, or store-bought frozen won tons.

30 uncooked won tons (page 56),
  fresh or frozen
2 quarts boiling water
6 cups chicken broth
1 tablespoon rice wine or
  vinegar

1 tablespoon soy sauce
1 2-inch piece green onion,
  minced
12 fresh spinach leaves, washed
  and stemmed

Drop the won tons one at a time into the boiling water over high heat, reduce the heat, simmer 5 minutes, or until cooked.

Meanwhile, in the wok at medium high (375°), combine the chicken broth with the rice wine, soy sauce, and green onion. Bring to a simmer, then add the won tons and the spinach leaves. Return the broth to a boil, turn off the heat, and prepare to serve the soup at once. The spinach should be just wilted and bright green. Serve five won tons and two spinach leaves with the broth for each guest.

Miso Soup

Prep. Time 5 minutes • Serves 4
Cooking Time 5 minutes

Authentic Japanese miso soup is made from a broth based on bonito flakes and dried seaweed. The key flavoring is miso, a fermented soybean paste which is sold in Oriental food shops that carry Japanese specialties. Here's a simple version, very easy to prepare, that makes a pleasant beginning for any meal.

2 cups bottled clam juice
2 cups chicken broth
½ teaspoon Japanese soy sauce
¼ cup miso

1 square tofu
1 green onion, trimmed to
  2 inches, in 1-inch shreds (see
  page 233)

In the wok over medium heat (350°), bring the clam juice and chicken broth to a simmer and stir in the soy sauce and miso. Cover the tofu with boiling water, drain, cut into ¼-inch-wide strips, and add to the broth. When it comes back to a boil, ladle the broth into serving bowls, garnish with green onion shreds, and serve.

Birds' Nest Soup

Prep. Time 10 minutes • Serves 4–6
Cooking Time 20–25 minutes

Birds' nests, sold whole or broken in specialty shops, are gelatinous material produced by swifts living in the South Sea islands. Birds' Nest Soup is a Chinese banquet item, not everyday fare. Soak the nests 3 hours or overnight, pick out any feathers, and rinse in clean cold water before using.

6 cups chicken broth
4–6 birds' nests, soaked and
  cleaned
½ teaspoon salt
1 teaspoon minced ham

4 tablespoons cooked shredded
  chicken breast
1 tablespoon soy sauce
1 tablespoon sesame oil or
  minced cilantro

In the wok at medium high (375°), heat the broth to a simmer. Add the birds' nests and salt, and when the broth returns to simmering, reduce the heat to simmer (about 200°) and simmer uncovered for 20 minutes. Add the ham, chicken, and soy sauce. Stir a moment more. Add the sesame oil and serve at once.

Hot and Sour Soup

Prep. Time 15 minutes • Serves 4–5
Cooking Time 15 minutes

This is a Sichuan specialty popular in cold weather all over China, except in the Canton region. It's the perfect final touch for a rich, spicy meal to help digestion.

¼ cup dried tree fungus
¼ cup tiger lily buds
4 dried Chinese mushrooms
4 cups beef broth
1 cake bean curd, cut into
    ¼-inch strips
2 tablespoons cornstarch
¼ cup cold beef broth

1 tablespoon soy sauce
½ teaspoon black pepper
1½ tablespoons rice vinegar or
    cider vinegar
1 egg
1 teaspoon water

Cover the tree fungus, tiger lily buds and mushrooms with boiling water and soak until soft, 5 to 15 minutes. Drain and squeeze dry. Sliver the fungus and mushrooms.

In the wok set at medium high (375°), combine the beef broth with the fungus, lilies, mushrooms, and bean curd, and bring to a simmer. Reduce the heat to simmer (about 200°), and cook 10 minutes. Combine the cornstarch with the cold beef broth, soy sauce, pepper, and vinegar, and stir into the soup.

Just before serving, reheat the soup to a simmer, mix the egg slightly with the water, and pour into the gently simmering soup in a slow, thin stream. Do not let the soup boil. Serve at once.

Winter Melon Soup, China

Prep. Time 20 minutes • Serves 6
Cooking Time 25 minutes

A banquet dish in China, served in the scooped-out shell of the winter melon at the end of the meal. The edges of the shell are serrated for the occasion, and at very special banquets a design is etched on the skin. In our markets, the big pale green melon is cut up and sold by the pound. This recipe was given to me by my friend, Alice Schryver, author of *Chinese Cooking for Beginners.*

2 teaspoons soy sauce
⅛ teaspoon pepper
½ teaspoon cornstarch
2 teaspoons water
6 cups chicken broth
¼ cup ground pork
1 pound winter melon, seeds and pulp removed, cut into 1-inch cubes
6 dried Chinese mushrooms, soaked in hot water to cover until soft, stems removed; halved

¼ cup canned, drained, rinsed bamboo shoots, cut into pieces ⅛ inch wide
8 water chestnuts, peeled, cut into ⅛ inch thick rounds
1–2 teaspoons chicken broth granules, if needed
1 green onion, trimmed to 3 inches, minced

In separate small bowls, combine the soy sauce and pepper, and the cornstarch and water. Heat the wok to medium high (375°), add the broth and bring it to a rapid boil. Add the pork, breaking it into crumbs in the broth, then add the melon, mushrooms, bamboo shoots, and water chestnuts. Bring the broth back to boiling, reduce the heat to simmer and cook, uncovered, until the melon is translucent, about 15 minutes. Add the soy sauce mixture. Stir in the cornstarch mixture. When the broth clears, taste, and add chicken broth granules a teaspoon at a time until you are satisfied with the flavor of the soup. Garnish with the green onion, and serve hot.

Dried Fruit Soup, Iran

Prep. Time 15 minutes • Serves 4–6
Cooking Time 1 hour 40 minutes

Delicious to serve before an Indian meal, or by itself with hot Indian bread or English muffins. Almost better the second day. This recipe is reprinted from my book *A Feast of Soups*.

¾ pound meaty lamb neck or
    shank
½ cup yellow split peas
1 onion, chopped
8 cups water (or more)
1 teaspoon salt
¼ teaspoon pepper
1 teaspoon turmeric
¼ teaspoon saffron threads

¼ teaspoon ground coriander
½ teaspoon ground cumin
¼ cup pitted, chopped dried
    prunes
¼ cup pitted, chopped dried
    apricots
1 tablespoon lemon juice
Salt

In the wok, combine the lamb and all the ingredients except the dried fruits, lemon juice, and extra salt. Heat the wok to medium high (375°), cover, bring to a boil, reduce the heat to simmer (about 200°), and cook 1 hour. Add the chopped fruit and simmer uncovered 30 minutes more. Stir often, and if the soup is getting too thick, add more water. Just before serving stir in the lemon juice; add more salt if desired. Serve hot.

Dhal Mulegoo Thani, India

Prep. Time 15 minutes • Serves 4–6
Cooking Time 1 hour 15 minutes

A beautiful orange-red soup made of lentils and flavored with Indian spices. It's thick enough to be a meal in itself. *Dhal* is the Indian for "pulse," the edible seeds of leguminous crops—peas, beans, and lentils, for instance. This is another recipe from my book *A Feast of Soups*.

1 cup red lentils	2 teaspoons turmeric
7 cups water	1 teaspoon ground coriander
1 small bay leaf	½ teaspoon ground cumin
1 small onion, chopped	1 teaspoon strained lime or
2 tablespoons butter	lemon juice
1 large clove garlic, minced	2 teaspoons salt
⅛ teaspoon red pepper or cayenne (or more)	

In the wok, combine the lentils with the water and bay leaf, heat to medium high (375°), cover, and bring to a boil. Reduce the heat to simmer (about 200°), and cook until the lentils are very soft, about 1 hour. Check often and stir to make sure the lentils aren't sticking to the bottom of the wok, and that the water isn't evaporating too quickly. Add more water if the soup is getting very thick and the lentils are uncooked. Evaporation in some woks is faster.

In a small saucepan over medium heat, sauté the onion in the butter with the garlic, red pepper, turmeric, coriander, and cumin for 5 minutes, stirring. Scrape this into the lentils with the lime juice and salt. Serve hot.

Five

Exotic Rice and Noodle Dishes

Rice is a staple of the Oriental diet and is integral to Oriental cuisine. It adds "filler" or bulk to Oriental meals which otherwise might leave one feeling hungry, and provides essential carbohydrates for a balanced meal. You may not want to serve rice with every Oriental meal, especially when preparing light meals for two, but it does enhance the flavors of many entrées, particularly those in a luscious sauce. Dishes like Lamb in Honey Sauce, Peking Style, or Shrimp with Coconut and Tamarind, Thai Style, just aren't satisfying without rice.

There are only 120 calories in a ⅔–cup portion of rice. Since the caloric content of many wok entrées is minimal, you can afford a little rice in your diet.

At a traditional Chinese dinner, a small bowl of plain rice is served to each person, while the entrées are set in the center of the table for everyone to dip into with chopsticks. Be aware that to leave even a grain of rice on the plate is considered a breach of etiquette by many Orientals. In India and countries in which curries predominate, rice is also served to each diner in an individual bowl. The rice may be either plain boiled or a pulao (pilaff). Some exotic rice dishes, like Philippine Nasi Goreng, are served as entrées.

Noodles, too, are integral to many Oriental recipes—for instance, Chicken Lo Mein. (The Chinese word for noodle is *mein*; all *lo mein* dishes are noodle-based.) In fact, in some regions of the Far East, noodles take the place of rice. In this country, Oriental markets offer a wide variety of noodles, among them rice stick noodles, which are narrow flat white sticks sold in neat bundles, and transparent bean thread or cellophane noodles, made from mung beans. Experiment with these noodles in recipes like Rice Stick Noodles with Shrimp, or Cellophane Noodles and Pork. Or try Fried Cellophane Noodles to add interesting texture to an entrée.

A Shopper's Guide to Rice

Converted long-grain rice: This is the "white" rice most of us are used to, and is the type usually offered with Chinese and Indian cuisine. It has been steam-treated or "polished" to remove the outer husk so that when cooked its grains will be tender and white, and, if properly prepared, will not stick together.

Brown rice: More nutritious than converted rice because it has not been polished and therefore retains the husk and all its nutrients. Unfortunately, however, the nutty flavor of brown rice does not complement delicately flavored Oriental foods the way white rice does.

Oval rice: Also called glutinous rice. A short-grain white rice that cooks up sticky—perfect when using chopsticks! It's the preferred rice in Japan. Available in Oriental specialty shops.

Menu Suggestions

Chinese Dinner for 4

Hot and Sour Soup
Chicken Lo Mein
Sichuan Shrimp
Radish Slices with Sesame Oil
Chilled canned lychee nuts

Chinese Dinner for 6

Spring Roll Miniatures, with Sweet and Sour Sauce
and Mustard Dipping Sauce
General Tso's Chicken
Shrimp with Vegetables
Steamed Rice
Fresh pineapple chunks
Strawberries, stems on

Indian Dinner for 6

Pakoras, India
Chicken and Shrimp Pulao, India
Raita
Onion Samball
Chilled mangoes

Basic Recipes for Cooking Rice

Rice	Yield	Serves 2–3	Water	Salt	Butter/Oil	Cook
Steamed rice	1½ cups	½ cup long-grain converted rice, raw	1¼ cups	½ tsp.	½ tbsp.	20–25 minutes
Sticky rice for chopsticks	1½ cups	½ cup oval, pearl, or short-grain rice, raw	1¼ cups	½ tsp.	½ tbsp.	20–25 minutes
Brown rice	2 cups	½ cup brown rice, raw	1¼ cups	½ tsp.	1 tbsp.	40–45 minutes

DIRECTIONS: In a medium-size saucepan that has a tightly fitting lid, bring the water, covered, to boiling. Add the salt, butter, and rice, stir a few seconds, then simmer, covered, for the time given above. Then remove the rice from the heat and keep covered until ready to serve. To reheat rice, place it in a steamer in the wok and steam until hot, about 10 minutes.

NOTE: Rinse oval rice in cold water until it runs clear. Converted and brown rice need not be rinsed. Allow ½ to ⅔ cup cooked rice per portion.

Saffron Rice, India

Prep. Time 10 minutes • Serves 4–6
Cooking Time 30 minutes

This beautiful golden rice, flavored with onion sautéed in butter and spices, is served as a main course for special occasions in India. Chutney is offered with it. You can serve it as either a main dish or an accompaniment.

½ teaspoon saffron threads
2 tablespoons hot water
1 teaspoon vegetable oil
½ stick butter
1 large onion, sliced
¼ teaspoon ground ginger
⅛ teaspoon ground clove
⅛ teaspoon ground cinnamon
¼ teaspoon ground cardamom

¼ teaspoon cumin seeds
1 cup raw converted long-grain rice
2½–3 cups chicken broth
3 tablespoons rice wine or dry sherry
Italian parsley or cilantro sprigs

Soak the saffron in the hot water. Heat the wok to medium (350°), swirl in the oil, stir in the butter, then add the onion and stir-fry until golden—about 3 minutes. Remove half the onion. Let the remaining onion brown while you add all the spices but the saffron. Stir in the rice and stir-fry 3 to 4 minutes, or until the rice is translucent. Stir in 2½ cups of the chicken broth, reduce the heat to simmer (about 200°), cover the wok, and cook until the broth has been absorbed, about 15 minutes. Check the broth level often and add more if it is evaporating too quickly.

When the broth is evaporated, the rice will be almost cooked. Stir in the saffron, its liquid, the onions, and the rice wine. Cover and cook another 3 minutes. Keep warm until ready to serve. Garnish with parsley or cilantro leaves.

Cantonese Shrimp Fried Rice

Prep. Time 15 minutes • Serves 4–6
Cooking Time 6–7 minutes

A traditional fried rice, rich with the flavor of shrimp, ham, and onions and crunchy with nut meats. A good second dish for dinner parties since it can be made ahead and kept warm without losing its quality. If you don't have dried shrimp, use more ham instead. Make the cooked rice a day or two before, and refrigerate to have on hand.

2 heaping tablespoons bacon fat
2 tablespoons dark seedless raisins, soaked in hot water until plump, then drained
½ cup dried shrimp, minced
⅓ cup Smithfield or boiled ham, minced
½ cup broken walnuts
½ cup slivered almonds

3 green onions, trimmed to 3 inches and chopped
2 tablespoons soy sauce
½ teaspoon salt
¼ cup thawed frozen peas
3 cups cooked converted long-grain rice

Heat the wok to medium high (375°), add the bacon fat, and stir until it melts. Add the raisins, shrimp, and ham, tossing for 1 minute after each addition. Stir in the walnuts and almonds. Add the green onions and stir-fry 1 minute. Stir in the soy sauce. Season with salt and mix in the peas. Add the cooked rice and stir-fry 2 minutes more, aiming to get each grain of rice separate and covered with sauce. Keep warm until ready to serve.

Variation:

Chicken Fried Rice—Use 1 to 2 cups of diced cooked chicken scraps (skin included) instead of ham and shrimp.

Pork Fried Rice

Prep. Time 10 minutes • Serves 4–6
Cooking Time 6–7 minutes

This tasty, classic fried rice is simple to make with leftover pork roast drippings. If this is not on hand, use 1 tablespoon vegetable oil or butter, and 1 tablespoon half and half. Make the cooked rice a day or two before, and refrigerate to have on hand.

2 heaping tablespoons fat of pork roast drippings
2 large cloves garlic, peeled and minced
1–2 cups diced pork roast
3 green onions, trimmed to 3 inches and chopped

¼ cup soy sauce, or to taste
About ¼ cup pork roast gravy, or beef broth
¼ cup thawed frozen peas
3 cups cooked converted long-grain rice

Heat the wok to medium high (375°) and stir in the pork roast drippings. Brown the garlic in the drippings, then add the pork and the green onions and stir-fry for 1 minute. Stir in the soy sauce and the pork roast gravy, then mix in the peas. Add the rice and stir-fry 2 minutes more, aiming to get each grain of rice separate and covered with sauce. Keep warm until ready to serve.

Philippine Nasi Goreng

Prep. Time 30 minutes • Serves 4
Cooking Time 6–8 minutes

This mélange of chicken, shrimp, and rice in a hot savory sauce topped by chopped peanuts can be prepared very quickly if you start with leftover cooked rice. It's particularly good with Orange Beef (page 130) and Vegetarian Delight (page 206).

1 small cucumber
2 tablespoons vegetable oil
1 pound skinned, boned chicken breast, cut into 1-inch cubes
½ pound small shrimp, shelled and deveined
1 cup cooked converted long-grain rice

1 egg scrambled loose with 3 tablespoons milk, mashed to a fine curd
5 ¼–inch wide strips sweet red pepper
2 tablespoons chopped raw peanuts

Sauce

¼ cup chicken broth
1 medium clove garlic, peeled and mashed
2 green onions, trimmed to 3 inches and minced

2 teaspoons shrimp paste in bean oil
1 teaspoon Hunan or chili paste
1 teaspoon soy sauce

Cut away the stem ends of the cucumber and 3 broad strips of the peel, then in a food processor or by hand, cut into thin slices. Arrange the cucumber rounds around the outside of a shallow circular serving dish. Mix the sauce ingredients together in a small bowl. Warm a medium-size bowl in a 250° oven.

Place each measured ingredient beside the wok in the order in which it is to be placed in the wok.

Heat the wok to medium low (300°) and swirl in the oil. Add the chicken and stir-fry for 3 minutes. Push to one side, add the shrimp, and stir-fry 3 minutes, or until pink and opaque. Push to one side. Pour in the sauce and when it is bubbling combine with the chicken and shrimp. Turn off the heat. Stir in the cooked rice and toss until it is well combined with the sauce. Turn the mixture into the warmed bowl and keep warm until ready to serve.

Unmold the rice into the center of the cucumber-circled dish and surround with the scrambled egg. Use the red pepper strips to make a decorative Chinese-style character in the center of the rice, and sprinkle with chopped nuts. Serve as soon as possible.

Chicken and Shrimp Pulao, India

Prep. Time 30 minutes • Serves 6
Cooking Time 30 minutes

An Indian-style rice pilaff—exotic, spicy, and fragrant! Serve with Tomato and Pepper Relish (page 223) and a salad, and finish off with chunks of fresh pineapple rolled in coconut.

½ teaspoon saffron threads
2 tablespoons hot water
1 pound skinned, boned chicken breast, cut into 2-inch pieces
1 teaspoon salt
3 large cloves garlic, peeled and minced
3 tablespoons dark, seedless raisins
¼ teaspoon ground cinnamon
¼ teaspoon ground cardamom
¼ teaspoon ground mace or nutmeg

1 teaspoon ground cloves
⅛ teaspoon pepper
1 teaspoon vegetable oil
1 stick butter
2 large onions, sliced in rings
2 cups raw converted long-grain rice
1 pound small raw shrimp, shelled and deveined
2 cups chicken broth
2 cups beef broth
2 tablespoons whole almonds

Soak the saffron in the water. Sprinkle the chicken with salt and set aside. In a small bowl, combine the garlic, raisins, and all the spices except the saffron.

Heat the wok to medium (350°), swirl in the oil, and melt in the butter. Stir-fry the onions until crisp, 4 to 7 minutes. Remove with a slotted spoon to a paper towel. Add the chicken pieces and stir-fry 1 minute. Add the garlic and spice mixture and stir-fry until the chicken browns, 4 to 5 minutes. Add the rice and stir-fry until it becomes opaque, 3 to 5 minutes. Stir in the shrimp, then the broths. Stir until they begin to boil, then cover, reduce heat to simmer (about 200°), and cook until most of the liquid is absorbed, about 10 minutes. Stir in the saffron and its liquid and the almonds. Cover and cook 5 minutes more, until all the liquid is absorbed and the rice is tender. Serve hot sprinkled with the fried onions.

Fried Rice Patties, Shanghai

Prep. Time 15 minutes • Serves 2
Cooking Time 6–8 minutes

Make these sizzling hot rice cakes flavored with ginger and shrimp from leftover or freshly cooked rice, either regular converted long-grain rice or Sticky Rice (page 77). This is a different version of fried rice, and one that is very good with meaty Chinese entrées and Indian curries.

1 ¼-inch piece fresh ginger,
  peeled
¼ pound small shrimp, shelled
  and deveined
1 egg white
1 tablespoon rice wine or dry
  sherry
1 teaspoon soy sauce

¼ teaspoon sugar
1½ cups cooked rice
Vegetable oil
1 green onion, trimmed to 3
  inches and cut into shreds
  (see page 233)

In the food processor or blender, or by hand, mince the ginger. Add the shrimp and chop coarsely. Turn the ginger/shrimp mixture into a small bowl and combine with the egg white, rice wine, soy sauce, and sugar. Mix in the rice until it is bound by the egg white mixture. Heat a serving dish lined with paper towels in a 250° oven.

Fill the wok with oil to a depth of 1½ to 2 inches. Heat the oil to high (400°), or until a day-old cube of bread browns in just under 1 minute. Heat another 4 minutes to stabilize the heat. Slide half the rice mixture into the oil. Without stirring, cook 3 minutes, or until golden along the edges. Use a sieve and spatula to turn the rice cake without breaking it. Cook 2 minutes more, or until golden brown. Transfer to the heated serving dish and keep warm while you cook the remaining half. Serve hot, sprinkled with onion shreds.

Rice Stick Noodles with Shrimp

Prep. Time 15 minutes • Serves 2–3
Cooking Time 10–14 minutes

Shrimp and Chinese cabbage enhance this delicious dish of rice noodles. Chinese cabbage (napa) shreds easily in the food processor or with a hand grater: discard the tough bottom part of the cabbage before grating. This is a good dish to serve with any of the Chinese chicken or pork entrées.

⅓ pound rice stick noodles
¼ Chinese cabbage, or small green cabbage
1 ¼-inch piece fresh ginger, peeled
1 green onion, trimmed to 3 inches
4 tablespoons vegetable oil

½ pound small shrimp, shelled and deveined
1 tablespoon rice wine or dry sherry
½ teaspoon salt
½ teaspoon sugar
1 tablespoon soy sauce
½ cup chicken broth

Soak the rice stick noodles in cold water to cover for 6 minutes, then drain. In a food processor, or by hand, shred the cabbage and turn into a bowl. In the processor, or by hand, mince together the ginger and onion.

Heat the wok to medium high (375°) and swirl in 2 tablespoons of the oil. Add the ginger/onion mixture and stir-fry 1 minute. Add the shrimp and stir-fry until pink, about 3 minutes. Sprinkle with the wine and push up onto the side of the wok. Pour the remaining 2 tablespoons of oil into the wok, and add the cabbage. Stir-fry for 2 minutes. Season with the salt, sugar, and soy sauce. Push up onto the side of the wok. Turn the noodles into the wok and stir-fry 1 minute. Pour in the broth and cook 3 minutes, stirring. Combine all the ingredients in the wok, heat through, and serve as soon as possible.

Chicken Lo Mein

Prep. Time 15 minutes • Serves 2–4
Cooking Time 15 minutes

This traditional Chinese fare of chicken and noodles served in a delicately flavored sauce with crunchy vegetables is a very good selection when you have leftover chicken or noodles. It can be prepared ahead and kept warm, so it's a good company recipe. Please be aware that these noodles are cooked before you begin the recipe.

1½ tablespoons cornstarch
3 tablespoons water
2 tablespoons chicken fat or vegetable oil
2 cups diced cooked chicken
½ cup shredded Chinese cabbage or cabbage
½ cup celery, shredded
½ cup bean sprouts

1 teaspoon sugar
1 cup chicken broth
2 tablespoons soy sauce
Salt and pepper
½ pound cooked narrow noodles
2 green onions, trimmed to 3 inches and minced

Combine the cornstarch with the water.

Heat the wok to medium high (375°), melt the fat in it or swirl in the oil, and add the chicken. Stir-fry 1 minute. Add the cabbage, celery, and bean sprouts, stir-frying 1 minute after each addition. Season with sugar. Push everything up the side of the wok and pour in the broth and the soy sauce. Cover the wok, reduce the heat to simmer (about 200°) and cook 10 minutes. Make a space in the center of the wok, pour in the cornstarch mixture, and stir until the sauce thickens and clears. Season with salt and pepper. Mix in the noodles, and keep warm until ready to serve. Garnish with minced green onion.

Cellophane Noodles and Pork

Prep. Time 15 minutes • Serves 2
Cooking Time 10–12 minutes

Bean thread is another name for these transparent noodles that cook into a silvery spaghetti, a bit slippery to eat but beautiful to serve. As a garnish to give the dish a crisp texture, you can top with more cellophane noodles, deep-fried for 30 seconds in hot oil—but you'll enjoy the dish even without this exotic topping.

6 dried Chinese mushrooms
2 ounces cellophane noodles (mung bean thread)
1 ¼-inch piece fresh ginger, peeled
1 green onion, trimmed to 3 inches
1 medium clove garlic, peeled
¼ pound boneless pork tenderloin
¼ pound small shrimp, shelled and deveined
2 teaspoons cornstarch
2 tablespoons cold water

2 tablespoons vegetable oil
1 tablespoon rice wine or dry sherry
2 tablespoons soy sauce (or more)
4 fresh water chestnuts, peeled and quartered, or 6 canned water chestnuts, drained, rinsed, and halved
¾ cup mushroom-soaking water
Fried Cellophane Noodles (page 87), optional

Soak the mushrooms in hot water to cover until soft—5 to 15 minutes. Cover the cellophane noodles with boiling water and soak 5 minutes. Drain the noodles and cover with cold water. Drain again. In a food processor or blender, or by hand, mince together the ginger, onion, and garlic and turn onto a plate. In the processor or by hand, mince the pork and remove to another plate, then mince the shrimp. Drain the mushrooms, reserving ¾ cup of the soaking liquid, discard the tough stems, and shred the mushrooms. Combine the cornstarch with the 2 tablespoons of cold water.

Place each measured ingredient beside the wok in the order in which it will be placed in the wok.

Heat the wok to medium high (375°). Swirl in the oil and stir-fry the ginger mixture 1 minute. Stir in the pork, and mash and stir-fry until all the pink is gone—2 to 3 minutes. Add the mushroom shreds and stir-fry 1 minute. Add and stir-fry the shrimp until cooked through, about 3 minutes. Season with the rice wine and soy sauce. Push the ingredients to the side, add the water chestnuts, and stir-fry 2 minutes more. Push everything up onto the side.

Pour in the mushroom water. Reduce the heat to simmer (about 200°) and mix the noodles into the sauce. Simmer 2 minutes. Stir in the cornstarch mixture, then toss everything together until well mixed. Taste, and add more soy sauce if desired. Keep warm until ready to serve. Serve with a handful of Fried Cellophane Noodles crushed over the top, if desired.

Fried Cellophane Noodles

Prep. Time 2 minutes • Serves for 2–4 as garnish
Cooking Time 1 minute

This is fun! Drop cellophane noodles into a wok with hot oil—they pop instantly into a crispy mass, like Medusa's hair. It's a nifty trick to display for guests, and adds a very satisfactory crunch to entrées like Cellophane Noodles and Pork (page 86).

½ cup cellophane noodles (bean   **Vegetable oil**
  thread) (about 2 inches from   **Salt**
  a 2-ounce package)

With a sharp carving knife, chop about 2 to 3 inches from the end of the package of cellophane noodles.

Fill the wok with oil to a depth of about 1½ inches. Heat the oil to high (400°), or until a day-old cube of bread browns in just under 1 minute. Throw the noodles into the hot oil. Almost immediately they'll pop up into a huge mass of twisted, crisped threads. At once, remove the mass with a sieve to paper towels. Sprinkle very lightly with salt and allow to drain until ready to serve. To serve, crumble by the handful over the entrée.

Sizzled Noodle Shreds

Prep. Time 15 minutes • Serves 2
Cooking Time 4–5 minutes

Leftover thin egg noodles are delicious flavored and deep-fried this way. Serve instead of rice or fried rice.

1 cup cooked thin noodles, cold
¼ cup raw shrimp, shelled and deveined
½ egg white
¼ teaspoon ground ginger
½ teaspoon salt
⅛ teaspoon pepper
Vegetable oil

Set the noodles in a medium bowl. In a food processor or by hand chop the shrimp into small pieces and combine with the egg white, ginger, salt, and pepper. Combine with the noodles without attempting to separate the noodles.

Fill the wok with oil to a depth of 1½ to 2 inches. Heat the oil to high (400°), or until a day-old cube of bread browns in just under 1 minute. Heat 4 minutes more to stabilize temperature. Lower the noodle clumps into the oil and cook without stirring until the edges begin to brown. Use a slotted spoon or a fork to break the clumps into 2- or 3-inch pieces, turn, and brown on the other side. Remove with a slotted spoon, drain on paper towels, taste, and add salt if desired. Serve hot.

Six

Fu Yungs and Bean Curd or Tofu Dishes

Fu yungs and dishes including wok-cooked bean curd or tofu are side dishes or luncheon or light supper entrées—they are delicious, easy to prepare, and lend a special Oriental touch to meals.

Fu yungs are somewhat like egg pancakes. They're sizzled in light oil and filled with good things like crabmeat, lobster, and savory bits of cooked pork, shrimp, or vegetables.

Cooking a fu yung presents the basic challenge offered by *omelettes fines herbes.* The cooking utensil must allow the beaten egg to congeal at once and slide around its surface to make a container for the filling ingredients. Put simply, your fu yung mustn't stick to the wok or you'll have scrambled eggs. A simple way out is to cook the fu yung in deep oil. That results in a delicious fu yung, but unfortunately one that is filled with oil!

Another way is to cook the fu yung in an omelet pan or a pan with a no-stick surface. The middle route is to cook the fu yung in 1 or 2 tablespoons of oil in a hot wok that lets things slide around (see Cleaning Your Wok, page 5). Beef Fu Yung is a good recipe to learn on, as is Crab Fu Yung, because both are fast and easy, and the results are delicious—a real reward for having learned a new egg trick.

Tofu and bean curd are used as a major nonmeat source of protein in the Far East. *Bean curd* is a cheeselike substance made of white soybeans which have been cooked, mashed, and pressed into cakes. *Tofu,* the Japanese version, is less firm. In this country, supermarket produce departments and Oriental greengrocers sell tofu and/or bean curd from water-filled tubs. Both are generally available in chunks 1 inch thick by 3 inches square. When my recipes call for a "piece" of bean curd or tofu, this is about the size meant.

Both bean curd and tofu are cooked products and need only to be heated through or tossed with hot ingredients or sauce long enough to absorb their flavor.

When planning a menu, consider tofu or bean curd as a meat dish. Use the recipe for Tofu with Vegetables as a guide to adding bean curd to stir-fried dishes. Add tofu to salads, as suggested in Chapter 11. Substantial salads and relishes are good side dishes for tofu entrées. And, since tofu and bean curd have practically no calories (72 calories per 3½ ounces), you can indulge in a rich dessert—bananas and cream or bananas in crushed pineapple, for instance.

The bean curd recipes in this book were supplied primarily by Bell Wong, my restaurateur friend, who hails from Shanghai and Canton.

A Shopper's Guide to Bean Curd and Tofu

As a rule of thumb, one piece of bean curd or tofu serves one person. Rinse with cold water and store in water to cover in the refrigerator. Change the water every day or so and always rinse again before using. It will keep about ten days. Fresh bean curd is firm and has no sour odor.

Bean curd: Chinese bean curd is best for stir-frying because it is firmer.
  SUBSTITUTE: Tofu.
Tofu: Japanese bean curd is best for salads.
  SUBSTITUTE: Bean curd.

Menu Suggestions

Light Luncheon for 2

Sichuan Bean Curd
Stir-fried Asparagus and Water Chestnuts
Sliced chilled grapefruit and oranges

Thai Luncheon for 2

Hot and Sour Soup (½ recipe)
Pork Fu Yung, Thailand
Steamed rice
Papaya halves served with lime

Chinese Luncheon for 4

Beef Fu Yung
Steamed rice for 4
Celery and Lettuce Salad (double recipe)
Fresh lychee nuts

Crab Fu Yung

Prep. Time 15 minutes • Serves 2
Cooking Time 10 minutes

This classic of Chinese restaurant menus is nice for lunch or a light supper, served with Cold and Spicy Relish with Sesame Oil (page 222).

1 ½-inch piece fresh ginger, peeled
1 green onion, trimmed to 4 inches
2 teaspoons vegetable oil
4 canned water chestnuts, drained and rinsed

4 ounces crabmeat or surimi crab slices salad style, thawed
4 eggs
1 tablespoon soy sauce
2 tablespoons vegetable oil
4 frilly green lettuce leaves

Sauce

½ cup chicken broth
1 teaspoon sugar
1 teaspoon oyster sauce or soy sauce

1 tablespoon chili sauce or tomato ketchup
2 teaspoons cornstarch

In a food processor or blender, or by hand, mince the ginger. Add the green onion and chop coarsely. Heat the wok to medium (350°), swirl in the 2 teaspoons oil, scrape the ginger mixture into the wok, and stir-fry 30 to 40 seconds. Scrape the ginger back into the processor or blender, or a bowl. Add the water chestnuts and chop coarsely. Add the crab and chop just enough to shred a bit. Add the eggs and soy sauce, and mix briefly. Heat a serving plate in a 250° oven. In a small saucepan over medium heat, combine the sauce ingredients and stir until the mixture thickens and clears. Pour into a bowl and keep warm in the oven.

Place the measured ingredients beside the wok in the order in which they are to be placed in the wok.

With the wok at medium heat (350°), swirl in 1 tablespoon of the oil and pour in half the crab-egg mixture. Push and scrape the sides up over the center of the mixture as it cooks. Lift the wok and swirl it around, extending any uncooked egg out around the sides, making a kind of pancake-scrambled egg. This will take about 2 minutes. Slide the fu yung onto the heated plate. Add the remaining oil and cook the remaining crab-egg mixture. Arrange on the serving plate with the lettuce leaves as garnish, pour the hot sauce over the fu yung, and serve at once.

Variations:

Shrimp Fu Yung—Substitute ¼ pound of small raw shrimp, shelled and deveined, for the crab. Chop the shrimp, then toss in the wok with the ginger and green onion until the shrimp is opaque and pink, about two minutes, before combining with the egg.

Pork Fu Yung—Substitute ½ cup shredded or chopped cooked pork for the crab and add 3 small stalks of celery, chopped, ½ cup chopped or shredded cabbage, 1 teaspoon sugar, and, if desired, ¼ cup chopped fresh mushrooms. Omit the sauce.

Lobster Fu Yung—Substitute cooked, shredded surimi lobster claws or shredded leftovers from a boiled lobster feast—including the meat from the lobster legs, the coral-hued roe, and the delicious tomalley or liver. (You don't have to have a whole 4 ounces of leftover lobster—use whatever you have; even half a cup is enough.) For a wonderful sauce, if there's more than a teaspoon or so of tomalley, instead of putting it into the fu yung, stir it into the sauce just before you turn it into the bowl to be kept warm until serving time.

Beef Fu Yung

Prep. Time 5 minutes • Serves 4
Cooking Time 10 minutes

Vietnamese dish, great for lunch or a light supper served with thick slices of vine-ripened tomatoes flavored with a little rice vinegar.

½ pound (1 cup) lean ground
  beef
1 teaspoon sesame oil
1 green onion, trimmed to
  4 inches and minced
½ teaspoon light soy sauce
¼ teaspoon sugar
½ teaspoon salt
4 large eggs, slightly beaten

1 tablespoon water
1 tablespoon mushroom soy or
  soy sauce
2 tablespoons vegetable oil
Spinach or Boston lettuce
  leaves, washed
Plum or sweet and sour sauce

Combine the beef, sesame oil, green onion, light soy sauce, sugar, and salt in a medium bowl. In another bowl, combine the eggs with the water and mushroom soy sauce. Heat a serving plate in a 250° oven.

Place the measured ingredients beside the wok in the order in which they are to be placed in the wok.

Heat the wok to medium (350°), swirl in the oil, and turn the beef mixture into the wok. Stir-fry using a slotted spoon until all surfaces are seared, about 2 minutes. With the slotted spoon, remove the meat to its mixing bowl. Leaving the oil in the wok, pour in half the egg mixture, then spoon half the meat mixture over the egg. As the egg cooks, push and scrape it up over the meat. As soon as the egg is dry, remove the mixture to the heated serving plate and keep warm. Repeat, using the remaining egg and meat mixtures. Arrange on the serving plate surrounded by spinach leaves or Boston lettuce leaves. Serve at once with a small bowl of plum sauce or sweet and sour sauce on the side.

Pork Fu Yung, Thailand

Prep. Time 15 minutes • Serves 2–3
Cooking Time 10 minutes

In this Thai fu yung the Chinese soy sauce is replaced by Thai fish sauce (nam pla), and garlic and coriander root or leaves (also called cilantro) are the key flavorings.

2 medium cloves garlic, peeled and sliced
2–3 small dryish coriander roots, sliced, or ½ teaspoon coriander (cilantro) leaves
4 peppercorns, crushed
2 teaspoons vegetable oil
½ cup ground pork
½ small onion, peeled
3–4 snow peas, strings removed

1 small ripe tomato, seeded and drained
½ teaspoon sugar
4 eggs
½ tablespoon fish sauce, Thai or other
2 tablespoons vegetable oil
Cilantro sprigs

In a mortar or a wooden bowl, mash together the garlic, coriander root or leaves, and the peppercorns to make a paste. Heat the wok to medium (350°), swirl in the oil, and stir-fry the garlic paste 30 seconds or until brown. Mash the pork into the wok and stir-fry until it is crumbly and brown, about 4 minutes. While it is cooking, coarsely chop the onion, snow peas, and tomato with the sugar in a food processor or blender, or by hand. When the pork is brown, mix in the onion mixture and stir-fry 2 minutes more. Return all of this to the processor, blender, or mixing bowl and clean the wok. Break the eggs over the pork mixture, add the fish sauce, and mix briefly. Heat a serving plate in a 250° oven.

Place the measured ingredients beside the wok in the order in which they are to be placed in the wok.

With the wok at medium (350°), swirl in 1 tablespoon of the oil and pour in half the pork-egg mixture. Push and scrape the sides up over the center of the mixture as it cooks. Lift the wok and swirl it around, extending any uncooked egg out around the sides, making a kind of pancake-scrambled egg. This will take about 2 minutes. Slide the fu yung onto the heated plate. Add the remaining oil and cook the remaining pork mixture. Arrange on the serving plate with cilantro sprigs as garnish.

Crab and Avocado Fu Yung

Prep. Time 15 minutes • Serves 2
Cooking Time 10 minutes

These pancakes stuffed with a soy sauce-flavored crabmeat, water chestnuts, and ginger are surrounded by thin slices of ripe avocado and frilly lettuce. A delicious combination for a special luncheon.

½ cup crabmeat or 4 ounces (½ package) surimi crab slices, salad style, thawed
1 tablespoon soy sauce
1 tablespoon rice wine or dry sherry
1 ¼-inch-thick piece fresh ginger, peeled and minced
2 fresh water chestnuts, peeled and shredded, or canned water chestnuts
1 teaspoon cornstarch

4 eggs
2 tablespoons water
½ teaspoon salt
¼ teaspoon pepper
2 tablespoons vegetable oil
2 green onions, trimmed to the white and shredded
1 ripe avocado, halved, peeled, seeded, and cut into 6 slices
6 frilly lettuce leaves
½ sweet red pepper, cut into thin strips

In a small bowl, toss the crabmeat with the soy sauce, rice wine, ginger, and water chestnuts. Sprinkle with cornstarch and toss again. In another bowl, beat the eggs with the water until bubbly. Season with salt and pepper. Heat two dinner plates in a 250° oven.

Place the measured ingredients beside the wok in the order in which they are to be placed in the wok.

Heat the wok to medium (350°), swirl in half the oil, and then add the onion shreds. Stir-fry 30 seconds, then scrape the onion into the crab mixture, retaining in the wok as much oil as you can. Pour half the eggs into the wok, pick the wok up, and swirl the egg around the side of the pan, spreading the egg as far as possible. Spoon half the crab mixture over the egg and cook without stirring until the egg looks set. Slide a thin spatula under the egg all around the wok, then push the sides down over the center and each other. Shake the wok until the egg is again centered. Let rest a moment, then slide onto a warm dinner plate. Add the remaining oil and cook the second fu yung. Garnish each with avocado slices, lettuce, and red pepper strips, and serve at once.

NOTE: To make this a *luncheon for 4*, double the recipe, cook the fu yung in two batches, then divide each large fu yung in half.

Hunan Bean Curd

Prep. Time 10 minutes • Serves 2
Cooking Time 15 minutes

A hot, spicy Chinese bean curd specialty created by Bell Wong at Hunan East. Serves as an entrée or as a side dish with a fish entrée and a chicken entrée.

2 pieces bean curd
2 teaspoons cornstarch
1 tablespoon water
1 tablespoon vegetable oil
1 ¼-inch piece fresh ginger, peeled and minced
2 green onions, trimmed to 3 inches and cut in 1-inch lengths

2 heaping tablespoons ground pork
2 small hot green peppers, seeded and shredded
2 tablespoons black beans, rinsed and drained
1 cup chicken broth
Cucumber fan (page 233), optional

Rinse the bean curd, cut it into 1-inch dice, and simmer it in boiling water 1 minute. Drain. Combine the cornstarch with the water.

Place the measured ingredients beside the wok in the order in which they are to be placed in the wok.

Heat the wok to medium low (300°) and swirl in the oil. Add the ginger and onion, and stir-fry 30 seconds. Add the pork and stir-fry until it is crumbly and brown. Add the peppers and black beans, stir once or twice, then add the broth and cook 5 minutes. Add the bean curd and cook 5 minutes more. Add the cornstarch and water and stir until the sauce thickens and clears. Serve hot, with a cucumber fan as garnish if you wish.

Sichuan Bean Curd

Prep. Time 10 minutes • Serves 2
Cooking Time 15 minutes

Another spicy bean curd entrée from Bell Wong's Hunan East. This is good with vegetable combination dishes, or a cool relish or salad.

2 pieces bean curd	**2 tablespoons ground pork**
2 teaspoons cornstarch	**1 tablespoon sesame oil**
1 tablespoon water	**Cucumber fan (page 233),**
1 teaspoon vegetable oil	**optional**
1 green onion, trimmed to	
3 inches and minced	

Sauce_____

1 tablespoon cooking wine	**1 tablespoon soy sauce**
1 tablespoon oyster sauce	**½ teaspoon hot chili paste**
1 tablespoon mushroom soy	**1 cup chicken broth**
sauce	

Rinse the bean curd, cut it into 1-inch cubes, and simmer in boiling water 1 minute. Drain. Mix together the cornstarch and water. In a small bowl, combine the six ingredients in the sauce. Heat a serving dish in a 250° oven.

Place the measured ingredients beside the wok in the order in which they are to be placed in the wok.

Heat the wok to medium low (300°) and swirl in the oil. Add the onion and stir-fry 1 minute. Add the pork and stir-fry until crumbly and brown. Pour in the sauce and stir for 5 minutes. Add the bean curd and cook 5 minutes more. Stir in the cornstarch and water, and cook until the sauce thickens and clears. Stir in the sesame oil. Turn into the heated serving dish and garnish with cucumber fan if desired. Serve hot.

Tofu and Vegetables, Japanese Style

Prep. Time 15 minutes • Serves 3–4
Cooking Time 15 minutes

Crunchy vegetables and protein-loaded tofu in a sauce made with light Japanese soy, if you have it, and vegetable broth or clam juice. Bean curd is a fine substitute for tofu. This is a meal-in-one, nice with a creamy dessert.

½ pound firm tofu
1 large clove garlic, peeled
3 green onions, trimmed to 3 inches
8 fresh water chestnuts, peeled, or canned water chestnuts, drained and rinsed

2 medium carrots, peeled
3 medium stalks celery
⅛ head Chinese cabbage or green cabbage
3 tablespoons vegetable oil

Sauce

½ cup vegetable broth or bottled clam juice
2 tablespoons Japanese soy sauce or soy sauce
1 tablespoon sake, rice wine, or dry sherry

1½ teaspoons sugar
2 teaspoons rice vinegar or cider vinegar
2 teaspoons cornstarch

Dip the tofu into boiling water, drain, and cut into strips ½ to ¾ inch wide. In a food processor, or by hand, mince together the garlic and onions and scrape onto a plate. One ingredient at a time, in the food processor or by hand, chop the water chestnuts coarsely, then slice the carrots, celery, and cabbage and set them on the plate. Combine the sauce ingredients in a small bowl. Heat a serving dish in a 250° oven.

Place the measured ingredients beside the wok in the order in which they are to be placed in the wok.

Heat the wok to medium (350°), swirl in the oil, and stir in the garlic and onions. Add the water chestnuts and carrots, stir-fry 2 minutes, and push up onto the side of the wok. Add the celery and stir-fry 2 minutes. Push up onto the side of the wok. Add the cabbage and stir-fry 1 minute, or until the color darkens. Add the tofu and stir-fry very gently 1 minute. Pour the sauce into the wok and stir until it thickens and clears. Toss the vegetables with the sauce. Remove to the heated dish, stir the pieces of tofu to the top, and serve at once.

Seven

Poultry Entrées

In Indian tradition, days when chicken was served were very special, even for the upper class, and in celebration, wonderful ingredients enhance chicken recipes from India. Coriander, cumin, nutmeg, coconut milk, jalapeño peppers, cashews, and exotic fruits are cooked into rich chicken casseroles served with chutneys, peanuts crushed with peppers, chopped apples, grated fresh coconut, and many other side dishes (see Chapter 11).

In China and other lands where soy sauce is the key flavor, chicken is just as special, and each bird is cut into lots of pieces so it can serve many. Recipes like two that follow, Chicken Uttar Pradesh, with its bite-size pieces of chicken, and Chicken Velvet, in which the chicken is pureed and shaped into chunks, serve far more in the East than they are likely to serve here. However, what the East lacks in the size of the portion, it makes up for in the variety of chicken dishes.

Supermarkets now provide us with birds already cut up for use, making preparation of these chicken recipes irresistibly easy. Chicken wings, chicken drumettes (the larger half of a chicken wing), drumsticks, thighs, boned and skinned breasts are plentiful and affordable. Thin turkey breast fillets are excellent for use in the wok.

Duck is the other bird for which wonderful recipes have been developed in the Orient. It is usually baked or braised in an exotic manner and presented with a grand flourish. Duck is sold in supermarkets, usually frozen, but fresh birds are better. Butchers will usually agree to cut up the duck, and now and then you'll find one who will skin and bone it for you, too. It isn't all that difficult to do yourself, and worth the effort. I'm partial to duck in bite-sized pieces that cook quickly and are accompanied by a rich sweet and sour sauce. You'll find my two favorite recipes on the following pages:

Duck with Pineapple and Cherries, and Duck with Raisins and Apricots.

A Shopper's Guide to Poultry

Always choose fresh rather than frozen poultry.

Boneless chicken breasts: Wok recipes call for these more often than for other cuts of poultry. Boned and skinned chicken breasts are offered in most markets—and it's the fastest (but most expensive) way to go. Whole breasts, with skin and bones intact, can be boned and skinned in 5 minutes with a sharp knife.
SUBSTITUTE: Skinned thigh meat or turkey breast fillet. But be aware that turkey meat is drier, and may need more sauce.

Chicken wings: A bargain at most supermarket counters. Choose wings with light skin; avoid those turning pink with age along the edges.
SUBSTITUTE: None.

Chicken drumettes: These are the larger half of the chicken wing, sold with the bone in, and skin on. Drumettes can also be used in recipes calling for drumsticks or thighs. They are often offered at bargain prices.
SUBSTITUTE: Small drumsticks; small thighs with as much fat as possible removed.

Leg and thigh of the chicken: Tastier and juicier than breasts, but harder to skin and bone. Many recipes call for leaving the skin on: where pockets of fat are visible under the skin, pull these out and discard.
SUBSTITUTE: Chicken breast or turkey breast fillet. Both are drier than chicken leg and thigh meat, so compensate with more sauce. Rabbit is also a good substitute.

Turkey breast fillet: Slices of boneless turkey breast are now available in most markets, fresh and frozen. Thin slices stir-fried just enough to color the flesh are tender and delicious. Do not overcook—the meat will become tough.
SUBSTITUTE: Boneless chicken breast.

Duck: Buy fresh duck, if you can, halved or cut up.
SUBSTITUTE: Duck has dark meat and a special flavor for which there is no substitute, but turkey fillets, chicken thighs, or rabbit can be used.

Menu Suggestions

Indonesian Dinner for 2

Chicken with Indonesian Spices
Steamed rice, optional
Three Color Salad (½ recipe)
Mangoes
Coconut sticks, served with Piña Colada Dressing

Malaysian Dinner for 4

Pakoras, India
Chicken with Almonds, Malaysia
Steamed rice
Raita
Red tomato slices
Chopped coconut
Peanuts Crushed with Pepper
Papaya halves, sprinkled with pomegranate seeds

Simple Curry Dinner for 4

Chicken Uttar Pradesh
Steamed rice
Chopped coconut
Tomato and Pepper Relish
Peanuts Crushed with Pepper
Fresh dates
Fresh figs

Chinese Dinner for 4

Turkey Breast in Orange Sauce
Sichuan Shrimp
Steamed rice
Two Sprout Salad
Lychee nuts
Kumquats

Chinese Dinner for 6

Duck with Pineapple and Cherries
Crispy Shrimp with Walnuts (double recipe)
Pork Fried Rice
Radish Slices with Sesame Oil
Orange sherbet
Fortune Cookies

Chinese Dinner for 6

Won Ton Soup
Chicken Stir-fried with Walnuts
Crispy Shrimp with Pineapple Sauce
Vegetarian Delight
Steamed rice
Oriental Fruit Cup

General Tso's Chicken

Prep. Time 15 minutes • Serves 4
Cooking Time 7–8 minutes

This crispy chicken dish in a glorious spicy sauce is one of Bell Wong's specialties. I recommend serving it with steamed rice.

4 large chicken legs including thighs, boned, cut into ½-inch pieces
1 egg, slightly beaten

½ tablespoon vegetable oil
½ tablespoon cornstarch
Vegetable oil

Sauce 1

2 green onions, trimmed to 4 inches
1½ tablespoons light soy sauce
1½ tablespoons mushroom soy sauce
1½ tablespoons rice wine or dry sherry

2 ½-inch thick pieces fresh ginger, peeled
Grinding of fresh pepper
3 tablespoons chicken bouillon
1 teaspoon brown sugar
1 tablespoon cornstarch

Sauce 2

1 teaspoon rice or cider vinegar
½ tablespoon chili paste (more, if you like hot food)

1 teaspoon sesame oil (optional)

In a medium bowl, combine the chicken with the egg, oil, and cornstarch. In a blender or food processor, or by hand, combine the ingredients for Sauce 1. In a small bowl, combine the ingredients for Sauce 2. Place the measured ingredients beside the wok in the order in which they are to be placed in the wok. Warm 2 serving dishes, one lined with paper towel, in a 250° oven.

Fill the wok to a depth of 1½ to 2 inches with vegetable oil. Heat the oil to high (400°), or until a day-old cube of bread browns in just under 1 minute. Heat another 4 minutes to stabilize the temperature. Put the chicken pieces into the oil one at a time until all are in. Stir-fry 3 minutes. Remove the pieces from the oil, draining well over the wok, and keep warm in the oven on the paper-lined dish. Empty the oil from the wok. Reduce the heat to medium (350°) and stir in Sauce 1. As soon as it bubbles, stir in the chicken. Sprinkle Sauce 2 over the chicken, stir-fry 1 minute more, then turn into the warm serving dish. Scrape the sauce over the chicken and serve at once.

Kung Pao Chicken

Prep. Time 15 minutes • Serves 2
Cooking Time 5–6 minutes

This popular Bell Wong recipe of crispy chunks of chicken and peanuts in a spicy red sauce gets its bite from the Hunan paste. If you buy boned, skinned chicken breast, the dish is ready in 20 minutes! Serve along with vegetable entrée and steamed rice.

1 whole chicken breast or 2 large legs including thighs, skinned, boned, and cut into 1-inch cubes
¼ cup cornstarch
1 ½-inch piece fresh ginger, peeled

3 green onions, trimmed to 3 inches
2 heaping tablespoons shelled raw peanuts
2 tablespoons vegetable oil

Sauce

2 tablespoons mushroom soy sauce or soy sauce
½ tablespoon sugar

½ tablespoon rice wine or dry sherry
1 teaspoon Hunan paste

Coat the chicken cubes well with cornstarch. In a food processor or blender, or by hand, mince the ginger; add and coarsely chop the onions. In a small bowl, combine the sauce ingredients. Heat a serving dish in a 250° oven.

Place the measured ingredients beside the wok in the order in which they are to be placed in the wok.

Heat the wok to medium high (375°), swirl in the oil, and add the chicken and peanuts. Stir-fry until the chicken is golden, no more than 2 minutes. Using a slotted spoon, transfer the chicken and nuts to the heated dish. Add the ginger and onions to the wok and stir-fry 1 minute. Stir in the sauce. When the sauce is bubbling, return the chicken and nuts to the wok and cook 1 minute more. Serve as soon as possible.

Ginger Chicken Wings Marcel

Prep. Time 5 minutes; Marinate 30 minutes • Serves 2
Cooking Time 30 minutes

Chef Marcel Stephan Hériteau, my father, made this delicious contribution to Oriental cooking. The chicken wings are exquisitely delicate, juicy, and rich in ginger flavor. Serve with rice.

8 chicken wings
4 large cloves garlic, peeled
1 ½-inch piece fresh ginger, peeled
¼ cup rice wine or dry sherry
¼ cup light soy sauce
½ teaspoon sugar

4 cups boiling water
2 tablespoons vegetable oil
½ sweet red or green pepper, seeded and shredded
1 teaspoon cornstarch

At the joint, cut the wing tip from each chicken wing and discard. (Or, freeze the tips with other chicken parts to make soup.) In a food processor or blender, or by hand, mince the garlic and ginger with the wine, soy sauce, and sugar. Marinate the wings in this sauce for half an hour or longer, turning now and then.

Half an hour before serving time, add the boiling water to the wok, remove the wings from the marinade—reserving the marinade—arrange them on the wok steaming rack, and put the rack in the wok. Cover, heat to a simmer (about 200°), and steam the wings 15 minutes, turning them once toward the end. Remove the wings to a serving dish. Turn off the heat. Pour the broth remaining in the wok—there should be about half a cup—into a measuring cup.

Place the measured ingredients beside the wok in the order in which they are to be placed in the wok.

Turn the heat to medium high (375°). Pour the oil into the wok, swirl it around, and when it is smoking hot, slide the wings, flat-side down, into the oil. Stir-fry 2 minutes on each side. Pour ¼ cup of the cooking broth, the pepper shreds, and the reserved marinade over the wings and stir-fry until the broth is almost all evaporated. Stir the cornstarch into the remaining ¼ cup of broth and pour down the side of the wok. Stir until the sauce has thickened and cleared. With tongs, remove the wings, flat-surface up, to the serving dish and scrape the sauce over them. Keep warm until ready to serve.

Chicken with Indonesian Spices

Prep. Time 15 minutes • *Serves 2*
Cooking Time 10–15 minutes

Serve these chicken chunks stir-fried in a savory sauce with a salad and fresh fruit for a fast and simple dinner. This is a good party dish, too: to multiply the number served, allow one chicken leg and thigh per guest, and have the butcher chop the chicken for you.

2 chicken legs including thighs
3 green onions, trimmed to
  5 inches
1 ½-inch piece fresh ginger,
  peeled
2 medium garlic cloves, peeled
1 teaspoon tapioca starch or
  cornstarch
1 tablespoon cold water
1 tablespoon vegetable oil

1 teaspoon ground cumin
1 teaspoon ground coriander
½ teaspoon sugar
1 tablespoon dark soy sauce or
  soy sauce
1 tablespoon lemon juice
½–1 cup chicken broth
Salt and pepper to taste

With a cleaver or a large knife and a mallet, chop the thighs into thirds, then the legs. Chop away the meatless ends of the legs. Be sure to rinse and remove any loose bits of bone. In a food processor or blender, or by hand, mince together the onions, ginger and garlic. In a small bowl, combine the starch with the water.

Place the measured ingredients beside the wok in the order in which they are to be placed in the wok.

Heat the wok to medium high (375°), swirl in the oil, and stir in the onion mixture. Stir a few seconds and then turn the chicken into the wok. Stir-fry 3 to 4 minutes. Sprinkle with the cumin, coriander, and sugar. Stir-fry 1 minute. Sprinkle with the soy sauce and lemon juice and stir-fry 1 minute. Stir ½ cup of chicken broth into the wok, scraping up the pan juices, and continue to stir-fry 2 to 3 minutes, or until the broth has reduced to make just enough sauce for the chicken. If needed, add more chicken broth. Taste and add salt and pepper if desired. Stir the starch mixture into the sauce and cook until it thickens, about 1 minute more. Serve hot.

NOTE: To serve four, use 4 chicken legs and increase recipe ingredients by 50 percent.

Chicken Thighs with Spices and Ginger

Prep. Time 15 minutes • Serves 4, with rice
Cooking Time 10–13 minutes

This combination of spices, ginger, and lime juice with tomato and yogurt is Indian cooking at its most exotic. You can also use chicken legs, or breasts cut into two or three pieces. Wonderful with rice, garden-ripe tomato slices, and corn on the cob.

8 small chicken thighs
4 large garlic cloves, peeled
2 ½-inch pieces fresh ginger, peeled
3 tablespoons water
3 tablespoons tomato sauce
3 tablespoons plain yogurt
1 tablespoon strained lime or lemon juice
½ cup chicken broth
2 tablespoons vegetable oil

⅛ teaspoon ground cinnamon
½ teaspoon crushed bay leaf, or 1 large dried bay leaf, crushed
¼ teaspoon ground cardamom
⅛ teaspoon ground clove
1 teaspoon turmeric
¼–½ teaspoon salt
Chutney with Peaches, Mango, and Ginger (page 218)

Prick the skin of the chicken all over. In a blender or food processor, or by hand, combine the garlic, ginger, and water and mince. In a medium bowl, combine the tomato sauce, yogurt, lime juice, and broth.

Place the measured ingredients beside the wok in the order in which they are to be placed in the wok.

Heat the wok to medium (350°) and swirl in the oil. Arrange the chicken thighs broad-side down in the wok and stir-fry until they are browned all over—about 5 minutes. Sprinkle the garlic and ginger mixture over the thighs and turn them once or twice. One by one, sprinkle the spices over the chicken. Add half the salt. Stir and toss the chicken with the spices, then add the tomato sauce mixture. Reduce the heat to a simmer (about 200°) and stir and cook 5 minutes more. The sauce should be the consistency of thick cream. Turn off the heat, taste, and add more salt if desired. Keep warm until ready to serve. Serve with chutney.

Chicken Stir-fried with Walnuts

Prep. Time 10 minutes • Serves 4–6
Cooking Time 10 minutes

My all-time favorite for company—perfect with Crispy Shrimp with
Pineapple Sauce (page 155) and steamed rice.

2 pounds chicken thighs and
breasts, boned, skinned, and
cut into 1-inch cubes
1 egg white
1½ tablespoons cornstarch
½ teaspoon salt
1 teaspoon cornstarch
½ cup chicken broth
4 tablespoons vegetable oil
1½ cups whole walnut meats

2 ½-inch pieces fresh ginger,
minced
2 large cloves garlic, peeled and
minced
1 tablespoon rice wine or dry
sherry
1 tablespoon sugar
2 tablespoons soy sauce

In a large bowl, mix the chicken cubes with the unbeaten egg white.
Mix the 1½ tablespoons cornstarch with the salt, add to the chicken,
and toss. In a small bowl, mix the 1 teaspoon cornstarch with the
chicken broth.

Place the measured ingredients beside the wok in the order in
which they are to be placed in the wok.

Heat the wok to medium high (375°), swirl in the oil, and count to
20. Add the walnuts and stir-fry until brown, about 3 minutes. (Stay
beside the wok stirring—otherwise, you're in danger of letting the
walnuts turn black and bitter.) As soon as they are browned,
remove them with a slotted spoon to a small bowl. Quickly add the
ginger and garlic to the wok; stir once or twice. Add the chicken
pieces and stir-fry until blanched on all sides, about 2 minutes. Add
the rice wine and toss the chicken pieces in it. Add the sugar and
soy sauce, turn the heat to medium (350°), and stir-fry 3 minutes
more. Push the chicken to one side. Stir the cornstarch mixture and
pour it down the side of the wok. Stir until the sauce thickens and
clears. Mix with the chicken, add the walnuts, and serve at once.

Chicken with Lemon Grass and Cashews, Vietnam

*Prep. Time 7–10 minutes; Marinate 10 minutes • Serves 4
Cooking Time 10 minutes*

Lemon grass is called xa in Vietnam, where this dish originated. It imparts to the chicken a subtle aroma that's a sheer delight. If you can't find fresh lemon grass, or powdered or dried lemon grass, grate and use the yellow part of the peel of a small lemon. Try Sweet Peppers in Sweet and Sour Sauce (page 199) as an accompanying entrée.

**2 stalks fresh lemon grass, or
 1 teaspoon powdered, or
 ¼ cup sliced dried
2 tablespoons nuoc mam or
 other fish sauce
2 teaspoons sugar
Grinding of fresh pepper
3 large cloves garlic, peeled and
 minced**

**4 large chicken legs and thighs,
 boned, and cut into 1–2-inch
 pieces
2 tablespoons vegetable oil
1 teaspoon mushroom soy or
 soy sauce
½ cup shelled unsalted cashews**

Peel away the dried outer stalks of fresh lemon grass until you reach the fresh inner stalks. Bruise the white base of the stalks slightly, then mince the stalks. Combine the lemon grass with the fish sauce in a small bowl, and stir in the sugar, pepper, and garlic. In a medium bowl, toss the chicken pieces with the lemon grass mixture. Ideally, the chicken should marinate in the lemon grass mixture for a while, especially if you are using dried lemon grass, so take your time getting ready to stir-fry it.

Heat the wok to medium high (375°) and swirl in the vegetable oil. Turn the chicken into the wok and stir-fry until the bits of garlic are well browned. Turn the heat down to medium low (300°) and continue to stir-fry for 5 minutes. Next, sprinkle with the mushroom soy sauce, stir and toss another minute, then stir in the cashews and heat another minute or so. Keep warm until ready to serve.

Chicken Uttar Pradesh

Prep. Time 15 minutes • Serves 2–3; 4 if rice is offered
Cooking Time 8–10 minutes

This exquisite golden curry always gets applause! Offer with it
Crisped Coconut Shreds (page 221) or a sweet and sour dish, such
as Crispy Shrimp with Pineapple Sauce (page 155), Orange Beef
(page 130), or Sichuan Shrimp (page 153).

1 pound chicken breast, skinned,
  boned, and cut into ½- or
  1-inch pieces
2 teaspoons ground coriander
1 rounded teaspoon grated fresh
  ginger
¼ teaspoon salt
Generous grinding of pepper
4 green onions, trimmed to
  4 inches and minced
8 ounces plain yogurt
½ cup heavy cream

1 teaspoon turmeric
1 firm ripe avocado, peeled,
  halved, and seeded
1 tablespoon vegetable oil
3 tablespoons butter
½ cup shelled, unsalted raw
  cashews
½ teaspoon ground cardamom
1 teaspoon minced fresh cilantro
Chutney with Peaches, Mango,
  and Ginger (page 218)

In a large bowl, toss the chicken with the coriander, ginger, salt, and
pepper. In a separate bowl, combine the onions, yogurt, cream,
and turmeric. Cut the avocado into eight long slices, and arrange
them around the edge of a round serving dish. Brush the top of
each avocado slice with just enough of the oil to keep it from
discoloring.

Place the measured ingredients beside the wok in the order in
which they are to be placed in the wok.

Heat the wok to medium (350°). Add the remaining oil (about 1
teaspoonful) and swirl it around the bottom and sides of the wok.
Melt the butter by swishing it around in the bottom of the wok. Add
the chicken and nuts and stir-fry until the chicken browns, about 2
minutes. Scrape the yogurt mixture into the wok and stir 2 minutes
more. Remove the chicken and nuts to their bowl. Turn the heat to
medium high (375°). Stir in the cardamom and boil, stirring, until
the mixture has thickened and reduced by about half. Return the
chicken and nuts to the sauce, then pour the contents of the wok
into the serving dish in the center, surrounded by the avocado
slices, and sprinkle with cilantro. Serve with chutney on the side.

Chicken with Almonds, Malaysia

Prep. Time 15 minutes • Serves 4
Cooking Time 12–15 minutes

A delicate, delicious mild curry to serve over steamed rice with Indian accompaniments like Chopped Apple Relish (page 220) and Tomato and Pepper Relish (page 223), or simply with Golden Tomato Salad (page 210). For a special touch, add ½ pound of shelled, deveined small raw shrimp for the last 4 minutes of cooking, and you have an elegant dinner for 6.

3 medium onions, peeled and
    sliced into ¼-inch rings
1 tablespoon ground coriander
1 teaspoon ground aniseed
½ teaspoon saffron threads
1 teaspoon ground ginger or 1
    thin piece fresh ginger peeled,
    minced
¼ teaspoon chili powder
2 cloves garlic, peeled and
    minced
2 tablespoons grated lemon rind
3 tablespoons lemon juice
2 tablespoons damson preserves
    or plum jam

1 teaspoon sugar
1 teaspoon salt
1 teaspoon vegetable oil
3 tablespoons butter
1 cup grated fresh coconut
2 pounds chicken breast,
    skinned, boned, and cut into
    1-inch cubes
2 cups Coconut Milk (page 34)
1 cup peeled whole almonds
Chutney

In a medium bowl, combine the onions with the spices, ginger, chili powder, garlic, lemon rind and juice, preserves, sugar, and salt, and toss.

Place the measured ingredients beside the wok in the order in which they are to be placed in the wok.

Heat the wok to medium (350°), add the oil, melt the butter, and stir-fry the coconut shreds until lightly browned, 2 to 3 minutes. With a slotted spoon, remove the coconut to a paper towel to drain. Add the chicken to the wok. Add the onion mixture and toss with the chicken. Add the coconut milk and almonds, bring to a rapid boil, then lower the heat and simmer covered, 8 minutes, or until the sauce is thick. Turn into a warm serving dish, sprinkle with crisped coconut shreds, and serve as soon as possible with chutney on the side.

Chicken and Shrimp, Indian Style

Prep. Time 30 minutes • Serves 2; 4 if rice is offered
Cooking Time 10–12 minutes

A spicy dish, especially delicious when served with peach and mango chutney. Wonderful with rice or ripe tomatoes. When doubling this recipe, be aware the curry paste yields 6 tablespoons.

2 tablespoons vegetable oil
2 medium, sweet red peppers, seeded and cut into 1-inch squares
2 big chicken legs including thighs, boned, skinned, cut into 1-inch cubes
⅓ pound medium or small shrimp, shelled and deveined

½ cup chicken bouillon
1 cup Coconut Milk (page 34)
Salt
Chutney, preferably Chutney with Peaches, Mango, and Ginger (page 218)

Curry Paste

3 stalks lemon grass, or 1 tablespoon grated lemon rind
1 bunch green onions, trimmed to 3 inches
1 ½-inch piece fresh ginger, peeled
4 large cloves garlic, peeled
1 jalapeño pepper, seeded

2 tablespoons vegetable oil
1 tablespoon ground cumin
1 tablespoon ground coriander
½ teaspoon ground nutmeg
½ teaspoon ground mace
1 teaspoon turmeric
⅛ teaspoon red pepper flakes

In a blender or food processor, or by hand, mix the curry paste: peel the lemon grass down to fresh inner stalks, and slice into the blender or processor (or add lemon rind). Mix with the next eleven ingredients to form a curry paste. Heat a bowl in a 250° oven.

Place the measured ingredients beside the wok in the order in which they are to be placed in the wok.

Heat the wok to medium high (375°), swirl in the oil, add the peppers, and stir-fry 2 minutes. Add the chicken and stir-fry 2 minutes. Add the shrimp and stir-fry 2 minutes. Scoop 3 tablespoons of the curry paste into the wok, add the bouillon and mash. Add the coconut milk and stir until combined. Remove the solid ingredients to the warm bowl. Stir and cook the sauce until it has thickened, about 4 minutes more. Return the solid ingredients to the sauce and heat through. Taste, and add more curry paste and salt if desired. Keep warm until ready to serve. Offer chutney.

Chicken Velvet with Snow Peas

Prep. Time 15 minutes • Serves 2–3
Cooking Time 20 minutes

Pureed chicken breast, deep-fried to a golden brown and combined with Chinese vegetables and almonds is a classic of Chinese restaurants. You must have a blender or food processor for this recipe. Serve with Sichuan Shrimp (page 153) and Lamb in Honey Sauce, Peking Style (page 141).

1½ whole chicken breasts, skinned and boned
1 tablespoon chicken broth
2 tablespoons rice wine or dry sherry
1 teaspoon salt
⅛ teaspoon pepper
1 tablespoon cornstarch
3 egg whites, beaten stiff
1 cup chicken broth
1 teaspoon soy sauce
1 tablespoon cornstarch
Vegetable oil
1 ½-inch piece fresh ginger, peeled and minced

5 medium mushrooms, wiped clean and cut into ¼-inch-thick T-shapes
¼ cup skinned whole almonds or almond slivers
12 snow peas, strings removed
8 canned whole water chestnuts, drained, rinsed, and sliced into ¼-inch-thick rounds
1 2-inch piece sweet red pepper, shredded
Carrot flowers (page 232), optional

Puree the chicken in a food processor or a blender. With the machine on, add the 1 tablespoon of chicken broth, the rice wine, salt, pepper, and cornstarch. Remove the chicken puree to a bowl and fold in the egg whites. Combine the 1 cup chicken broth, the soy sauce, and the cornstarch in a small bowl. Place a paper towel-lined serving bowl in a 250° oven.

Place the measured ingredients beside the wok in the order in which they are to be placed in the wok.

Fill the wok to a depth of 1½ to 2 inches with oil. Heat the oil to high (400°), or until a day-old cube of bread browns in just under 1 minute. Heat another 4 minutes to stabilize the temperature. Add the chicken puree by tablespoonfuls, placing in the oil at one time only as many tablespoonfuls as can float freely. Fry until golden brown. Lift the cooked pieces from the oil and keep warm in the paper-lined bowl. When all the chicken is cooked, empty the wok, reserving the oil, then return to it 2 tablespoons of the oil. Reduce heat to medium high (375°), add the ginger, mushrooms, and almonds, and stir-fry 1 minute. Add the snow peas and chestnut slices and stir-fry until the snow peas are bright green, about 3 minutes. Stir in the red pepper shreds, then push the ingredients to one side and pour in the broth and cornstarch mixture. Stir until thick and clear. Pull the paper out from under the chicken morsels, pour the contents of the wok over them, and serve at once with carrot flowers as a garnish, if you wish.

Chicken and Fruit Curry, Java

Prep. Time 10 minutes • Serves 4, with rice
Cooking Time 10 minutes

A rich fruit-filled curry to make with leftover chicken. If you want to serve more than 4, add Sichuan Shrimp (page 153)—a wonderful combination. Ginger Ice Cream (page 241) makes a nice dessert.

1 tablespoon vegetable oil	¼ teaspoon pepper
¼ cup tomato sauce	4 tablespoons white vinegar
1 tablespoon lemon juice	1 ripe mango, peeled and sliced
1 cup canned coconut milk or Thick Coconut Milk (page 34)	½ cup canned pineapple chunks in their own juice
1 small onion, minced	1 ripe banana, peeled and sliced
1 clove garlic, peeled and minced	Honey, optional
½ tablespoon ground coriander	Salt, optional
1 teaspoon turmeric	2 cups cooked chicken, skinned, boned, cubed
1 teaspoon ground cumin	8 maraschino cherries, drained (optional)
⅛ teaspoon chili powder	
¼ teaspoon fennel seeds	

Place the measured ingredients beside the wok in the order in which they are to be placed in the wok.

Heat the wok to medium (350°) and swirl in the oil. Stir in each of the ingredients except the last four, one at a time. Cover, reduce the heat to simmer (about 200°), and cook 5 minutes, or until the sauce is thick. Taste, and add honey for more sweetness, if desired, and/or salt if desired. Add the chicken, and the cherries if you wish, and simmer until the chicken is heated through, about 3 more minutes. Keep warm until ready to serve.

Chicken in Sweet and Sour Sauce, with Vegetables

Prep. Time 15 minutes • Serves 4; 6 with rice
Cooking Time 10–12 minutes

Tender strips of chicken breast in a sweet and sour sauce with crispy Chinese vegetables; maraschino cherries and pineapple chunks add color and flavor. Nice with Bean Sprout Salad (page 211) and Fortune Cookies (page 239) for dessert.

2 whole chicken breasts, skinned and boned
1 egg white
1½ tablespoons cornstarch
½ teaspoon salt
1 10-ounce can pineapple chunks, canned in its own juice, drained, reserve the juice
½–⅔ cup reserved pineapple juice
2 tablespoons packed light brown sugar
½ teaspoon salt

⅛ teaspoon pepper
2 tablespoons cider vinegar
1 cup chicken broth
1½ tablespoons cornstarch
2 tablespoons cold water
3 tablespoons vegetable oil
1 cup Chinese cabbage, shredded
8 canned whole water chestnuts, drained, rinsed, and halved
½ cup canned bamboo shoots, drained and rinsed
8 maraschino cherries

Cut the chicken into strips about ½ by ¼ by 2 inches thick. In a medium bowl, toss the strips with the egg white, cornstarch, and salt. Measure the reserved pineapple juice: if you have less than ½ cup, add a little chicken broth. In a small bowl, mix together the pineapple juice with the sugar, salt, pepper, vinegar, and broth. In a cup, combine the cornstarch and the water.

Place the measured ingredients beside the wok in the order in which they are to be placed in the wok.

Heat the wok to medium high (375°), swirl in the oil, then add the chicken strips and stir-fry until they are blanched, about 2 minutes. Add the cabbage, chestnuts, bamboo shoots, and pineapple chunks, tossing after each addition. Pour the pineapple juice mixture into the wok and stir-fry until the syrup is almost reduced by half. Push solid ingredients up onto the sides of the wok. Pour the cornstarch mixture into the bottom of the wok, stir and cook until the sauce thickens and clears, then mix well with the contents of the wok; add the maraschino cherries and toss one more time. Keep warm until ready to serve.

Chicken Stir-fried with Tomatoes, Vietnam

Prep. Time 15 minutes • Serves 4; 6 with rice
Cooking Time 25 minutes

Chicken parts simmered with tomatoes in a rich Vietnamese sauce. Serve with steamed rice, stir-fried bean sprouts, Radish Slices with Sesame Oil (page 209), and chilled canned palm seed fruit in syrup or lychee nuts.

1½ pounds cut-up chicken parts (12 pieces)
2 large shallots or 4 green onions, minced
1 teaspoon salt
¼ teaspoon pepper
3 tablespoons vegetable oil
2 large cloves garlic, peeled

2 large garden-ripe tomatoes, chopped
1 large shallot, minced or 1 large green onion
1 tablespoon tomato paste
1 tablespoon nuoc mam or other fish sauce
Tomato juice or water

In a large bowl, toss the chicken pieces with the shallots, salt, and pepper.

Place the measured ingredients beside the wok in the order in which they are to be placed in the wok.

Heat the wok to medium high (375°), swirl in the oil, and add the chicken pieces. Toss once, lower the heat to medium (350°), and stir-fry 5 minutes. Cover, simmer 10 minutes. Using a garlic press, crush the garlic over the chicken; stir-fry 30 seconds. Add the tomatoes, shallot, and tomato paste. Mash around until the tomatoes render their juice. Cover and cook another 5 minutes. Add the fish sauce and stir-fry 2 minutes more. If the sauce appears to be evaporating, add a few tablespoons of tomato juice or water. Keep warm until ready to serve.

Chicken with Peppers and Onions

Prep. Time 10–15 minutes • Serves 2
Cooking Time 10 minutes

A Chinese recipe, light, easy to make, and very popular with everyone. When yellow tomatoes are in season, slice a big one into rounds and arrange it with Boston lettuce leaves as a garnish.

1 tablespoon soy sauce
1 tablespoon rice wine or dry sherry
1 large chicken breast, skinned and boned and cut into 1-inch cubes
2 medium-size ripe sweet red peppers

1 medium onion, peeled
1 teaspoon black beans
3 tablespoons vegetable oil
2 large cloves garlic, peeled and minced

Sauce

½ cup chicken broth
1 tablespoon soy sauce

½ tablespoon cornstarch
¼ teaspoon sugar

In a medium bowl, combine the soy sauce and rice wine with the chicken and toss well. Slice the peppers into lengths 1-inch wide, discarding core and seeds, then cut crosswise into 1-inch squares. Cut a thin slice off either end of the onion then divide it into eight wedges and separate the layers. Rinse and drain the beans and mash them in a small bowl with the back of a fork. Mix the sauce ingredients together in a small bowl.

Place the measured ingredients beside the wok in the order in which they are to be placed in the wok.

Heat the wok to medium high (375°). Swirl in 2 tablespoons of the oil. Add the garlic and stir-fry until it begins to brown. Mash the beans into the oil, stir with the garlic, then add the chicken and stir-fry 3 minutes. Lift the chicken onto a plate with a slotted spoon. Add the remaining tablespoon of oil to the wok and stir in the sweet pepper pieces. Stir-fry 1 minute. Add the onion and stir-fry 2 to 3 minutes. Slip the chicken and its juices back into the wok, stir-fry 1 minute, then pour the sauce mixture down the side of the wok and stir with the other ingredients until the sauce thickens and clears, about 1 minute. Keep warm until ready to serve.

Chicken Stir-fried with Chinese Mushrooms

Prep. Time 20 minutes • Serves 4; 6 with rice
Cooking Time 15 minutes

Savory pieces of dark chicken meat stir-fried with Chinese vegetables and flavored with ginger and soy. Serve with Cantonese Shrimp Fried Rice (page 79) and a basket of exotic fruits for dessert.

12 dried Chinese mushrooms
2 cups very hot water
8–12 small chicken thighs
1 tablespoon soy sauce
½ teaspoon salt
1 tablespoon cornstarch
2 tablespoons water
2 tablespoons vegetable oil
3 ½-inch-thick pieces fresh ginger, peeled and minced
2 green onions, trimmed to 3 inches and cut into 1-inch lengths

¼ pound fresh water chestnuts, or canned water chestnuts, drained and rinsed, halved
¼ pound snow peas, strings removed
¼ teaspoon pepper
½ teaspoon sugar
1 tablespoon oyster sauce

Soak the mushrooms in the hot water until soft, 5 to 10 minutes. Drain, reserving the liquid, and remove and discard the stems. While they soak, chop the chicken thighs into thirds and remove the bones. Rinse to wash away bits of broken bone and toss the pieces in a medium bowl with the soy and salt. In a cup, combine the cornstarch with the water.

Place the measured ingredients beside the wok in the order in which they are to be placed in the wok.

Heat the wok to medium high (375°), swirl in the oil, add the chicken pieces, and stir-fry 2 minutes. Add the ginger and stir-fry 1 minute. Add the mushroom water, mushrooms, green onions, water chestnuts, snow peas, pepper, and sugar. Cover, reduce heat to simmer (about 200°), and cook 10 minutes. Stir in the oyster sauce. Pour the cornstarch mixture down the side of the wok and stir until the sauce thickens and clears. Keep warm until ready to serve.

Chop Suey Chimney Hill, Party Recipe

Prep. Time 30–40 minutes • Serves 16, with rice
Cooking Time 30 minutes

Here's a stir-fry recipe to feed a crowd. The stir-frying method given here shows how you can cook for a crowd in a standard 14-inch wok. You can also make it outdoors in a giant wok which can handle all the ingredients—add the oil, then the ingredients one at a time in the sequence given, placing each in its own space. Keep all the pieces moving so they won't burn. As soon as the last ingredient is in, begin mixing together the first ingredients added until all are combined.

A good companion dish for this recipe is Surimi in Malaysian Curry (page 166), which also serves 16. A basket of exotic finger fruits makes a perfect dessert. Chimney Hill is the name of the house we lived in in Sharon, Connecticut, when I first began to experiment with Oriental cooking.

8 dried Chinese mushrooms
4 large pieces tree fungus
½ cup vegetable oil
1 3-inch piece fresh ginger, peeled and minced
1 Bermuda onion, sliced in ¼-inch rounds
8 large garlic cloves, peeled, minced
¼ head small cabbage, shredded
2 heads broccoli, cut in 1-inch florets

1 pound button mushrooms, wiped clean
3 sweet red peppers, seeded and shredded
1 cup (8 ounces) bean sprouts, fresh or canned, drained and rinsed
4 cups shredded cooked chicken (1 broiler baked and cut up, including skin and drippings)

Sauce

4 tablespoons soy sauce (or more)
1 tablespoon sugar (or more)
1 tablespoon rice wine or dry sherry (or more)

1 tablespoon rice vinegar (or more)
1 tablespoon salt (or more)
½ teaspoon pepper

Thickener

6 cups chicken broth

6 tablespoons cornstarch

Soak the mushrooms and fungus separately in boiling water to cover until soft, 5 to 15 minutes. Drain, remove and discard the stems, and shred. In a bowl, combine the sauce ingredients (leave the containers handy in case you need more later). In a large bowl, combine the chicken broth and cornstarch. Heat a large pan, such as a turkey roasting pan, in a 250° oven.

Place the measured ingredients beside the wok in the order in which they will be placed in the wok.

Heat the wok to medium high (375°) and swirl in the oil. While the oil heats, get the heated pan from the oven and set it by the wok. Add the ginger into the oil and stir-fry 1 minute. Add the onion slices and stir-fry 1 minute. Add the garlic and stir-fry 1 minute. Use a slotted spoon to lift about half the onion and garlic from the wok and spread them over the heated pan. Push the remaining vegetables up onto the side of the wok and add the cabbage to the oil. Stir-fry 2 minutes. Spoon over a fifth of the sauce. With the slotted spoon, remove the cabbage to the heated pan and spread it around. Repeat the procedure, stir-frying the broccoli 2 minutes, the mushrooms 4 minutes, the peppers 3 minutes, fresh bean sprouts 2 minutes or canned bean sprouts 1 minute, and the Chinese mushrooms and tree fungus together 2 minutes. Spoon a fifth of the sauce over each batch before you remove it to the pan, except for the mushrooms and fungus. Stir up the thickener, pour it into the wok, and cook, stirring, until the sauce thickens and clears; if it fails to thicken, add 1 tablespoon cornstarch mixed with 1 tablespoon water. Taste the sauce and add more of the sauce seasonings if desired. Mix in the chicken shreds and heat through—about 2 minutes. Turn all the vegetables back into the wok and combine with the sauce. Taste again and add seasonings if desired. Serve as soon as possible from the wok.

NOTE: *To make chop suey for 6, see page 135.*

Duck with Pineapple and Cherries

Prep. Time 15 minutes • Serves 4
Cooking Time 25 minutes

Juicy chunks of savory duck in a sweet and sour sauce with golden pineapple and bright red maraschino cherries—a real party dish, and the fastest way you ever saw to prepare duck! Serve with rice and a salad.

1 4–4½-pound duck, cut into 2–2½-inch chunks, mostly boneless and free of fat but with skin on
1 20-ounce can pineapple chunks in their own juice, drained, reserve the juice
1 ½-inch piece fresh ginger, peeled
4 green onions, trimmed to 4 inches
3 large cloves garlic, peeled
1 tablespoon tapioca starch or cornstarch

1 tablespoon cold water
1 teaspoon vegetable oil
1½–2 cups chicken broth
½ cup rice wine or dry sherry
1 tablespoon thick soy sauce or soy sauce
2 tablespoons lemon juice
Salt and pepper (optional)
12 maraschino cherries, drained
½ bunch watercress, or a green garnish of your choice

In a medium bowl, toss the duck pieces with the reserved pineapple juice. In a food processor or blender, or by hand, mince together the ginger, green onions, and garlic. In a small bowl, combine the starch with the water. Heat a serving dish in a 250° oven. Have handy a receptacle into which excess hot fat can be poured.

Place the measured ingredients beside the wok in the order in which they are to be placed in the wok.

Heat the wok to medium high (375°), swirl in the oil, and, skin-side down, brown the duck pieces on all sides—about 8 minutes. Pour off all the fat. Sprinkle the ginger mixture over the duck and stir-fry together 1 minute. Pour 1½ cups of the broth and the wine into the wok, cover, reduce the heat to simmer (about 200°), and cook 10 minutes. Check the sauce level and replenish with broth as needed. Stir the duck pieces often, making sure each is getting its share of the hottest part of the wok. Push the meat to one side and stir in the pineapple juice, soy sauce, and lemon juice.

Simmer 2 minutes. Stir in the starch mixture and stir until it thickens. Taste, and add salt and pepper if desired. Stir in the pineapple chunks and cherries, cook half a minute, toss with the duck pieces, and turn into the warm serving dish. Keep hot until ready to serve. Garnish with greens and serve.

NOTE: Unless you have an accommodating butcher, you'll have to thaw and cut up the duck yourself: halve the duck; remove the legs and breast meat; cut the breasts into 4 to 5 pieces each, removing some of the fat under the skin; cut the thighs from the legs and cut each into three pieces—twelve pieces in all; find a few more pieces that are mostly meat; remove and discard as much fat as possible without eliminating all the skin, which is good. You should have twenty-four to twenty-eight pieces of duck meat not more than 2½ inches thick, not counting skin and fat.

Duck with Raisins and Apricots

Prep. Time 15 minutes • Serves 4
Cooking Time 20 minutes

This dish—juicy chunks of duck in a rich sauce—is Indian in origin. Serve with boiled plantains or rice, Onion Samball (page 215), and Tomato and Pepper Relish (page 223).

1 4–4½-pound duck cut into 2–2½-inch chunks, mostly boneless and free of fat, but skin on

1 ½-inch piece fresh ginger, peeled
1 medium onion, peeled
Salt and pepper, optional

Sauce

1½–2 cups chicken broth
3 tablespoons tomato sauce
1 teaspoon ground cumin
1 teaspoon fennel seeds

1 tablespoon lemon juice
4 tablespoons golden seedless raisins
6 dried apricots, minced

Heat the wok to medium high (375°), then put a few pieces of duck that have fat showing into the bottom of the wok and slide them around to grease the metal. Add the remaining duck and brown, turning often, for 6 minutes. While the duck is browning, in a food processor or blender, or by hand, mince together the ginger and onion. In a medium bowl, combine 1½ cups of the broth with the remaining sauce ingredients. Heat a serving dish in a 250° oven. Have handy a receptacle for excess hot fat.

When the duck is well browned, drain off all the fat, push the duck to one side, stir in the ginger-onion mixture, and stir-fry 2 minutes with the duck pieces. Pour in the sauce, scrape up the pan juices, cover, reduce the heat to simmer (about 200°), and cook 10 minutes. Check the sauce level and if it is disappearing, add more broth. Taste, and add salt and pepper if needed. Keep hot until ready to serve.

NOTE: If you can't get cut-up duck from your butcher, follow the instructions on page 123.

Eight

Meat Entrées

In countries where soy flavors the cooking, pork is the most commonly used meat. Although it is a main ingredient, at least as often it appears as one of a medley of flavoring agents. The recipes for Spring Rolls and Won Tons in Chapter 3—both combinations of ground pork and shrimp—are classic examples.

In India, the heart of the curry-cooking cultures, the meat most used is young goat, which is translated into American and British recipes as lamb. Beef is eaten by the Muslims and Christians in India, though not by the Hindus, who make up the largest percentage of the population.

As Eastern cooking has become Americanized in our restaurants, more beef dishes have come into the repertoire. The recipes in this chapter reflect that development. Exotic Orange Beef can take the place of a sweet and sour dish as one of three entrées. Two Japanese classics that each make a whole meal are Sukiyaki and Teriyaki. And a good family recipe for leftover beef or steak is Chop Suey Chimney Hill—a favorite with the Hériteau children.

The pork entrées given here are specialties at Bell Wong's Hunan East: Moo Shu Pork, which is fun because you get to stuff your own pancake wrappers, and Peking Style Pork, a savory dish.

The lamb recipes in this chapter are very special: Lamb in Honey Sauce, Peking Style, is sweet and wonderful with rice and any well-sauced soy-flavored dish including vegetables. Lamb Korma is a creamy curry made with yogurt, a great entrée to serve with rice and a crispy relish.

A Shopper's Guide to Meats

Beef steak: Boneless flank steak, strip steak, tenderloin, quality chuck, eye of the round, or filet mignon are the most successful cuts of beef for wok cooking because they're tender and best when cooked fast. Markets now offer packaged chunks of beef intended for satés and kebabs which are often suitable for stir-fries and other wok-cooked dishes. For tender little shreds and strips, cut across the grain. Choose beef a light cherry-red in color.

SUBSTITUTE: Any boneless beef cut your butcher recommends as tender—or, tenderize by marinating in meat tenderizer. (Indians used mashed green papayas to tenderize tough meats.) Flank steak is excellent flash-cooked, as long as it is cut across the grain—as in Orange Beef and Beef in Ginger Curry, Sumatra.

Leg of lamb: The best lamb for quick cooking is sliced from the leg. Blade and shoulder chops are too tough and take too long to cook—loin chops are too expensive. Buy a whole leg and butcher it into 1-pound and ½-pound steaks to freeze for Oriental recipes.

SUBSTITUTE: Boned lamb breast is suitable in recipes that cook a little longer. Lamb shank may be used in the wok, but first the meat must be boned, and then the sinews and film sheathing the meat must be removed. That leaves it in shreds suitable for wok cooking. (Save the bones to make soup.)

Pork tenderloin: The cut used when pork is a main ingredient. This is now often sold packaged in chunks, boneless and perfect for use in wok dishes that use bite-size pieces of meat.

SUBSTITUTE: There is no substitute for pork meat; it has its own special flavor. However, any boneless tender cut of pork, such as pork loin, may be used in recipes calling for tenderloin.

Ground pork: Used when pork is a flavoring agent instead of a main ingredient. Make your own from inexpensive blade steaks and other lean cuts. Boned, these may be divided into ¼-pound lots and chopped or ground in a food processor or blender or shredded or minced by hand (¼ pound will make roughly ½ to ¾ cup of ground meat). Stored in plastic in the freezer, ground pork will keep for many months.

SUBSTITUTE: Any ground or chopped pork—but not sausage, which is highly flavored—may be used in recipes calling for ground pork, as long as it is mostly lean.

Menu Suggestions

Chinese Luncheon for 2

Moo Shu Pork
Sweet and Sour Broccoli
Steamed rice
Kumquats

Japanese Dinner for 2

Miso Soup (½ recipe)
Beef Teriyaki, Japan
Stir-fried shiitake mushrooms
Steamed rice
Radish Slices with Sesame Oil
Fresh figs, strawberries, carambola, with day lily garnish

Indian Dinner for 4

Shrimp Balls, India
Lamb Korma, India
Steamed rice
Onion Samball
Tomato and Pepper Relish
Mangoes, strawberries, and kiwi fruit slices

Chinese Dinner for 6

Spring Rolls, Cantonese Style
Chicken Velvet with Snow Peas
Lamb in Honey Sauce, Peking
Sichuan Shrimp
Steamed rice
Ginger Ice Cream
Fortune Cookies

Japanese Dinner for 6

Miso Soup
Sukiyaki, Japan
Steamed rice
Cold and Spicy Relish with Sesame
Platter of exotic finger fruits

Hunan Beef

Prep. Time 10 minutes • Serves 2
Cooking Time 10 minutes

Strips of steak in a spicy red sauce—another favorite from Bell Wong's repertoire! Great with plain steamed rice and entrées that include lots of vegetables.

½ pound boneless steak, cut
    into ¼-inch-thick slices
¼ cup cornstarch
1 ½-inch piece fresh ginger,
    peeled
1 green onion, trimmed to
    3 inches
3 medium cloves garlic, peeled
2 tablespoons vegetable oil

1 head broccoli, cut into
    1-inch-wide florets
¼ cup button mushrooms
    (¼ pound), wiped clean
2 ounces canned bamboo
    shoots, drained and rinsed
Green onion brushes (page 233),
    optional

Sauce

½ cup chicken broth
1½ tablespoons mushroom soy
    or soy sauce
1½ tablespoons soy sauce
½ tablespoon rice wine or cider
    vinegar

½ teaspoon sugar
½ teaspoon Hunan paste (or
    more)
1 teaspoon cornstarch

In a large bowl, toss the steak with the cornstarch. In a food processor or blender, or by hand, mince the ginger, then add and mince the onion and garlic. Combine the ingredients for the sauce in a medium bowl. Heat a plate in a 250° oven.

Place the measured ingredients beside the wok in the order in which they are to be placed in the wok.

Heat the wok to medium high (375°) and swirl in 1 tablespoon of the oil. Add the steak, and stir-fry until the white of the cornstarch has gone—about 1 minute. Push to the side. Add the broccoli and stir-fry 2 minutes. Scrape the steak and broccoli onto the warm plate. Add the other tablespoon of oil to the wok, stir in the ginger mixture, and stir-fry 1 minute. Stir in the sauce and cook until it thickens and clears, about a minute. Stir in the mushrooms and bamboo shoots, heat a moment, then return the steak and broccoli to the wok and toss all ingredients together until heated through—about 1 minute. Serve as soon as possible, with green onion brushes as garnish if you wish.

Beef Teriyaki, Japan

Prep. Time 5 minutes; Marinate 15 minutes • Serves 2
Cooking Time 5 minutes

Tender, savory strips of beef marinated in a Japanese sauce, then stir-fried. Serve with rice. As a second dish, choose any seafood and vegetable entrée or steamed fresh asparagus and a tossed salad.

½ pound flank steak, or any
  tender cut of beef cut across
  the grain into ⅛ inch slices

3 tablespoons vegetable oil
Radish flowers (page 235),
  optional

*Marinade*_____

1 1-inch piece fresh ginger,
  peeled
½ cup Japanese soy sauce or
  soy sauce
⅓ cup sake or rice wine

3 tablespoons loosely packed
  brown sugar
1 large clove garlic, peeled
½ teaspoon Chinese prepared
  mustard

In a blender or a food processor, or by hand, mince the ginger and process with the soy sauce, sake, sugar, garlic, and mustard. Toss the meat with the marinade and allow to marinate 15 minutes.

Heat the wok to medium high (375°), swirl in the oil, and stir in the meat and marinade. Stir-fry only until the red is gone—1 minute or 2 at most. Serve at once, garnished with radish flowers if you wish.

Variation:

Chicken Teriyaki—Substitute for the beef 2 chicken legs with thighs, separated at the joint, boned, and cut into shreds ½-inch thick.

Orange Beef

Prep. Time 15 minutes; Marinate 2–4 hours • Serves 4–6
Cooking Time 8–10 minutes

Tender strips of flank steak with carrots and celery in an orange sauce that makes this recipe a favorite. It's a good choice for any multi-entrée meal because it can be kept warm 15 to 20 minutes before serving without losing its quality. Great with Philippine Nasi Goreng (page 81) and Sichuan Shrimp (page 153).

1 flank steak (about 1½ pounds)
¼ cup all purpose flour
¼ cup vegetable oil
2 medium carrots, peeled and cut into long ovals ¼ inch thick
2 large celery stalks, cut into ½-inch rounds

3 fat green onions, trimmed to 4 inches
4 thin orange slices, optional
4–6 mint or basil or parsley sprigs, optional

Marinade
½ cup rich marmalade
½ cup orange juice
2 teaspoons orange rind

¼ cup soy sauce
1 teaspoon Hunan or chili paste

In a large bowl, combine the marinade ingredients. Lay the steak flat and, with the knife at a slight angle, cut it into strips 2 inches wide. Mix the steak into the marinade and marinate at room temperature for 2 to 4 hours. Scrape the marinade from the steak strips, reserving the marinade. Wipe the steak with paper towel and dredge it in the flour until well coated. Heat a large serving dish in a 250° oven.

Place the measured ingredients beside the wok in the order in which they are to be placed in the wok.

Heat the wok to medium high (375°) and swirl in the oil. Lay the steak strips one at a time across the hottest part of the wok until half are in. Turn until brown on all sides. Push up onto the side of the wok and repeat until all the strips are browned. This should not take more than 3 to 5 minutes—don't overcook; the strips should be rare inside. When the steak strips are browned, push them all up the side of the wok and add the carrots. Stir-fry 1 to 2 minutes and push to the side. Add the celery, stir-fry 1 or 2 minutes, and push to the side. Add the green onions, stir-fry 1 minute. Scrape the marinade into the wok and stir until it bubbles and thickens. Combine the meat and vegetables thoroughly with the sauce. Keep warm until ready to serve in the heated dish, garnished with orange slices and herb sprigs if you wish.

Variation:

Turkey Breast in Orange Sauce—Substitute for the beef strips 4–6 large fillets of turkey breast ¼-inch thick. Brown in batches 1–2 minutes on each side, then remove to a warm serving dish. Pour the prepared vegetables and sauce over the turkey.

Sha Cha Beef

Prep. Time 10 minutes • Serves 2–3
Cooking Time 7 minutes

Sha Cha Beef is another specialty of my friend, restaurateur Bell Wong. Sha cha sauce is for barbecues, he tells me, and he uses one made in Taiwan of fish, garlic, chili pepper, dried shrimp, and soybean oil. The flavor is mild and uniquely Chinese. Serve the dish with rice.

1 tablespoon vegetable oil
½ flank steak (¾–1 pound), sliced into shreds ½ inch thick
12 pieces canned baby corn, drained and rinsed
1 sweet green pepper, seeded and cut into strips ½ inch wide

1 medium carrot, peeled and sliced into long ovals ¼ inch thick
2 green onions, trimmed to 3 inches and minced

Sauce_____

½ cup chicken broth (or more)
1 tablespoon sha cha sauce or oyster sauce
½ tablespoon soy sauce

1 tablespoon rice wine or dry sherry
2 teaspoons cornstarch

In a small bowl, combine the sauce ingredients. Heat a serving dish in a 250° oven.

Place the measured ingredients beside the wok in the order in which they are to be placed in the wok.

Heat the wok to medium high (375°) and swirl in the oil. Turn the steak into the wok and stir-fry just long enough to have the meat lose its red color, 1 to 2 minutes. Push the steak up the side of the wok. Add the corn and peppers and stir-fry 2 minutes. Add the carrots and stir-fry 1 minute. Push the vegetables up the side of the wok. Add the onions, stir once, and push to the side. Pour in the sauce and stir until it bubbles and thickens. If the sauce is too thick, add more broth. Push all the ingredients down into the sauce, stir once or twice, and turn into the warm dish. Serve at once.

Beef in Ginger Curry, Sumatra

Prep. Time 15 minutes • *Serves 2; 3 with rice*
Cooking Time 15 minutes

Tender strips of stir-fried flank steak topped with an aromatic, spicy chili sauce. I've made this with ground beef patties, too, and it's delicious. Serve with rice and Tomato and Pepper Relish (page 223) or a tossed salad.

½ **flank steak (¾–1 pound)**
½ **cup tamarind liquid (page 36),**
 or 2 tablespoons lemon juice
1 **1-inch piece fresh ginger,**
 peeled
1 **small onion, peeled**
2 **medium cloves garlic, peeled**
1 **tablespoon ground coriander**
1 **teaspoon ground cumin**
¼ **teaspoon cinnamon**
½ **teaspoon pepper**

½ **teaspoon ground cloves**
½–1 **teaspoon chili paste or red**
 pepper flakes
½ **teaspoon shrimp paste in**
 bean oil
1 **cup coconut milk (page 34)**
2 **tablespoons vegetable oil**
6 **leaves frilly lettuce**
Chutney

Holding a sharp knife at a slight angle, cut the meat into ¼-inch-thick slices and toss with the tamarind liquid. In a food processor or blender, or by hand, mince the ginger, then add and coarsely chop the onion and garlic. Measure the five spices into a small bowl, along with the two pastes, and mix together. Warm a serving dish in a 250° oven. Remove the steak strips from the tamarind liquid and dry with paper towel.

Place the measured ingredients beside the wok in the order in which they are to be placed in the wok.

Heat the wok to medium high (375°) and swirl in the oil. Add the steak and stir-fry until the red is gone—but not more than 1 minute. Remove to the warm serving dish. Reduce the heat to simmer (about 200°), add the ginger mixture to the wok, and stir-fry 2 minutes. Add the spice and paste mixture and cook 5 minutes, stirring. If the mixture gets too dry, add a little coconut milk. Add the remaining coconut milk and cook, stirring often, until the sauce is thick. Reheat the steak strips in the sauce, stirring together for about 1 minute. Serve at once on lettuce, with chutney on the side.

Steak, Peppers, and Eggplant, Cantonese Style

Prep. Time 15 minutes • Serves 2
Cooking Time 8–10 minutes

Steak stir-fried with vegetables in a tangy sauce—great with rice. A good companion dish is Sichuan Shrimp (page 153).

1 strip or blade steak (about ½ pound), cut into strips ⅛–¼ inch thick
1 medium onion, peeled
1 small Chinese eggplant or eggplant
½ cup beef broth
½ tablespoon cornstarch

2 tablespoons vegetable oil
⅓ each red, yellow, green sweet pepper, seeded and cut into 1-inch squares
Radish flowers (page 235), optional
Parsley sprigs, optional

Marinade

2 tablespoons soy sauce
1 tablespoon hoisin sauce, or soy sauce mixed with plum sauce
2 tablespoons rice wine or dry sherry

½ teaspoon sugar
2 big cloves garlic, peeled and crushed
¹⁄₁₆ teaspoon pepper

Combine the marinade ingredients in a bowl, mix well with the steak, and marinate until ready to cook, 5 minutes or more. Slice the top and bottom from the onion, divide it into eight wedges, then separate the leaves. Stem the eggplant and slice it into ½-inch-thick rounds or pieces about ½ inch by 2 inches. In a small bowl, combine the broth and the cornstarch. Warm a serving dish in a 250° oven.

Place the measured ingredients beside the wok in the order in which they are to be placed in the wok.

Heat the wok to medium high (375°) and swirl in the oil. Push the steak into the wok, retaining in the bowl as much marinade as possible. Stir-fry 1 minute, then lift the steak onto the warm serving dish. One at a time, add the vegetables to the wok, stirring briefly after each addition. Stir-fry until the onions are crispy tender, 3 to 4 minutes. Stir up the cornstarch mixture and pour into the wok. Pour the remaining beef marinade into the sauce and cook, stirring, until the sauce thickens and clears. Stir the steak into the sauce, then combine the vegetables with the sauce, turn onto the serving dish, garnish with radish flowers and parsley if you wish, and serve as soon as possible.

Chop Suey Chimney Hill

Prep. Time 10–15 minutes • Serves 6, with rice
Cooking Time 15 minutes

This savory meat and vegetable mélange has always been a favorite in my family. Serve it with boiled rice, tossed green salad, and fruit for dessert. One of the great things about this dish is that it is also good made with leftover meat from a pork or chicken roast, from tips from beef steaks, or from almost any scraps of beef cut into thin shreds.

1 cup beef broth
1 tablespoon cornstarch
2 tablespoons vegetable oil
1 medium onion, sliced thin
2 large cloves garlic, peeled and minced
4 medium stalks celery, cut into strips ¹⁄₁₆ by 5 inches
3 tablespoons soy sauce (or more)
½ teaspoon sugar (or more)
½ teaspoon salt (or more)

½ teaspoon pepper (or more)
1 medium sweet pepper, seeded and cut in long shreds
1 cup canned bean sprouts, bamboo shoots, or baby corn, drained and rinsed
½ pound large mushrooms, wiped and cut in T-shapes
1–2 cups cooked or raw beef, shredded

Place the measured ingredients beside the wok in the order in which they are to be placed in the wok.

Combine the broth with the cornstarch in a small bowl. Heat the wok to medium high (375°) and swirl in the oil. Add the onion and garlic and stir-fry 1 minute, then push up onto the side of the wok. Add the celery and stir-fry 2 minutes, or until the strips are soft and pliable. Season with a bit of the soy, sugar, salt and pepper. Repeat the procedure with the rest of the ingredients, stir-frying about 1 to 2 minutes and then seasoning. Push everything up onto the side of the wok (as best you can), pour in the broth and cornstarch mixture, and stir until the broth thickens and clears. Push everything into the broth, and stir to combine well. Taste, and add more soy, sugar, salt, or pepper if you wish. Serve at once.

NOTE: *To feed 16,* see Chop Suey Chimney Hill, Party Recipe (page 120).

Sukiyaki, Japan

Prep. Time 30 minutes • Serves 6
Cooking Time 10 minutes

Sukiyaki is one of Japan's best-known dishes. Cook it at the table in front of dinner guests if you own an electric wok. Also a great choice for a beach party or picnic where you can cook over an open fire. Serve with individual bowls of rice.

1 package bean threads
2 pounds sirloin or chuck steak, cut into 2-inch by 1-inch strips
4 medium carrots, peeled and cut into matchstick shreds
2 bunches green onions, trimmed to 3 inches and cut into matchstick shreds
½ pound big mushrooms, wiped clean and sliced in ½-inch-thick T-shapes

1 16–ounce can baby corn, drained and rinsed
2 squares tofu, cut into 1-inch cubes
4 cups washed spinach leaves
Radish flowers (page 235)
Parsley sprigs
½ cup vegetable oil

Sauce

2 cups beef broth
¾ cup Japanese soy sauce
¼ cup sugar

3 tablespoons rice wine or dry sherry

Soak the bean threads in hot water 20 minutes, drain, and pat dry. Combine in a bowl the four sauce ingredients. In the center of a very large platter, arrange the bean thread in a row and set the meat slices on top. Arrange the vegetables in rows on either side and garnish with radish flowers and parsley. Bring to the table with the oil and sauce and with tongs or chopsticks (if you can, cook with chopsticks).

Heat the wok to medium (350°) and swirl in about 1 tablespoon of the oil. Lay a third, or less, of the meat pieces across the bottom of the wok and brown quickly on each side—1 to 2 minutes. Push them high on the side of the wok and add a third of the sauce. Scrape up the pan juices and add a third of the carrots, onions, mushrooms, and corn to the wok. When the ingredients boil, place a portion of the tofu, bean thread, and raw spinach over this layer, and place the browned meat on top. When the sauce returns to a boil, invite guests to help themselves to its contents. As soon as the wok is empty, repeat the process, and continue until all the ingredients have been cooked.

Sukiyaki

Moo Shu Pork, Northern China

Prep. Time 30 minutes • Serves 2; 4 with a second dish
Cooking Time 10 minutes

This dish is very popular in Bell Wong's restaurants. Each guest gets a plate with heaps of savory pork, scrambled eggs, and shredded onion, which he rolls up in thin pancakes. To serve two people, allow three pancakes per plate; use two pancakes per plate if three or four people are being served. The recipe looks complicated, but once you understand that the pancakes steam while you stir-fry the stuffing, you'll see it's easy and fast. This makes a delightful luncheon or dinner with salad and chilled fruit.

6–8 Chinese pancake wrappers, thawed
1 piece tree fungus (2 by 1½ inches)
3 dried Chinese mushrooms, or fresh mushrooms
¼ cup loosely packed tiger lily buds
3–5 green onions, trimmed to 3 inches

¼ small head green cabbage, shredded (1½–2 cups)
2 tablespoons vegetable oil
2–3 ounces pork loin, shredded by hand
2 eggs (3 if serving 4) beaten with 2 tablespoons water (or more)
Hoisin sauce
Cilantro sprigs

Sauce

⅓ cup chicken broth
1½ tablespoons mushroom soy or soy sauce

1½ teaspoons sugar
1 tablespoon cornstarch

Organize the steaming of the wrappers: set the stack of wrappers on moistened paper towel on a steaming rack and cover with three sheets of damp paper towel. Place the rack in your second wok, if you have one, or over a large pot that has a domed lid.

Set the fungus, dried mushrooms, and tiger lily buds to soak separately in boiling water to cover for 5 to 15 minutes, or until soft. Mince 1 green onion and set near the cabbage. Shred the others and reserve until serving. In a small bowl, mix the ingredients for the sauce. Just before you start to cook, squeeze the fungus, mushrooms, and lily buds dry. Cut away and discard the tough fungus core and mushroom stems. Shred the fungus and mushrooms and halve the lily buds. Set the dinner plates to warm in a 250° oven.

Place the measured ingredients beside the wok in the order in which they are to be placed in the wok.

Pour boiling water to a depth of 1 inch into the steaming pot, uncover the pancakes, and turn the heat to simmer (about 200° in an electric wok). Heat the wok to medium high (375°) and swirl in 1 tablespoon of the oil. Add the pork and stir-fry 2 minutes. Add the cabbage and stir-fry 2 minutes. Stir in the minced onion. Stir in the fungus, mushrooms, and lily buds and stir-fry 1 minute more. Push the ingredients to one side and pour the sauce down the side of the wok. Stir as it cooks and clears, and combine well with the pork mixture. Divide among the warmed dinner plates and keep warm. Cover the pancakes again with the damp paper towel, and continue steaming.

Wipe out the wok, swirl in the second tablespoon of oil, and scramble the eggs until barely set—don't cook them dry. Turn off the heat and divide the eggs among the warmed plates. Divide the pancake wrappers among the plates. Arrange a little bundle of the reserved shredded green onions, a small dish of hoisin sauce, and 3 pancakes on each plate. Garnish with cilantro sprigs. Serve at once. NOTE: *To eat*—heap half or a third of the pork mixture, eggs, and shredded onion onto each pancake, with a bit of cilantro if desired, and roll up like a spring roll leaving the top open. Dip in hoisin sauce.

Peking Style Pork

Prep. Time 10 minutes • Serves 2
Cooking Time 5–6 minutes

A very fast, very easy dish of sweet shreds of pork and crisp bean sprouts in a tangy sauce. Serve with Crispy Shrimp with Walnuts (page 154), or fried rice. This is another of Bell Wong's favorites.

2 tablespoons vegetable oil
1 large garlic clove, peeled
½ pound boneless pork tenderloin, cut across the grain
into ¼- by 1½-inch slices

1 16-ounce can bean sprouts,
drained and rinsed, or 2 cups
fresh bean sprouts, rinsed
Snow pea fan, optional

Sauce

1 tablespoon rice wine, or dry
sherry
1 tablespoon soy sauce

1½ tablespoons hoisin sauce
1 teaspoon cornstarch
1 tablespoon water

In a small bowl, combine the sauce ingredients. Heat the wok to medium high (375°) and swirl in the oil. Slice the garlic into the oil, add the pork, and stir-fry 2 minutes. Push the pork up onto the side of the wok and add the bean sprouts. Stir-fry 1 minute and push up onto the side of the wok. Add the sauce and stir until it thickens and clears. Combine with the pork and sprouts and keep warm until ready to serve. Garnish the serving plate with a snow pea fan if you wish.

Lamb in Honey Sauce, Peking Style

*Prep. Time 10–12 minutes; Marinate 30 minutes • Serves 2; 3 with rice
Cooking Time 10–12 minutes*

Nuggets of sweet, spicy lamb in a most unusual dish that is an adaptation of an ancient Manchu recipe. The "honey" in the title indicates the delightful flavor rather than an actual ingredient. This is great with Crispy Shrimp with Walnuts (page 154), Philippine Nasi Goreng (page 81), Peking Style Pork (page 140), or fried rice.

½–¾ pound boneless leg of
   lamb, cut into shreds ¼ inch
   by 2 inches
2 tablespoons hoisin sauce
1 tablespoon soy sauce

1½ tablespoons cornstarch
Vegetable oil
2 tablespoons sesame oil
Fruit garnish (see list pages
   247–250), optional

*Sauce*_____

1 ½-inch piece fresh ginger,
   peeled and minced
2 tablespoons soy sauce
3 tablespoons rice wine or dry
   sherry

2 tablespoons rice vinegar or cider vinegar
1 teaspoon molasses
1 tablespoon sugar

In a large bowl, toss the lamb shreds with the hoisin and soy sauces, then mix in the cornstarch and marinate 30 minutes. Combine the six sauce ingredients in a blender or food processor, or by hand. Heat a serving dish lined with paper towels in a 250° oven. Have handy a container for excess hot oil.

Fill the wok with oil to a depth of 1½ to 2 inches. Heat the oil to high (400°), or until a day-old cube of bread browns in just under 1 minute. Heat another 4 minutes to stabilize the temperature. Scrape the lamb into the oil and stir to separate the shreds. Cook about 2 minutes. Lift the lamb onto the heated dish and keep warm. Turn off the heat. Pour off oil, wipe out the wok, and reheat to medium high (375°). Swirl in the sesame oil. Pour the sauce into the wok and stir until it bubbles and begins to thicken a little. Turn the meat into the wok, heat through, and scrape into the serving dish. Keep warm until ready to serve with a garnish of fruit, such as mango slices or mandarin orange segments, if you wish.

NOTE: *To serve 10*, multiply all ingredients by 4.

Lamb Korma, India

Prep. Time 10 minutes; Marinate 15 minutes • Serves 4
Cooking Time 20–30 minutes

Tender lamb chunks in a creamy, aromatic curry sauce that is wonderful with rice and chopped fresh coconut, chopped apple, or Onion Samball (page 219). A favorite in my family.

1 pound boneless leg of lamb
   or boned lamb breast, cut into
   1-inch cubes
½ teaspoon salt
1 pint plain yogurt
1 8-ounce can tomato sauce
1 tablespoon ground coriander
1 tablespoon ground cumin
¼ teaspoon ground cardamom
½ teaspoon ground ginger

Pinch of ground clove
¼ teaspoon red pepper flakes
1 tablespoon vegetable oil
3 tablespoons butter
1 large onion, peeled and sliced
1 large clove garlic, peeled and
   sliced
Chutney

In a large bowl, combine the lamb with the salt and yogurt and marinate 15 minutes. Pour the tomato sauce into a small bowl and stir into it the six spices.

Place the measured ingredients beside the wok in the order in which they are to be placed in the wok.

Heat the wok to medium (350°) and swirl in the oil. Melt the butter, add the onion and garlic, and stir-fry until the onion is golden, 3 to 5 minutes. Add the lamb and the tomato sauce mixture and stir together. Cover, reduce the heat to simmer (about 200°), and cook until the meat is tender, 20 to 30 minutes. If the sauce seems thin, remove the cover and raise the heat for the last few minutes of cooking. Serve hot, with chutney on the side.

Lamb Curry with Lima Beans

Prep. Time 10 minutes • Serves 4, with rice
Cooking Time 30 minutes

A rich curry highlighted by baby lima beans. This dish is a good choice for parties, because it can be made ahead and reheated.

1 teaspoon vegetable oil
2 tablespoons butter
1 pound boneless leg of lamb or boned lamb breast, cut across the grain into shreds ½ inch by 2 inches
¼ teaspoon salt
Grinding of pepper
1½ cups beef broth (or more)

10 ounces thawed frozen baby lima beans
2 tablespoons Curry Paste (page 35)
4 ounces vanilla yogurt
Chutney with Peaches, Mango, and Ginger (page 218) or fruit chutney

Place the measured ingredients beside the wok in the order in which they are to be placed in the wok.

Heat the wok to medium (350°), swirl in the oil, then melt the butter in the wok and brown the meat strips on all sides. Season with the salt and pepper and push up the side of the wok. Pour in the 1½ cups of broth and when it boils, add the lima beans. Put the meat on top of the beans, reduce the heat to simmer (about 200°), cover the wok, and cook 10 minutes. Stir in the curry paste and yogurt, cover, and simmer 10 minutes more. Check often to make sure the sauce isn't drying out. If it does, add a little more broth. When the beans are cooked and the sauce is thick the dish is done. Serve hot, with chutney on the side.

NOTE: Thai curry paste tends to be hot. For a milder curry paste, prepare my recipe on page 35.

Nine

Seafood and Surimi Entrées

Seafood entrées are among the best in the Oriental repertoire. Each Far Eastern culture seems to have produced its own fish sauce, oyster sauce, and shrimp paste; in addition, shrimp is often included as a flavoring in meat and vegetable dishes. Anyone looking for light meals has probably already discovered that fish and shellfish are nutritionally very sound, providing all the nutrients of meat—without the calories—as well as some meat does not supply, like phosphorus and Vitamin B. Many of the recipes that follow are under 200 calories per portion, including their sauces.

Fish in Your Wok

Fish cooked in a wok are most often marinated and steamed, or batter-dipped and deep-fried, or cut into bite-size pieces and gently stir-fried.

Steaks of firm-fleshed fish such as salmon, swordfish, and tuna can be ready in minutes when marinated briefly in a sauce and steamed, as in the recipe for Swordfish in Tamarind Sauce. Large fish fillets—1-inch-thick fillets of cod and haddock, for instance—may also be steamed, about 6 to 8 minutes per pound. Smaller fillets are ready in 6 minutes per pound. Test the fish gently with a fork before removing it from the steamer. If the flesh separates cleanly into flakes, it's cooked. Err on the side of underdone.

For stir-frying in bite-size pieces, the fish must have flesh that is somewhat firm. Monkfish is a good choice. Softer-fleshed fish, such as flounder, are excellent batter-dipped and deep-fried.

Small whole fish may be dredged in cornstarch and deep-fried briefly, as in the recipe for Sea Bass Hunan Style. As a rule of thumb, small fish and chunks of batter-dipped fish are cooked after 3 to 4 minutes in hot oil.

Freshwater fish, whose flesh tends to be soft, may be pureed and used as stuffing, as in the recipe for Cod-stuffed Peppers in Oyster Sauce.

Surimi

Surimi is a new and excellent addition to the Oriental larder in this country, although it has been used in Japan for centuries (since 1100 A.D.). A cooked fish paste, surimi in America is shaped, flavored, and colored to look like crabmeat, lobster, and shrimp. It includes a percentage of the "real" thing plus pollock, whiting, croaker, or hake, and flavoring agents. The flavor resembles the seafood being imitated with a hint of something Japanese—soy sauce perhaps?

Baked and steamed fish "cakes" are yet another surimi product; they can simply be thawed and served as appetizers, and are especially good with gingery sauces like Teriyaki Sauce (page 225).

Because surimi is already cooked, it makes preparation and cooking of any dish it is used in very fast indeed. And surimi costs about half as much as the foods it imitates while offering a higher protein content and a slightly lower calorie count. I like to use surimi because the flavor is a bit more robust than the flavor of the real thing, and stands up well to the strong flavorings in many stir-fry recipes.

One warning: never deep-fry or boil surimi. It is meant to be served either just warmed or cold in salads and appetizers.

The recipes in this book use surimi "lobster claws," "crab slices" ("salad style crab"), and "crab legs," but you can use other forms if the one called for isn't available. Surimi "shrimp" cannot be used as a substitute for raw shrimp to flavor recipes and for that reason has not been called for in any of the dishes in this section.

Handle surimi products as you do fresh fish: use as soon as possible after purchase, and if frozen, right after thawing.

A Shopper's Guide to Fish and Shellfish

Apart from surimi, there is no such thing as a bargain in seafood. A bargain usually means a not-so-fresh product. Seafood deteriorates much faster than meat, and can't be stored several days without developing the "fishy" odor that has made many people dislike fish. Really fresh fish has a briny, not fishy, smell.

In the days when my father, Chef Marcel Stephan, went to market to buy his seafood, he could tell fresh fish by the clarity of the eyes as well as by the smell. Filmed-over, glazed eyes meant an old catch. Today we must often choose from filleted pieces, sometimes packaged in plastic, so it isn't easy to judge whether the fillet is dried out or smells "fishy." That means you must rely on the fish merchant. Before you buy, ask specifically whether the fish is fresh. If the merchant says, "Fresh thawed," he's being honest. Most fish we buy—unless we're near the sea—comes from big fishing fleets that freeze their catches at sea. It is good unless it's been thawed for more than a day.

Selecting Shellfish

Crab: Most of the recipes here use either cooked shelled fresh hardshell crabmeat or surimi forms. Shelled fresh crabmeat is sold by the pound and half pound. The only way to get crabmeat out of the shell is to cook it, cool it and pick it out. This entails much work, so the product is expensive. I've paid anywhere from $8 to $16 a pound. Many fish markets offer up to four types of shelled fresh crabmeat in half-pound and pound cartons. Lump crabmeat is large chunks taken from the crab body. Backfin is taken from the body but in smaller pieces. Claw meat is taken from the pincers. Flake crabmeat is made up of bits taken from the body and the claws. Lump is the most expensive—flake the least. Whichever you buy, pick it over with your fingers, removing any bits of shell and cartilage overlooked by the packers.

SUBSTITUTE: Surimi crab in salad slices, sea legs, sticks. Recipes for crab will also be good for lobster.

Softshell crab: During the spring on the East Coast, 4- to 6-inch crabs that have shed their old shells but not yet hardened new ones, come on the market. Since they are sold by the piece, always select the largest.
SUBSTITUTE: None.

Lobster: The recipes here use fresh Maine lobsters, and surimi lobster claws. Maine, or *Homarus*, lobster is the East Coast type with large claws and modest tails, rather than the spiny lobster of European and southern waters, which has small pincers, and is often sold as "lobster tails." Buy live lobster and have the merchant bag them separately—so they won't eat each other. And check the pincers to make sure they are pegged to keep them from pinching you. Lobsters from Maine and Canada are the best. The shell of a live lobster is dark, mottled, greenish. The lobsters from the northern waters are lighter than those from farther south—that's how you can guess whether the lobster being sold as a Maine lobster really is from Maine, rather than from the waters off Cape Cod. These are excellent, too. Buy live lobster no more than a day before you will cook it: store it in its bag in the refrigerator, preferably in the crisper.
SUBSTITUTE: Spiny lobster of equal weight; frozen, thawed raw lobster tail; surimi lobster "claws."

Prawns: Very big shrimp often are billed as prawns, but there's a difference. Prawns are closer to the lobster than to the shrimp, but have thick antennae that flop back over the body where lobsters have pincers. The flesh of a prawn is finer and sweeter than shrimp, but prawns and shrimp are so similar in every respect that restaurants use whichever is easier to find and most reasonably priced. I prefer shrimp, whose flavor seems to me stronger, for Oriental cooking. There are no prawn recipes in the book. If prawns are easier for you to find than shrimp, you may use them in any recipe here that calls for shrimp.
SUBSTITUTE: Shrimp.

Scallops: The shellfish itself is rarely offered on the market because it dies quickly once out of the water. Instead, what is offered is the cream-colored muscle that closes the shells of this bivalve. The sea scallops are large, about 1½ inches in diameter, shaped rather like a marshmallow, and are strongly flavored. This type is most often offered in Oriental restaurants. Bay scallops are ½ inch in diameter, and sweeter. The recipes here call for the larger type, sold by the pound. Sea scallops are quite a bit less expensive. Look closely before you buy—fresh scallops are firm, have little odor; older scallops seem to mush together, have a strong smell. Fresh sea scallops are a definite cream-color; small bay scallops tend toward pink. Big sea scallops that are very white may have been soaked in water to increase their weight, and may spoil more quickly.

SUBSTITUTE: For many recipes, bay and sea scallops may be interchangeable, but not in the recipes here.

Shrimp: Most recipes here call for fresh, small raw shrimp, which are sold by weight. There are about 26 to 30 in one pound. Medium-size shrimp have about 20 to 24 in a pound. Big shrimp are about 12 to a pound. The larger the shrimp, the more expensive—that's why when the shrimp will be cut up or pureed, or used as a flavoring agent, recipes call for the smaller size. Larger sizes may be used when small sizes are called for, but small shrimp get even smaller after cooking, so don't buy these to serve as appetizers or when an impressive display of shrimp is wanted. Raw fresh shrimp and just-thawed frozen shrimp have tight skins and feel plump and full. The odor is briny and shrimpy, but not very strong. Older shrimp have loose shells, feel a bit mushy, and in a handful there will be several broken pieces. Buy shrimp the day you plan to use them, if possible. You can keep them one or two days in the refrigerator, but no longer. Since many of my recipes call for shrimp as a flavoring and as a main ingredient, you may want to buy very fresh shrimp and freeze them in the shell in quarter-pound lots, labeled with the date. Large fish merchants often stock 5- and 10-pound bags of raw frozen shrimp in the shell—called green shrimp—but I avoid these since to get them into smaller lots, I would have to break up the frozen block or thaw and refreeze. For instructions on the fast way to shell and devein shrimp, see below.

SUBSTITUTE: Prawns. Small canned shrimp may be used to flavor a recipe. Shelled deveined cooked shrimp are a rubbery substitute, only suitable for use as a flavoring agent. Don't use Oriental dried shrimp—they taste like smoked ham.

How to Shell and Devein Shrimp

In timing recipes, I have allowed about 5 minutes to shell and devein ¼ pound of small raw shrimp. Medium and large shrimp will take less time (since there are fewer shrimp per pound), very small shrimp maybe more time. It also takes less time per quarter pound to do a whole pound—you get into the rhythm of it, and it moves fast. You may find it slow going until you've shelled your first batch, then it will become easy and fast.

Place the shrimp in the sink with two bowls; one to hold the discarded shells; the other to hold the prepared shrimp. Take a shrimp in both hands, belly facing you. With both thumbnails, gently break the shell segments in the center of the belly and pull the center segment off the body. Then hold the shrimp in one hand and, working from belly to back with your fingers, peel away the remaining shell segments. Gently tug on the tip of the tail shell until it comes away, leaving the tail intact. (Sometimes, especially working with small shrimp that aren't too fresh, the tail will come away with the shell—this can't be helped.) On very large shrimp, the tail shell is usually left on because it makes a better presentation.

When all the shrimp are shelled, devein them with a small, sharp knife. Hold the shrimp under cold running water in one hand, body curled around so the back faces you. Starting at the top, or head end, make a very shallow incision all along the center back to just above the tail. In small shrimp the force of the running water is often enough to dislodge the dark or light pink vein. If not, use the tip of the knife to push the vein free and rinse the shrimp under the water. Drain the shrimp, then set them on paper towel so the last of the excess moisture can be absorbed. The shrimp are now ready to cook.

Selecting Fish

Cod: A large Atlantic fish that can weigh between 40 and 60 pounds. Buy fillets and make sure they are boneless.
SUBSTITUTE: Scrod, lufish, cush are other varieties of cod. But any boned white-fleshed fish will be a suitable substitute.

Flounder: A light-fleshed, or white, flat fish, resembling sole and halibut, but having slightly coarser flesh, and less expensive. I use it for my wok recipes whose strong flavors tend to drown rather than bring out the delicacy of the more expensive fish. Flounder is sold filleted in sizes from 4 ounces to almost a pound. If the fillet is to be cooked and served whole, choose individual fillets each four to six ounces in weight for each serving. If the fish is to be cut into bite-sized portions, or pureed, choose pieces of fillet about 1-inch thick.
SUBSTITUTE: Sole varieties and halibut, fluke, petrale, round nose, dab, rock turbot—some of the latter are types of flounder, while others are regional varieties with different names. A delicious but expensive substitute is orange roughy. Monkfish is an excellent substitute for stir-fried recipes.

Monkfish: This relative of the grouper is new to our fishmarkets, though a treasured staple in France where it is known as *lotte*. Other local names for it are angler-fish, belly fish, goosefish. It's big—3 to 5 feet—with a head so big it seems to take up half the tapered body. Sold in thick fillets, monkfish flesh is light-colored, firmer than flounder, and tastes a bit like lobster. The firmness makes monkfish ideal for use in stir-fry recipes. Rather inexpensive.
SUBSTITUTE: Haddock, flounder, orange roughy.

Salmon: Big, pink-to-coral-fleshed fish of the cold Pacific and Atlantic waters. The types sold as Atlantic salmon and chinook have the finest texture, color, and flavor. For the recipes here, buy fresh steaks, or just-thawed steaks, about 1-inch thick and weighing 4 to 6 ounces. Use the same day if possible, though salmon will keep a day or two.
SUBSTITUTE: No substitute, but a salmon steak recipe will be good made with fresh swordfish or tuna.

Sea bass: A smallish saltwater fish weighing about half a pound and served whole in Chinese restaurants. My recipe—and most calling for sea bass—serves one whole fish per guest. The flesh is delicate. Sold by the pound in most big fish markets, including supermarket fish shops. Black sea bass is easiest to find on the Atlantic Coast.
SUBSTITUTE: Small tunny, horse mackerel, bluefin, yellowfin, skipjack, and albacore.

Swordfish: Related to the mackerel, this is a big saltwater fish whose flesh is almost as firm as meat. Swordfish steaks have two dark spots near the tail. Buy fresh fish, if possible, about 1-inch thick, and allow 4 to 6 ounces per serving. Prices are high.
SUBSTITUTE: Mako, tuna.

Tuna: Another relative of the mackerel. Albacore is the expensive variety; bluefin, yellowfin are similar. Bonito is the strongest-flavored and least desirable. Buy steaks as fresh as possible, and allow 4 to 6 ounces per person.
SUBSTITUTE: Swordfish.

Menu Suggestions

Cantonese Luncheon for 4

Monkfish in Sweet and Sour Sauce
Steamed rice
Won Ton Soup
Exotic Finger Fruits

Elegant Malaysian Dinner for 2

Spring Roll Miniatures
Softshell Crabs and Shrimp, Malay Style
Steamed rice
Crisped Coconut Shreds
Wilted Green Vegetable Salad (½ recipe)
Peaches with Honey-Lime Sauce

Polynesian Dinner for 2

Spring Rolls, Cantonese Style (4)
Lemon Sole Polynesian Style
Steamed rice
Chopped Apple Relish
Garden-ripe yellow tomatoes
Papaya halves sprinkled with pomegranate seeds

Elegant Chinese Dinner for 2

Won Ton Soup
Steamed Swordfish Steaks with Spinach and Ginger
Vegetarian Delight
Chilled canned lychees in syrup
Fortune Cookies

Thai Dinner for 4

Lobster Claws with Coconut Sauce
Chutney-stuffed Won Tons
Steamed rice
Garden-ripe tomatoes, red and yellow
Basket of exotic finger fruits

Japanese Dinner for 4

Miso Soup
Tempura Dinner, Japan
Steamed rice
Ripe honeydew melon with lime wedges

Indonesian Dinner for 4

Hot and Sour Soup
Cod-Stuffed Peppers in Oyster Sauce
Steamed rice
Vegetable Salad with Shrimp Dressing
Sliced bananas and mangoes with yogurt topping

Bengalese Dinner for 4

Cod Fillet Curry, Bengalese Style
Steamed rice
Tomato and Pepper Relish
Wilted Green Vegetable Salad
Basket of exotic finger fruits

Light Supper for 2, Thailand

Swordfish with Tamarind Sauce, Thai
Steamed rice
Peanuts Crushed with Pepper
Mushroom and Alfalfa Sprout Salad
Chopped coconut
Pineapple chunks and mangoes

Light Supper for 2, Indonesia

Salmon in Spice Sauce with Papaya
Celery and Lettuce Salad
Chilled Fruit Cream, India

Sichuan Shrimp

Prep. Time 25 minutes • Serves 4, with rice
Cooking Time 6 minutes

Plump shrimp steamed, then stir-fried for a moment in a spicy, savory sauce from Bell Wong's kitchen. This is a great dish for ginger lovers and goes well with Orange Beef and lots of hot rice. Serve an icy fruit dessert such as Fruit Platter with Yogurt Topping (page 244).

1 pound small shrimp, shelled and deveined
1 2-inch piece fresh ginger, peeled

½ small onion
1 green onion, green part only
2 tablespoons vegetable oil

*Sauce*_____

5 tablespoons ketchup
3 tablespoons rice wine or dry sherry

2 tablespoons sugar
2 tablespoons Hunan paste

Prepare the shrimp and set on the wok steaming tray. In a food processor or blender, or by hand, mince the ginger and then the onion with it. Mince the green onion separately. Combine the sauce ingredients in a small bowl.

Fill the wok with hot water to within 1 inch of the rack. Cover and heat the wok to simmer (about 200°). After steam begins to escape, set the rack with the shrimp into the wok, cover, and steam 3 minutes. Remove the rack, empty the wok, and wipe it out with a paper towel. Raise the temperature to medium high (375°) and when it is hot, swirl in the oil, then the ginger mixture. Stir-fry 1 minute, then pour in the sauce and heat until bubbling. Add the shrimp, mix well with the sauce, then turn into a serving dish, garnish with minced green onion, and serve at once.

Crispy Shrimp with Walnuts

Prep. Time 10–12 minutes • Serves 2
Cooking Time 8–10 minutes

A delicious combination, wonderful with rice and a salad and a great companion for any of the vegetable mélanges in Chapter 10. Bell Wong cooks this dish differently: he deep-fries the shrimp, and sprinkles commercial sugar-coated walnuts over the shrimp and the sauce. Either way, it's good!

½ pound small shrimp, shelled, deveined, and halved lengthwise
1 egg white
½ teaspoon salt
⅛ teaspoon pepper

1½ tablespoons cornstarch
4 tablespoons vegetable oil
6 ounces whole walnut meats
Frilly green lettuce

*Sauce*_____
1 teaspoon chili paste
¾ tablespoon sugar
½ tablespoon rice wine or dry sherry

1½ tablespoons ketchup
1 tablespoon soy sauce

Toss the shrimp halves with the egg white and mix in the salt, pepper, and cornstarch. In a small bowl, combine the five sauce ingredients. Heat a serving dish lined with paper towel in a 250° oven.

Heat the wok to medium high (375°), swirl in the oil, and stir in the walnuts. Stir-fry 3 minutes or until brown. Do not overcook—they'll turn black and bitter! Remove the walnuts to the paper-lined plate and keep warm. Turn the shrimp into the wok and stir-fry 3 minutes, separating the shrimp from each other as you cook them. Push the shrimp up onto the side of the wok and pour in the sauce. When it bubbles, mix in the shrimp and the walnuts. Stir just long enough to coat with the sauce, and serve as soon as possible with frilly lettuce as a garnish.

Crispy Shrimp with Pineapple Sauce

Prep. Time 20 minutes • Serves 4, with rice
Cooking Time 10–12 minutes

Sweet, crispy, deep-fried shrimp in a mouth-watering sweet and sour sauce that is wonderful with fried rice. Can be made up to half an hour ahead without losing quality.

1 cup all-purpose flour
1 teaspoon salt
1 cup water
1 tablespoon vegetable oil
1 pound medium shrimp, shelled and deveined

1 16-ounce can pineapple tidbits in their own juice, drained, reserve the juice
8 maraschino cherries, drained
Vegetable oil

Sauce

½ cup reserved pineapple juice
¼ cup water
1½ tablespoons vegetable oil
3 packed tablespoons brown sugar

¼ teaspoon black pepper
2 tablespoons rice vinegar or cider vinegar
1 tablespoon cornstarch

In a medium bowl, combine the flour, salt, water, and oil, and while the batter sets, prepare the shrimp, pineapple, and cherries. In a small saucepan, stir together the eight ingredients for the sauce over medium-low heat until the sauce thickens and clears. Turn off the heat. Heat a serving dish lined with paper towel in a 250° oven.

Fill the wok with oil to a depth of 1½ to 2 inches. Heat the oil to 400° or until a day-old cube of bread browns in just under 1 minute. Heat another 4 minutes to stabilize the temperature. Blot the moisture from the shrimp and mix them into the batter. Scoop the shrimp out one at a time and drop into the oil (I confess—I use my fingers). Fry at one time only as many as can float freely on the surface. Scoop out when shrimp are golden brown—2–3 minutes—and set on the paper-lined plate. Keep warm until all shrimp are done. Reheat the sauce, stir in the pineapple and cherries, then the shrimp, and serve at once.

Shrimp with Coconut and Tamarind, Thai

Prep. Time 25 minutes • Serves 2–3; 4 with rice
Cooking Time 10–12 minutes

Shrimp in a curry that is tart, fragrant, lemony and wonderful over boiled rice. Serve with a savory second entrée, such as Chicken Stir-fried with Walnuts (page 109), or Lamb in Honey Sauce, Peking Style (page 141).

12 ounces shrimp
1 ½-inch piece fresh ginger, peeled
1 bunch green onions, trimmed to 4 inches
2 large garlic cloves, peeled

4 tablespoons vegetable oil
½ cup grated coconut, fresh or packaged
Chutney, preferably Chutney with Peaches, Mango, and Ginger (page 218)

Sauce

1 tablespoon ground coriander
½ teaspoon turmeric
2 tablespoons tamarind liquid (page 360) or lime juice

½ cup tomato juice
1 cup coconut milk (page 34)

Steam the shrimp in their shells until pink, about 3 minutes, then shell and devein.

Mince the ginger, green onions, and garlic together in a processor or blender or by hand. Combine the sauce ingredients in a small bowl. Have handy a bowl lined with paper towel.

Heat the wok to medium (350°), swirl in half the oil, then the coconut, and stir-fry until it browns, 3 to 4 minutes. Transfer the coconut to the paper-lined bowl. Add the remaining oil to the wok, reduce the heat to simmer (about 200°), and set the ginger mixture to brown. Turn the sauce into the ginger mixture and simmer until it is thick. Turn the shrimp into the sauce and heat through—about 2 minutes. Serve sprinkled with the coconut, with chutney on the side.

Variation:

Swordfish with Tamarind Sauce, Thai—While the sauce thickens, steam four 1-inch-thick fresh swordfish steaks, about 1–1½ pounds total, 6 minutes or until they flake. Pour the sauce over the steaks, garnish with cherry tomatoes, and serve with chutney, grated fresh coconut and Peanuts Crushed with Pepper (page 221).

Shrimp with Vegetables

Prep. Time 30 minutes • Serves 4
Cooking Time 10–12 minutes

A fast, easy, tasty dish that goes with any of the more exotic entrées, like Lamb in Honey Sauce, Peking Style (page 141), Hunan Beef (page 128), or Kung Pao Chicken (page 105).

1 ½-inch piece fresh ginger, peeled
4 green onions, trimmed to 3 inches
1 large garlic clove, peeled
2 tablespoons vegetable oil
1 pound small shrimp, shelled and deveined
1 cup Chinese cabbage or other cabbage, shredded

2 tablespoons shredded sweet red or green pepper
½ pound medium mushrooms, wiped clean and sliced into ¼-inch T-shapes
¼ pound snow peas, strings removed

Sauce
2 teaspoons rice vinegar or cider vinegar
2 teaspoons sugar

1 cup chicken broth
2 tablespoons soy sauce

Thickener
1 tablespoon cornstarch

3 tablespoons water

In a food processor or blender, or by hand, mince the ginger, then add and coarsely chop the green onions and the garlic. In a medium bowl, combine the sauce ingredients, and in a small bowl, the thickener ingredients.

Place the measured ingredients beside the wok in the order in which they are to be placed in the wok.

Heat the wok to medium high (375°) and swirl in the oil. Stir in the ginger mixture and stir-fry about 1 minute. Add the shrimp and stir-fry 2 minutes. Push the shrimp up onto the side of the wok and add the vegetables, one at a time, stir-frying 1 minute after each addition, or until the vegetable changes color and brightens. Push each vegetable up onto the side of the wok before adding the next. Pour the sauce into the wok and stir until it bubbles. Stir up the cornstarch mixture, add to the sauce, and cook until it thickens and clears. Mix the shrimp and vegetables into the sauce, and serve as soon as possible.

Tempura Dinner, Japan

Prep. Time 30 minutes • Serves 4–6
Cooking Time 25 minutes

A classic of Japanese cuisine—seafood and vegetables fried to a golden crisp in batter. This is a recipe to prepare at the table, or at a kitchen counter with guests standing by waiting to gobble up the crispy nuggets as they come ready from the wok. Serve with Miso Soup (page 70), steamed rice, iced honeydew melon with lime wedges for dessert.

2 cups all-purpose flour
1 teaspoon baking powder
2 teaspoons salt
1 teaspoon paprika
2 cups water less 4 tablespoons
2 tablespoons oil
1 tablespoon rice wine or dry sherry
6–12 large shrimp, deveined, or rock lobster tails, shelled, tails on
3 inches fresh ginger, peeled and minced
½ cup daikon shreds or prepared horseradish
1 pound fillet of flounder, haddock, sea scallops, or firm white fish, cut into 2- by 1-inch strips

4–6 large mushroom caps, wiped clean and halved
4–6 tiny eggplants, stemmed and cut into ¼-inch-thick lengths (skin on)
2 sweet red or green peppers, seeded and cut into 1-inch-wide strips
6 winged beans, stemmed and halved, or ¼ pound snow peas, stems removed
Vegetable oil

Sauce

1 cup beef broth
¼ cup oyster sauce or soy sauce
4 tablespoons rice wine or dry sherry

In a medium-large bowl, combine the flour, baking powder, salt, and paprika. Combine the water, oil, and rice wine in another bowl, then mix into the flour to form a lumpy batter (I use my fingers). Let the batter set while you prepare the other ingredients.

Slit the shrimp or lobster tails along the back to make them lie flat, but don't cut all the way through. In a small bowl, combine the sauce ingredients, then divide the sauce among smaller bowls, one for each guest. Put the minced ginger and the daikon or horseradish each into a small bowl. Arrange all the other ingredients on a tray and set by the wok—which will be where the guests are. While the wok heats, distribute the individual sauce bowls among the guests and pass around the ginger and daikon or horseradish, inviting each guest to add a little of each to their dipping sauce. Keep handy the oil bottle, so you can add more to the wok as the level lowers, and a little extra flour.

Fill the wok with oil to a depth of 1½ to 2 inches and heat to high (400°), or until a day-old cube of bread browns in just under 1 minute. Heat 4 minutes more to stabilize the temperature. Dip each piece of seafood and vegetable into the batter, allow excess batter to drip off, and place in the oil. Add only as many pieces as can float freely. Separate pieces with tongs if they stick together. When the batter turns golden brown, the pieces are ready. Divide among the guests, and continue to cook. If batter thins because of liquid from fish, add a little flour. Add oil as the level lowers, but make sure the heat stays constant, or the batter will become oily and soggy.

Triple Delight

Prep. Time 30 minutes • Serves 2; 3 with rice
Cooking Time 12–15 minutes

Beef, chicken, and shrimp in a savory sauce rich in green vegetables. This Bell Wong recipe goes well with rice and a spicy dish like Shiitake Mushrooms (page 48).

2 pieces dried tree fungus
2 tablespoons vegetable oil
½ pound small shrimp, shelled and deveined
½ chicken breast, skinned, boned, and cut into strips ¼ inch thick
¼ flank steak (about ⅓ pound), cut into strips ¼ inch thick
1 green onion, trimmed to 3 inches

½–1 cup broccoli florets, 1 inch across
¼ pound snow peas, strings removed
Parsley sprigs or frilly lettuce
Red pepper flowers (page 234) or tomato roses (page 235), optional

Sauce
3 tablespoons chicken broth
1 tablespoon soy sauce
1 tablespoon mushroom soy sauce or soy sauce
½ tablespoon sugar

⅛ teaspoon pepper
1 teaspoon sesame oil
1 tablespoon rice wine or dry sherry

Thickener
2 teaspoons cornstarch

2 tablespoons water

Soak the fungus in hot water to cover until soft, 5 to 10 minutes. Drain, discard the hard parts, and cut into strips. In one small bowl, combine the seven sauce ingredients, and in another, the two thickener ingredients. Heat a serving dish in a 250° oven.

Place the measured ingredients beside the wok in the order in which they are to be placed in the wok.

Heat the wok to medium high (375°), swirl in half the oil, add the shrimp, and stir-fry 2 minutes. Push shrimp up onto the side of the wok. Add the chicken and stir-fry 2 minutes, then push up the side of the wok. Stir-fry the beef 2 minutes. Remove the shrimp, chicken, and beef to the warm serving dish. Add the remaining oil to the wok and in it stir-fry the onion 1 minute, then the broccoli florets 2 minutes. Push them onto one side. Stir-fry the snow peas 2 minutes, then add the fungus. Push the ingredients aside. Pour the sauce into the wok and cook until it bubbles. Add the thickener and cook, stirring, until it thickens and clears. Push the vegetables down into the sauce, then combine the shrimp, chicken, and beef with the vegetables and sauce. Turn into the serving dish and serve as soon as possible garnished with greens and vegetable flowers, if you wish.

Scallops and Shrimp in Garlic Sauce

Prep. Time 30 minutes • Serves 4
Cooking Time 6–8 minutes

Tender little bay scallops and baby shrimp steamed and served in a gingery sauce. Serve with fried rice and Two Sprout Salad (page 211). This is a Bell Wong recipe and very popular in his restaurants.

2 dried tree fungus (optional)
½ pound small shrimp, shelled and deveined
½ pound bay scallops
1 cup broccoli florets 1 inch across (about 1 head)
6 fresh water chestnuts, peeled and sliced in ¼-inch rounds, or canned water chestnuts, rinsed

1 ¼-inch piece fresh ginger, peeled
1 green onion, trimmed to 3 inches
2 large cloves garlic, peeled
2 tablespoons vegetable oil
½ tablespoon sesame oil
2 tomato roses (page 235), optional

Sauce

4 tablespoons chicken broth
1¼ tablespoons mushroom soy sauce or soy sauce
1½ tablespoons soy sauce
1 tablespoon rice wine or dry sherry

1½ tablespoons rice vinegar or cider vinegar
½ teaspoon chili powder
2 teaspoons cornstarch

Soak the fungus, if you are using it, in hot water to cover until soft, 5 to 10 minutes. Arrange the shrimp, scallops, broccoli, and chestnuts on the steaming rack. Drain the fungus, discard the tough parts, and slice it into ½-inch strips. Add to the steaming rack. Fill the wok with hot water to within 1 inch of the rack. Cover and heat the wok to simmer (about 200°). After the steam begins to escape, cook the ingredients 3 to 5 minutes, or until the shrimp are opaque. Meanwhile, in a blender or food processor, mince the ginger, add the onion and garlic, and chop. In a small bowl, combine the sauce ingredients.

When the steaming is complete, remove the rack and its contents. Wipe out the wok with paper towel and reheat it to medium (350°). Swirl in the vegetable oil, add the ginger mixture, and stir-fry 1 minute. Add the sauce and stir until it thickens and clears. Slide the ingredients from the steaming rack into the sauce, stir once, add the sesame oil, stir to combine everything with the sauce. Serve as soon as possible, with tomato roses as garnish if you wish.

Variation:

Surimi Crab in Garlic Sauce—For the scallops and shrimp, substitute 1 pound surimi crab—either sea legs or sliced salad style—heated for 1 or 2 minutes in the sauce.

Softshell Crabs and Shrimp, Malay Style

*Prep. Time 20 minutes • Serves 2
Cooking Time 10–12 minutes*

The ultimate luxury combination—softshell crab and shrimp in a tart Malaysian curry. The secret ingredient is coconut milk. (Half-and-half cream is a substitute, but it won't be quite the same.) Serve with rice, chopped apple, Raita (page 220), and Onion Samball (page 219).

2 softshell crabs
¼ pound small shrimp
1 1-inch piece fresh ginger, peeled
1 tablespoon ground coriander
1 tablespoon ground cumin
½ teaspoon turmeric
2 tablespoons water
4 green onions, trimmed to 3 inches
3 big cloves garlic, peeled
¼ teaspoon mustard powder, or ½ teaspoon good prepared mustard

2 tablespoons vegetable oil
1 cup coconut milk (page 34), or more
½ teaspoon salt
1 big meaty tomato, cut into 4 or 6 wedges
Chutney, preferably Chutney with Peaches, Mango, and Ginger (page 218)

Reserve any liquid the crabs and shrimp may have rendered before preparing them. Rinse and drain the crab. Shell and devein the shrimp. In a food processor or blender, or by hand, mince the ginger. Turn it into a small bowl and mash together with the coriander, cumin, and turmeric, then mix with the water. In the processor or blender, or by hand, mince together the green onions and garlic, place in a small bowl, and sprinkle the mustard over them.

Place the measured ingredients beside the wok in the order in which they are to be placed in the wok.

Heat the wok to medium low (300°) and swirl in the oil. Stir-fry the onion-garlic mix for about 2 minutes, or until the onions show a bit of browning. Stir in the spice paste, and stir-fry 1 minute. Stir in the coconut milk and cook until the mixture begins to thicken, about 3 minutes. Slide the crabs into the sauce on their backs, legs up. Spoon the simmering sauce over the tops and stir them around while they cook 2 minutes. Turn them over and stir the shrimp into the sauce. Add any liquid the crab and shrimp have rendered—the sauce should be thickening, and the liquid will thin it out a bit. It should be thin enough and plentiful enough so the seafood is surrounded by simmering sauce. If necessary, add a little more coconut milk, or water. The curry should cook 3 minutes more after the shrimp are added. Stir, scraping up the bottom to keep it from sticking and burning. Stir in the salt. Turn off the heat. Arrange the tomato wedges around the edge of the wok, cut ends in the sauce, and serve at once. Offer chutney on the side.

NOTE: *To serve four*, double the crabs, add ¼ pound of shrimp, 1 more tomato, ¼ cup more milk, and a bit more salt.

Surimi in Malaysian Curry

Prep. Time 30 minutes • Serves 14–16
Cooking Time 30 minutes

This is a wonderful party curry entrée, rich in seafood and aromatic spices. Serve with little side dishes of Crisped Coconut Shreds (page 221), Peanuts Crushed with Pepper (page 221), Raita (page 220), and Onion Samball (page 219). You can make the sauce hours ahead, heat the surimi in it, and cook the shrimp at the last minute.

4 cups raw converted long-grain rice, cooked
1 3-inch piece fresh ginger, peeled and minced
3 tablespoons ground coriander
3 tablespoons ground cumin
1 teaspoon ground cardamom
1½ teaspoons turmeric
6 tablespoons water
2 bunches green onions, trimmed to 4 inches
8 big cloves garlic, peeled
¾ teaspoon mustard powder, or 1½ teaspoons good prepared mustard
4 cups coconut milk (page 34), or half-and-half cream
4 tablespoons vegetable oil
1½ teaspoons salt (or more)
3 tablespoons tamarind liquid (page 36) or lemon juice

1 pound raw small shrimp, shelled, deveined, and halved lengthwise
1 8-ounce package surimi lobster claws, thawed and cut into 6–8 slices each
1 8-ounce package surimi crab legs, thawed and cut into 4 pieces each
1 8-ounce package surimi crab salad style, thawed and shredded
4 large garden-ripe tomatoes, cut into 8 wedges each
Chutney, preferably Chutney with Peaches, Mango, and Ginger (page 218)

While cooking the rice, prepare the other ingredients. In a small bowl, mash together the ginger and the four spices, then mix in the water. In a food processor or blender, or by hand, mince together the green onions and the garlic, and sprinkle the mustard over them.

Place the measured ingredients beside the wok in the order in which they are to be placed in the wok.

Heat the wok to medium low (300°) and swirl in the oil. Stir in the onion mixture and fry for 4 minutes, or until it begins to brown. Mash in the spice paste and stir-fry 3 minutes. Stir in the coconut milk and cook until the sauce begins to thicken. Add the salt and tamarind liquid, cook 2 minutes, and taste. If you wish, add more salt. Mix the shrimp into the sauce and cook until they turn pink, about three minutes. Add the surimi pieces and combine well with the sauce. Scrape into a serving dish and line the edges of the plate with the tomato wedges, cut side in the sauce. Serve with the hot rice and chutney.

Surimi Crab Legs Sichuan

Prep. Time 15 minutes • Serves 2
Cooking Time 4 minutes

Exotic and piquant. Serve with steamed rice. This can be made with fresh crab meat, but Sichuan seasonings are better suited to the more robust flavor of the surimi product.

8 ounces surimi crab salad style, thawed
2 ounces (about ¼ cup) thawed frozen peas
6–8 shreds red or yellow sweet pepper
1 large garlic clove, peeled
1 green onion, trimmed to 4 inches
1 ½-inch piece fresh ginger, peeled
½ teaspoon chili paste (more if you like it hot)

2 tablespoons ketchup
3 tablespoons beef bouillon
1 tablespoon rice wine or dry sherry
1½ tablespoons brown sugar (dark or light)
1 teaspoon cornstarch
1 tablespoon water
2 tablespoons vegetable oil
1 teaspoon rice vinegar or cider vinegar (or more)

Arrange the crab, peas, and sweet pepper on a small plate. Mince the garlic, onion, and ginger together and place on a saucer. In a small bowl, combine the chili paste and ketchup. In another bowl, combine the bouillon, rice wine, and brown sugar. In a third bowl, dissolve the cornstarch in the water.

Place the measured ingredients beside the wok in the order in which they are to be placed in the wok.

Heat the wok to medium high (375°). Swirl in the oil and stir-fry the garlic, onion, and ginger until brown—1 to 2 minutes. Add the chili paste and ketchup mixture. Turn off the heat. Stir in the bouillon, wine, and sugar mixture, and stir and cook until bubbling stops. Turn the heat back on and stir in the crab, the peas, the peppers, and the onion mixture. Stir-fry 30 seconds. Stir in the cornstarch mixture and as soon as it thickens, sprinkle with the vinegar. Turn off the heat. Taste, and if desired add a bit more vinegar. Serve at once.

Curried Crab and Cucumber, India

Prep. Time 10 minutes • Serves 2
Cooking Time 13 minutes

Crab makes a wonderful main ingredient for this delicious curry, crunchy with cucumber slices. With a food processor, preparation takes no time at all. Wonderful with rice, a tossed salad, and thick slices of golden or red tomatoes. Offer any of the relishes in Chapter 11, or Onion Samball (page 215), as side dishes, along with chopped coconut.

1 medium cucumber
1 ½-inch piece fresh ginger, peeled
1 large onion, peeled
1 large clove garlic, peeled
3 tablespoons vegetable oil
1 tablespoon ground coriander
1 teaspoon ground cumin
1 teaspoon turmeric
½ teaspoon salt
½ cup coconut milk (page 34), or more
8 ounces cooked, shelled fresh crab, surimi crab legs, or surimi crab slices
Parsley or cilantro sprigs
Chutney

With a potato peeler, remove the stem ends and three broad stripes of peel from the cucumber. In a food processor or by hand, slice the cucumber into thin rounds and spread on paper towels. In the processor, or by hand, mince the ginger, then add and chop the onion and garlic.

Place the measured ingredients beside the wok in the order in which they are to be placed in the wok.

Heat the wok to medium (350°) and swirl in the oil. Add the ginger-onion mixture and stir-fry until golden, 3 to 4 minutes. Reduce the heat to simmer (about 200°) and stir in the spices and salt. Stir and cook 2 minutes more. Add the coconut milk and stir and cook 3 minutes more. Add the cucumber and cook until it is barely tender, about 2 minutes. If the sauce dries out, add more coconut milk. Add the crab and simmer until it is warmed through, about 2 minutes. Garnish with parsley or cilantro and serve hot with chutney on the side.

Lobster with Coconut Sauce

Prep. Time 30 minutes • Serves 2; 4 with rice
Cooking Time 14 minutes

Thai in origin, this is a delicately flavored curry that enhances the flavor of fresh Maine lobster. Delicious with steamed rice and slices of ripe tomatoes.

2 live lobsters (about 1 pound each), steamed, halved, or 4 surimi lobster claws, thawed
⅔ cup clam juice or chicken broth
1 teaspoon cornstarch
1 tablespoon coconut milk (page 34)
2 tablespoons butter
3 green onions, trimmed to 3 inches and minced
1 ½-inch piece fresh ginger, peeled and minced
2 large cloves garlic, peeled and minced

8–10 medium mushrooms, wiped clean and sliced into ½-inch-thick T-shapes
½ cup broccoli florets, 1-inch wide
½ teaspoon turmeric
1 tablespoon ground coriander
½ cup coconut milk (page 34), or more
Salt and pepper
Chutney
4 sprigs cilantro (optional)

Place the live lobsters in warm tap water 10 minutes to put them to sleep. Set them on the steamer rack of the wok above 1½ inches of hot water, cover, set the heat to simmer (250°), and steam the lobsters 20 minutes after steam starts to escape from under the wok lid. Remove the lobsters. Set them on their backs, and with a big carving knife, cut them in half down the center all the way to the tip of the tail. Crack the claws. Reserve the liquids that escape from the lobsters as they are halved, and any of the greenish tomalley, and add it to the clam juice. Remove the claws, keeping them as whole as possible. Pull the tail meat free. Discard the claw and tail shells, but reserve the bodies of the lobsters. In a small bowl, mix the cornstarch and 1 tablespoon coconut milk.

Place the measured ingredients beside the wok in the order in which they are to be placed in the wok.

Heat the wok to medium low (300°) and melt the butter in it. Add the onions, and stir-fry 1 minute. Add the ginger and garlic and stir-fry 1 minute. Add the mushroom pieces and stir-fry 2 minutes. Add the broccoli florets and stir-fry a moment, then sprinkle the turmeric and coriander over the ingredients in the wok, stir once or twice, and pour in the clam juice and coconut milk. Cook, stirring, until the sauce has reduced by about a third. Stir in the cornstarch mixed with coconut milk, and cook, stirring, until the sauce thickens.

Taste and add salt and pepper if desired. Turn off the heat. Gently place the lobster meat in the sauce, and allow to heat through, about 2 minutes. Meanwhile, arrange the body sections of the lobsters on warm dinner plates, one half to each of four plates, or two halves to each of two plates. Lift the claws and tails from the sauce and arrange at the head and tail of the body sections. Scrape the sauce and vegetables from the wok over the lobster, including the body sections. Serve with chutney and cilantro sprigs as garnish, if desired.

Salmon in
Spice Sauce with Papaya

*Prep. Time 10 minutes; Marinate 5 minutes • Serves 2; 4 with rice
Cooking Time 10 minutes*

A very simple entrée of pink salmon steaks and golden papaya slices enhanced by a delectable Indian sauce. Nice with a green salad and fresh pineapple.

2 ½-pound salmon steaks
1 teaspoon vegetable oil
½–1 cup chicken broth
½ teaspoon ground cumin
½ teaspoon ground coriander
¼ teaspoon ground cardamom

1 teaspoon rice vinegar or cider vinegar
2 tablespoons butter
16 large spinach leaves, washed
1 ripe papaya, peeled, seeded, and cut into 8 thin slices

Marinade_____

1 ½-inch piece fresh ginger, peeled
3 tablespoons rice wine or dry sherry
1 tablespoon soy sauce

2 tablespoons piña colada frozen concentrate or packed brown sugar
1 teaspoon sesame oil

In a processor or blender, or by hand, mince the ginger with the rice wine, soy sauce, piña colada, and sesame oil. Set the salmon steaks in a shallow bowl, pour the ginger marinade over them, and marinate 5 minutes. Turn once. Put the dinner plates in the oven at 250° to warm.

Heat the wok to medium high (375°), swirl in the oil, add the steaks and the marinade, and sear the steaks on both sides—about a minute a side. Pour in half a cup of broth and reduce the heat to barely simmering (about 200°). Cook 4 minutes, then turn the steaks gently, and add the three spices and vinegar. Cover and simmer another 4 minutes. If necessary, add more chicken broth to make sauce for both steaks. Turn off the heat, stir the butter into the sauce, cover, and keep warm until ready to serve. Line the warm dinner plates on one side with spinach leaves. Place the steaks on the leaves. Arrange the papaya slices on the other side of the steaks. Pour the sauce over all, and serve.

Salmon Steamed with Two Sauces

Prep. Time 3 minutes • Serves 2; 4 with rice
Cooking Time 10 minutes

This is the fastest, easiest way to prepare salmon—delicious with buttered rice or baked potatoes, or a salad of tossed greens in Soy and Sesame Salad Dressing (page 216).

2 ½-pound salmon steaks
Soy sauce
Sesame oil or melted butter
1 green onion, trimmed to
   3 inches, minced
1 ripe papaya or avocado,
   peeled and seeded

6–8 leaves Boston or Bibb
   lettuce
½ recipe Vietnamese Dipping
   Sauce (see page 229)
1 recipe Piña Colada Dressing
   (see page 217)

Brush the salmon steaks on both sides with soy sauce, then with sesame oil. Set on the steaming rack and sprinkle with minced green onion.

Set the steaming rack in the wok and fill the wok with hot water to within 1 inch of the rack. Cover and heat the wok to simmer (about 200°). After steam begins to escape, cook the steaks 10 minutes. Meanwhile, cut the papaya into eight crescent-shaped slices. Arrange the lettuce leaves on one side of each plate, and the papaya or avocado slices on the other. Divide the sauces among small sauce bowls, and arrange one of each sauce on each plate or at each place setting. Transfer the cooked salmon to the lettuce leaves and serve at once.

NOTE: *To serve 4*, double the recipe.

Steamed Swordfish Steaks with Spinach and Ginger

Prep. Time 5 minutes · Serves 2
Cooking Time 8 minutes

These fish steaks are steamed with a dash of soy sauce atop a heap of bright green spinach, then drizzled with a gingery lemon sauce! Perfect with a flavored rice and salad, and fresh fruit for dessert.

¼ pound fresh spinach, washed
Mushroom soy sauce or soy sauce
2 ½-pound swordfish steaks (about 1 inch thick)
1 ¼-inch piece fresh ginger, peeled and minced

1½ tablespoons strained lemon juice
2 tablespoons butter or sesame oil
Lemon wedges (optional)

Remove the coarse stems from the spinach and heap the leaves on the steaming rack. Sprinkle lightly with soy sauce. Arrange the steaks on the spinach and sprinkle with soy sauce. Combine the ginger, lemon juice, and butter or oil in a small saucepan. Put two dinner plates in a 250° oven to warm.

Set the steaming rack in the wok and fill the wok with hot water to within 1 inch of the rack. Cover and heat the wok to simmer (about 200°). After steam begins to escape, steam the fish 6 to 8 minutes depending on its thickness. Meanwhile, if you have an electric stove, turn a small burner on the stove to high heat, but don't put the sauce on it yet. Transfer the cooked fish and spinach to the warmed plates, and garnish with lemon wedges if you wish. Put the sauce on the burner over high heat and stir until it froths. Cook 30 seconds, then drizzle over the fish. Serve at once.

Tuna with Saffron and Rice, Vietnam

Prep. Time 30 minutes; Marinate 30 minutes • *Serves 2–3*
Cooking Time 5–6 minutes

This exotic creamy dish glows with the gold of saffron.

1 cup long-grain converted rice
1 pound tuna (slices about 1 inch thick)
2 tablespoons vegetable oil

1 clove garlic, peeled
½ cup heavy cream (or more)
Cucumber fan (page 233), optional
Parsley sprigs

Marinade_____

3 tablespoons heavy cream
½ teaspoon saffron
½ teaspoon salt

2 teaspoons nuoc mam or fish sauce
¼ teaspoon chili powder

Cook the rice while preparing the rest of the ingredients. Cut the tuna into small ¼-inch-thick pieces. Combine the cream, saffron, salt, nuoc mam, and chili powder, and smear the fish shreds with this marinade. Marinate 30 minutes.

Heat the wok to medium high (375°), swirl in the oil, and crush the garlic into the oil with a garlic press. Stir-fry until the garlic begins to brown. Reduce the heat to medium (350°), add the fish and marinade, and stir-fry 2 minutes. Push the fish up the side of the wok, add the cream, mix with the pan juices, then stir in the fish. Simmer a minute more, stirring. If the sauce gets too dry, add a little more cream. Mound the rice on a heated serving dish. Pour the fish and sauce over the rice, garnish with parsley, and the cucumber fan if you wish, and serve at once.

Flounder Steamed Cantonese Style

Prep. Time 5 minutes; Marinate 20 minutes • Serves 2
Cooking Time 8 minutes

Flounder marinated in rice wine and ginger, steamed on a bed of cabbage, then drizzled with a scallion and sesame oil sauce. Very good with a flavored rice and salad, and carambola for dessert.

½ pound flounder fillet, or Boston blue, sole, lingcod, or scrod	1 tablespoon vegetable oil
	1 tablespoon sesame oil
1 cup shredded cabbage	Green onion bundles (page 233), optional
1 green onion, trimmed to 3 inches, minced	Parsley sprigs

Marinade

3 tablespoons rice wine or dry sherry	1 tablespoon soy sauce
1 ½-inch piece fresh ginger root, peeled	

Blend the wine with the ginger and soy sauce and marinate the fish in it for about 20 minutes. Arrange the cabbage on the steaming rack. Set the fish on the cabbage and scrape the marinade over it. Combine the green onion with the vegetable and sesame oils in a small saucepan and set on the stove. Warm two plates in a 250° oven.

Set the steaming rack in the wok and fill the wok with hot water to within 1 inch of the rack. Cover and heat the wok to simmer (about 200°). After steam begins to escape, steam the fish 6 to 8 minutes depending on its thickness. Meanwhile, turn a small burner on the stove to high heat, but don't put the sauce on yet. Transfer the cooked fish and cabbage to the warmed plates, and arrange the green onion bundles if you wish. Put the sauce on the burner over high heat and stir until it froths. Cook 30 seconds, then drizzle over the fish. Garnish with parsley and serve.

Flounder Flavored with Garam Masala

Prep. Time 5 minutes • Serves 4
Cooking Time 15 minutes

This tomato and spice sauce will enhance any firm-fleshed white fish fillets, such as orange roughy, sole, or haddock.

2 medium-size yellow onions,
  peeled
2 large cloves garlic, peeled
2 big juicy ripe tomatoes,
  chopped
2 tablespoons vegetable oil
1 ½-inch piece fresh ginger,
  peeled and minced
½ teaspoon chili powder
½–1 cup bottled clam juice, or
  water

½ yellow or red sweet pepper,
  seeded and slivered
½–1 teaspoon salt
4 medium-thick flounder fillets
  (about 1¼ pounds)
1 teaspoon garam masala (page
  36)
Grated fresh coconut (optional)
Raita (page 220), optional

In a food processor or blender, or by hand, chop the onions coarsely with the garlic. Cut up the tomatoes, taking care not to lose the juice. Heat a serving dish in the oven at 250°.

Place the measured ingredients beside the wok in the order in which they are to be placed in the wok.

Heat the wok to medium low (300°), swirl in the oil, add the onion mixture, and stir-fry as it browns—about 4 to 5 minutes. Reduce the heat to simmer about halfway through. Add the ginger, tomatoes, and chili powder. Continue to stir-fry until the tomatoes are becoming mushy. Add the clam juice, pepper, and ½ teaspoon of salt. Scrape the bottom often to keep it from sticking. When the sauce is thick, slide in the fish fillets, cover, and cook until the fish flakes easily, about 5 minutes. If the sauce dries, add more clam juice or water. Remove the fish to the heated serving dish. Stir the garam masala into the sauce and heap the sauce over the fillets. Serve at once with side dishes of grated fresh coconut and Raita, if you wish.

Sea Bass Hunan Style

Prep. Time 15 minutes • Serves 2
Cooking Time 3–4 minutes

Sea bass are the size of an average dinner plate, and you use the whole fish, from head to tail. Deep-fried to a crispy gold and ladled with black bean sauce, they make an elegant dinner with rice and greens tossed with Soy and Sesame Salad Dressing (page 216). Sea bass come complete with bones, so this is not a good choice for children or people who hate bones or don't have the knack of eating fish that aren't boneless fillets. This is one of Bell Wong's wonderful ways with fish!

2 whole sea bass about ½ pound each, cleaned and scaled
¼ cup cornstarch

Vegetable oil
1 green onion, trimmed to 3 inches and shredded

*Sauce*_____

1 cup chicken broth
1 tablespoon rice vinegar or cider vinegar
1½ tablespoons rice wine or dry sherry
2 teaspoons Hunan paste
½ teaspoon soy sauce

2½ tablespoons mushroom soy or soy sauce
1 tablespoon grated lemon rind
1 ¼-inch piece fresh ginger, peeled
1 tablespoon cornstarch

In a blender or food processor or by hand, combine the nine sauce ingredients until the ginger is minced. Turn the sauce into a small saucepan and stir over medium-low heat until it thickens and clears. Warm a serving plate in a 250° oven. Slash the fish at right angles to the backbone—gashes that go through almost to the backbone, but not quite. Dredge the fish in cornstarch.

Fill the wok to a depth of 1½ to 2 inches with oil and heat to 400° (high), or until a day-old cube of bread browns in just under 1 minute. Heat another 4 minutes to stabilize the temperature. Put the fish into the oil and cook 3 to 4 minutes, or until the fish begins to turn golden brown. Lift the fish from the oil and drain on the paper towel while you reheat the sauce to bubbling. Arrange the fish on the serving plate, ladle with sauce, and serve at once, garnished with green onion shreds.

Variation:

Surimi Lobster Claws with Black Bean Sauce—Heat surimi lobster claws for 1 to 2 minutes in the sauce for Sea Bass Hunan Style. An 8-ounce package of surimi lobster claws serves 4 with rice and a second entrée.

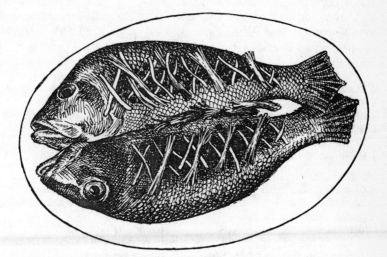

Steamed Sea Bass

Cod-stuffed Peppers
in Oyster Sauce

Prep. Time 15 minutes • Serves 2; 4 with a second dish
Cooking Time 15 minutes

These peppers are stuffed with fish puree, then seared in the wok and simmered until tender. Makes a complete meal for two served with Mushroom and Alfalfa Sprout Salad (page 213) with Soy and Sesame Salad Dressing (page 216). You need a food processor to make this.

2 small or 1 large sweet green
  or red pepper
Tapioca starch or cornstarch
1¼ teaspoons tapioca starch or
  cornstarch
1 tablespoon cold water

2 tablespoons vegetable oil
1–1½ cups chicken broth
2 teaspoons oyster sauce or soy
  sauce
8 thin rounds yellow or red
  tomatoes (2 tomatoes)

Stuffing

1 ½-inch piece fresh ginger,
  peeled
2 green onions, trimmed to
  4 inches
½ pound fillet of cod, scrod,
  Boston blue, or other white
  fish

1 tablespoon cold water
2 teaspoons tapioca starch or
  cornstarch
2 teaspoons sesame oil
½ teaspoon soy sauce
¼ teaspoon sugar
½ egg white

In a food processor, mince together the ginger and green onions, then add and puree the fish. Combine the water and starch, then mix in the sesame oil, soy sauce, sugar, and egg white, and beat into the puree. Halve small peppers, or quarter large ones, at points that create pepper cups for stuffing. Seed and discard the stems. Dust the interiors of the pepper cups with starch. Stuff the pepper cups with fish puree, using all the puree and pressing it firmly into the cups. Flatten the puree surface. Combine the 1¼ teaspoons starch and the 1 tablespoon water. Warm a serving dish in the oven at 250°.

Heat the wok to medium high (375°), swirl in the oil, and set the peppers into it, puree side down. Cook for 3 minutes, sliding the peppers around often until the puree is dark brown. Add 1 cup of the broth, cover, reduce the heat to simmer (about 200°), and cook stirring now and then for 8 minutes. Add more broth as needed to keep sauce simmering around the peppers; there should never be less than ⅓ cup. When the peppers begin to look a duller color and a bit shriveled (thinner-walled peppers cook faster than thick-fleshed peppers), the dish is done. Stir in the oyster sauce and the starch mixture, and stir until the sauce has thickened. Turn the peppers, puree side up, onto the warm serving dish, garnish with tomato slices, and pour the sauce over top. Serve hot.

Cod Fillet Curry, Bengalese Style

Prep. Time 10 minutes • Serves 4
Cooking Time 7 minutes

A mild, creamy gold and green curry fragrant with coconut. Serve with rice and a chilled relish, such as Tomato and Pepper Relish (page 223), and a fruit salad for dessert. Monkfish or haddock are also suitable for this recipe.

1¼ pound thin cold fillets, cut into 1-inch chunks
1 tablespoon turmeric
¼ teaspoon salt
2 cups coconut milk (page 34)
1 teaspoon ground coriander
1 teaspoon ground cumin

2 tablespoons tamarind liquid (page 36) or lemon juice
½ sweet green pepper, seeded and shredded
2 tablespoons butter
Chutney

In a large bowl, toss the fish fillets with the turmeric and sprinkle with the salt. Heat a serving dish in a 250° oven.

Place the measured ingredients beside the wok in the order in which they are to be placed in the wok.

Heat the wok to simmer (about 200°). Pour in the coconut milk and bring to a simmer. Turn the fish into the milk and stir gently 2 minutes. With a slotted spoon, lift the fish onto the heated serving dish. Raise the heat for the wok to medium high (375°). Stir the coriander, cumin, and tamarind liquid into the milk and cook 2 minutes. Stir in the pepper shreds and cook until the sauce is thick, 2 to 3 minutes more. Pour the sauce over the fish, scraping the wok clean with a rubber spatula. Reduce the heat to medium (350°) and heat the butter in the wok until it turns golden brown. Pour over the fish at once and serve. Offer chutney on the side.

Lemon Sole Polynesian Style

Prep. Time 10 minutes • Serves 2
Cooking Time 6–8 minutes

Delicate lemon sole in an exquisite cream sauce flavored with fennel, saffron, and orange rind. Serve with boiled rice and garden-ripe yellow or red tomatoes, and a platter of exotic fruits for dessert.

1 ½-inch piece fresh ginger, peeled and minced
2 tablespoons butter or sesame oil
¾ pound lemon sole or sole fillet

½ head Bibb or other looseleaf green lettuce
Salt and pepper
Orange slices, thin, seeded
Chutney

Sauce

⅔ cup coconut milk (page 34) or heavy cream
1 tablespoon grated orange rind
¼ teaspoon saffron threads

½ teaspoon ground fennel or anise seeds
1 medium clove garlic, peeled
Salt and pepper

Sprinkle the ginger over the bottom of a baking dish that will fit on your wok steaming rack, and add the butter to the dish. Set the steaming rack and the baking dish in the wok. Fill the wok with hot water to within 1 inch of the rack. Cover and heat the wok to simmer (about 200°). Heat until the butter has melted. Remove the baking dish. With a fork, stir the ginger and butter together. Lay the sole on its gray side in the butter, then turn it over—coating both sides well with the butter-ginger mixture. Remove the sole. Line the dish with lettuce leaves, frilled side outward. Lay the sole, pale side up, on the lettuce. Season lightly with salt and pepper and return the baking dish to the steamer. Cover, and steam 6 to 8 minutes, or until the fish is opaque and flakes easily.

While the fish is steaming, in a small saucepan over medium heat, stir together the coconut milk, orange rind, saffron, and fennel. Crush in the garlic with a garlic press and add salt and pepper to taste. Stir until the sauce has reduced by about a quarter and is slightly thick. Remove from the heat. When the fish is done, garnish the sides of the baking dish with orange slices, and pour the hot sauce over the fish. Serve at once, with chutney.

Monkfish in Sweet and Sour Sauce

*Prep. Time 15 minutes; Marinate 20 minutes • Serves 4, with rice
Cooking Time 8 minutes*

This is an adaptation of a Cantonese recipe for flounder fillets. Nice with steamed rice and a curry, such as Beef in Ginger Curry, Sumatra (page 133).

1½ pounds monkfish fillets, cut into 1½-inch chunks
2 tablespoons cornstarch
2 tablespoons water
2 eggs, slightly beaten

1½ tablespoons vegetable oil
1 10-ounce can pineapple chunks in their own juice, drained and halved; reserve the juice

Marinade

2 tablespoons soy sauce
½ teaspoon salt
1 tablespoon rice wine or dry sherry

1 green onion, shredded
1 ½-inch piece fresh ginger, peeled and grated

Sauce

Reserved pineapple juice
¼ cup water, or more
3 packed tablespoons brown sugar

¼ teaspoon black pepper
2 tablespoons rice vinegar or cider vinegar
1½ tablespoons cornstarch

In a large bowl, combine the marinade ingredients. Add the monkfish chunks and marinate. In another bowl, combine the cornstarch, water, and eggs. Combine the sauce ingredients in a cup (add more water if needed, to make 1 cup liquid). Place a serving dish lined with paper towel in a 250° oven.

Place the measured ingredients beside the wok in the order in which they are to be placed in the wok.

Heat the wok to high (375°) and swirl in the oil. Stir up the egg mixture. Dip each chunk into the egg mixture and place in the wok; keep the pieces in the wok stir-frying as you add more. Stir-fry about 4 minutes. Add to the wok only as many pieces as will fit in one layer. Transfer the cooked pieces to the serving dish and keep warm. When all are done, add the sauce and remaining marinade to the wok and stir until the sauce thickens and clears. Stir in the pineapple chunks. Remove the paper from the serving dish, pour the sauce over the fish, and serve as soon as possible.

Fish Balls, Burma

Prep. Time 20 minutes • Serves 4–6
Cooking Time 20 minutes

Curry-flavored fish balls cooked in a rich tomato sauce. Serve with rice and a tossed salad. You need a food processor to prepare this dish.

3 medium onions, peeled
4 large cloves garlic, peeled
1 tablespoon grated lemon rind
¼ teaspoon chili powder
2 teaspoons curry powder
2 teaspoons salt
1½ pounds cod fillets, or haddock, Boston blue, or flounder, cut in 2-inch pieces

All-purpose flour
¼–½ cup vegetable oil
3 medium-size ripe tomatoes, chopped, or 2 cups tomato sauce
Parsley sprigs
Chutney

In a food processor mince the onions and garlic. Scrape the mixture into a small bowl and combine with the next four ingredients. Put the fish into the food processor, grind, and leave in processor. Line a large plate with about an inch of flour.

Heat the wok to medium (350°), swirl in about 4 tablespoons of oil, and stir in the onion mixture. Stir-fry 2 to 3 minutes, or until golden brown. With a slotted spoon return the mixture to its bowl. Put a third of the onion mixture into the food processor with the fish, and process until the mixture becomes a fluffy mass. Scoop the fish mixture onto the flour-lined plate. Between your palms, roll the mixture into balls the size of a small cherry tomato, then roll in the flour.

Add 1 to 2 tablespoons of oil to the wok and, in batches, stir-fry the balls until golden brown. Add more oil as needed. Keep the cooked balls warm. When all are done, stir in the tomatoes, scraping up the pan juices. Add a little water if the tomatoes are dry. Simmer the tomatoes 5 minutes. Add the reserved onion mixture and simmer 10 minutes until the tomatoes have cooked down. Pour over the fish balls. Keep warm until ready to serve. Add the parsley as a garnish and offer chutney on the side.

Ten

Vegetable Dishes

Oriental vegetable dishes, particularly those from China, often are not intended as side dishes, but as entrées. My friend restaurateur Bell Wong's Vegetarian Delight not only showcases the exotic Oriental uses of vegetables, but it is satisfying enough to serve as a main dish. In India, dishes like Lentils with Garam Masala are served as a main course with bread or rice. In China these vegetable entrées are enhanced with meat or seafood, as in Broccoli in Crab Sauce and Green Beans Fukien. Most of the recipes in this chapter can be served as an entrée, or as an accompaniment to meat or fish entrées. To add meatless protein to any of the recipes that follow, mix in rinsed, dried, bean curd. See pages 89–90 for a discussion of bean curd and tofu.

Steaming and stir-frying are now such popular ways to cook vegetables that I've begun this chapter with guides to steaming and stir-frying vegetables featuring the 17 most common vegetables. Following the basic steps in these guides, you will be able to create an exciting entrée or side dish easily in minutes.

Also in this chapter you'll find a list to introduce you to some of the exotic new vegetables that have recently begun to appear in your local supermarket. The list is arranged alphabetically and is intended to help you identify as well as use them.

Menu Suggestions

Vegetarian Dinners for 4

Chutney-stuffed Won Tons
Hot and Sour Soup
Vegetarian Delight, garnished with Fried Cellophane Noodles
Lentils with Garam Masala
Chilled Fruit Cream, India

Shrimp Toast
Dhal Mulegoo Thani, India
Broccoli in Crab Sauce (double recipe)
Steamed rice
Bean Sprout Salad
Fruit Platter with Yogurt Topping

Rice Chips (1–1½ cups rice)
Stir-fried Broccoli and Button Mushrooms (double recipe)
Sweet Peppers in Sweet and Sour Sauce
Saffron Rice, India
Crushed Pineapple with Coconut Cream Topping

Basic Recipe for Steaming Vegetables

Follow the steps below in conjunction with the chart on pages 187–188 to steam and season the vegetable of your choice. If you like, omit the basic sauce suggested in the chart and use one of the sauce recipes in Chapter 11 instead. Depending upon the vegetable you've chosen, cooking time will range from 1 to 12 minutes. *The amounts given serve 2.*

(1) Prepare 1 to 1⅓ cups of the vegetable you've chosen as specified in the PREP. column of the chart.

(2) Fill the wok with hot water to about 1 inch below the steaming rack. Set the vegetable on the rack. Cover the wok and heat to simmer (about 200°). When steam escapes from under the cover, begin counting the steam time specified for the vegetable you've chosen.

(3) While the vegetable steams, in a small saucepan combine the basic sauce ingredients given in the chart, plus any additional ingredients specified in the SAUCE column opposite your vegetable. Cook, stirring constantly, until the sauce thickens and clears. Remove from heat.

(4) *To serve at once*, combine the steamed vegetable with the sauce, and add garnish if desired. *To keep warm*, put the cooked vegetable in a heated serving dish in a 250° oven. Just before serving, heat the sauce to boiling, combine with the vegetable, and garnish if desired.

Vegetable	Prep.	Steam Time	Sauce
			1–1½ cups chicken broth, 2 tsp. cornstarch, 1 tbsp. soy sauce, ¼ tsp. sugar, salt & pepper
			add:
Asparagus	roll-cut, or whole	6–9 minutes	*Omit sauce:* Use 4 tbsp. melted butter mixed with ¼ tsp. minced fresh ginger
Beans	roll-cut	5–6 minutes	

Vegetable	Prep.	Steam Time	Sauce add:
Bean sprouts	as is	2 minutes	1 tbsp. rice wine
Broccoli	1" florets	2–3 minutes	1 clove garlic, peeled and minced
Cabbage	shred	3–4 minutes	½ tsp. roasted sesame seeds
	⅛ head	10–12 minutes	
Carrots (and parsnips)	¼" slices	3–4 minutes	¼–½ tsp. grated orange rind
Cauliflower	1" florets	5–6 minutes	1 tsp. rice vinegar
Celery	¼" slices, or roll-cut	6–8 minutes	
Eggplant, unpeeled	3" × 1" fingers	7–8 minutes	1 clove garlic, peeled and minced
Lettuce	shred	2–3 minutes	1 tsp. minced fresh dill
Mushrooms	whole	4–6 minutes	1 clove garlic, peeled and minced, 2 tsp. rice wine
Peppers, sweet	¼" shreds	2–3 minutes	1 clove garlic, peeled, minced, + 1 green onion, minced
Snow peas	strings removed	3–4 minutes	1 clove garlic, peeled and minced
Spinach (and other leafy greens)	stemmed	1–2 minutes	1 clove garlic, peeled and minced
Summer squash, unpeeled	⅛" rounds	2–3 minutes	1 clove garlic, peeled and minced
Zucchini, unpeeled	⅛" rounds	2–3 minutes	1 clove garlic, peeled and minced

Basic Recipe for Stir-Frying Vegetables

Follow the steps below in conjunction with the chart on the opposite page to stir-fry and season the vegetable of your choice. Depending upon the vegetable you've chosen, cooking time will range from 1 to 8 minutes. *The amounts given serve 2.*

(1) Prepare 1 to 1⅓ cups of the vegetable you've chosen as specified in the PREP. column of the chart.

(2) Heat the wok to medium high (375°). While wok is heating, in a small bowl combine the basic sauce ingredients given in the chart plus any additional ingredient specified in the SAUCE column opposite your vegetable. Set aside.

(3) To the wok add 1 to 2 tablespoons vegetable oil and stir-fry the vegetable for the time specified in the STIR-FRY TIME column.

(4) While stir-frying, add the basic SEASONINGS plus any additional ingredients, specified one at a time.

(5) When the vegetable is within 1 minute of being done, push it to the side of the wok. Stir up the sauce from Step 2 and pour it down the inside of the wok. Cook, stirring constantly, until the sauce thickens and clears.

(6) Mix the vegetable in with the sauce. Garnish if desired, and serve immediately.

Vegetable	Prep.	Stir-Fry Time	Seasonings	Sauce
		in 1–2 tbsp. vegetable oil	½ tsp. sugar 1 tsp. soy sauce *add:*	½–1 cup chicken broth, 2 tsp. cornstarch, salt & pepper *add:*
Asparagus	roll-cut, or whole	4–5 minutes		
Beans	roll-cut	3–5 minutes		1 tsp. minced fresh dill
Bean sprouts	as is	1 minute		1 tbsp. rice wine
Broccoli	1" florets	1½ minutes	1 garlic clove, peeled and minced	
Cabbage	shreds	2–3 minutes		1 tsp. sesame oil
Carrots (and parsnips)	¼" slices	2–3 minutes	1 tsp. minced fresh ginger	
Cauliflower	1" florets	3–4 minutes		1 tsp. rice vinegar
Celery	¼" slices, or roll-cut	2–3 minutes 6–8 minutes		
Eggplant, unpeeled	3" × 1" fingers	3–4 minutes	1 green onion, minced, + 1 clove garlic, peeled and minced	

Vegetable	Prep.	Stir-Fry Time	Seasonings	Sauce add:
Lettuce	shred	1–2 minutes		
Mushrooms	¼" slices, quarters	1½–2 minutes 2–3 minutes	1 clove garlic, peeled and minced	2 tsp. rice wine
Onions	quartered in length, then halved, leaves separated	1–2 minutes	1 clove garlic, peeled and minced	Pinch ground clove
Peppers, sweet	¼" shreds	1–2 minutes	1 clove garlic, peeled and minced, + 1 green onion, minced	
Snow peas	strings removed	1½–3 minutes	1 clove garlic, peeled and minced	
Spinach (and other leafy greens)	stemmed	1 minute	1 clove garlic, peeled and minced	1 tbsp. sesame oil, optional
Summer squash, unpeeled	⅛" rounds	2–3 minutes	1 clove garlic, peeled and minced	
Tomatoes	discard seeds, chop coursely	2–3 minutes	1 clove garlic, peeled and minced	
Zucchini, unpeeled	⅛" rounds	2–3 minutes	1 clove garlic, peeled and minced	

A Guide to Preparing and Serving Exotic New Vegetables

Over the last decade many new vegetables have become available on the American market. Exotic vegetables from around the world that once were available only in specialty shops—if at all—can now be found in the local supermarket. Some of these vegetables and legumes are from Europe: celeriac (which looks like a root and tastes like celery), fennel, and radicchio. Many are from the Far East: Chinese cabbage, chard, eggplant, okra, and turnip; snow, sugar, and China peas; daikon (white Japanese radish), snow puff mushrooms, winged beans, and winter melon. The vegetables I have listed here are useful in Oriental cooking—for stir-frying or steaming, in entrées, for shredding over salads and as garnishes, and for use on crudités platters. Some will find a more comfortable place in your cooking experience than others, but all are fun to try, just to learn what mysterious flavors lurk beneath fascinating new shapes.

Beans, long: These snap green beans usually grow to 12 to 24 inches. They should be handled and cooked as ordinary green beans. Cut 4- to 6-inch lengths and steam until just tender. Serve as ordinary green beans; stir-fried in Chinese recipes such as Green Beans Fukien (page 205) or Long Beans and Pork Shreds (page 204); or steamed, with dipping sauce.

Beans, winged: About the length of your hand, this legume appears now and then on produce shelves in supermarkets. Choose crisp rather than withered specimens, rinse in cold water, and refrigerate until ready to use. Serve steamed until tender, 6 to 8 minutes and offer as a crudités with sauce; or stir-fried until just tender, 5 to 6 minutes when they are large.

Black radish: Large and turnip-like, with a pungent flavor. Carve like a carrot flower (page 232), or shred over salads, or stir-fry as carrots.

Bok choy: See CHARD, CHINESE.

Broccoli, Chinese: Also called *chum soy* and Chinese flowering cabbage, this looks like a very leafy broccoli with sparse buds. It is prized in Chinese and Italian cuisine for its faintly bitter turnip-like taste. Choose small stems that are firm with relatively few buds and open flowers. Serve stir-fried 2 to 4 minutes, or steamed 4 to 6 minutes, as an accompaniment to strongly flavored dishes such as Kung Pao Chicken (page 105) or Sichuan Shrimp (page 153).

Cabbage, Chinese: Also called celery cabbage or napa cabbage. These greens are long like romaine lettuce and packed tight like a cabbage head. Choose pale colors. Discard the tough bottom. Serve shredded in salads, stir-fried, or steamed as cabbage.

Cardoon: A celery-like vegetable with a flavor like an artichoke. Use a potato peeler to remove the stringy part of the ridges. Serve shredded as a relish, particularly with curry dishes and over salads.

Celeriac: Also called celery knob or celery root. It is rootlike and tastes like the sweet, dense root at the bottom of celery. Select small specimens. Serve peeled, grated, or diced; in salads; cut into fingers, with dipping sauces; or cut into shreds and stir-fried, as celery. As a side dish, slice thin and steam 10 to 12 minutes, until tender.

Chard, Chinese: Also called bok choy. A longer version of our familiar Swiss chard. Serve as described for Chinese cabbage, above.

Chayotte: Known as mirliton among Creoles, and vegetable pear in Florida. A South American pale green squash shaped like an animal paw. It's rather tasteless, like most summer squashes, but firmer, so you can do more with it. While chayotte is young, the seed in the middle is edible. Young chayotte also doesn't need peeling. Serve steamed: slice into lengths 2 inches wide, cook 8 to 10 minutes, and serve with a sauce.

Corn, baby: See Oriental Staples, page 17.

Cucumber, lemon: A yellow cucumber that is round like a lemon and has a mild flavor. Serve as cucumbers, sliced, iced, shredded, in salads and relishes and on crudités platters.

Cucumber, long: There are several types of long cucumbers available. One is virtually seedless and ideal for use shredded and on crudités platters. Ask the grocer for this type. Remove seeds and serve cut into sticks with dipping sauce, add shreds to stir-fries at the last minute for a touch of crispness. Serve chilled with curries.

Daikon: A large, mild Oriental radish, often shredded and sliced with Japanese foods, particularly sushi and sashimi. Serve chilled and shredded, with tempura and in salads, or use to make radish fans (page 235).

Eggplant, Chinese: Chinese or Japanese eggplants can be long and curved or small and round, white or pink, as well as the beautiful aubergine of the common varieties. Choose the smallest, because seeds are smaller and flesh firmer. Always remove the stem. Leave the skin on the eggplant if it is to be sliced into rounds for stir-frying—they'll be prettier. Serve stir-fried (see page 185) or steamed with a sauce (see page 188). A nice addition to a tempura meal: slice long, sausage-like eggplant into ½-inch rounds or cut small egg-shaped eggplant into strips ½-inch thick, steam, serve with Peanut Sauce (page 224) in a platter of crudités.

Fennel: A bulbous celery-like head that tastes of licorice. Serve as celery, shredded as a relish or cut into strips as part of a crudités platter. Snip the delicate ferny green leaves over salads, and chew the seeds as an appetite suppressant and breath sweetener.

Jerusalem artichoke: Sunflower tubers with a flavor similar to artichokes. Serve peeled and shredded in salads, or slice, steam 8 to 10 minutes until tender, and serve with butter or curry sauce.

Kohlrabi: Looks like a flying saucer with leaves, tastes like a delicious turnip, and has a great crisp texture. Peel before using.

Serve shredded, stir-fried with a sauce, or steamed until just tender, 3 to 4 minutes.

Long beans: See BEANS, LONG.

Mushrooms: *Dried Chinese or black mushrooms, see* Oriental Staples, page 18.

Enoki, or snow puff, a mushroom with a tiny head and a willowy thread-like stem, sold prepackaged in Oriental markets. Serves as a garnish for salads.

Shiitake mushrooms also are called golden oak on the East Coast, and black forest on the West Coast. They have a superb wild, piney flavor and shouldn't be drowned in strong sauces. Delicious stir-fried in a little butter and served as a side dish.

Common mushroom (Agaricus bisporus): The type most-often called for in recipes. Wipe clean with paper towel. If really soiled, scrub gently with a mushroom brush or wadded paper towel under cold running water. Drain and set on paper towel to dry. Slice off the tough end of the stem before using. Cut into ¼-inch-thick T-shapes.

Button mushrooms are small *"champignons de Paris,"* our common mushrooms in 1-inch sizes. They're sold in supermarkets and are ideal for stir-frying.

Stuffing mushrooms are big (2–3 inches across), beautiful, heavy common mushrooms with white skins, marvelous for slicing onto crudités platters and for stuffing. Or, fill with butter and minced garlic, season with a grating of lemon grass or lemon rind, salt, and pepper, and bake at 375° for 20 minutes, or until withered and juicy.

Mustard, Chinese: A mustard green more pungent than domestic varieties. A few leaves add flavor to soups. Good steamed 5 to 7 minutes and served with butter, or stir-fried as spinach.

Okra, Chinese: A large okra, up to 12 inches long. Scrape away the tops of the ridges and serve steamed or stir-fried. To steam: cut into 1-inch slices and steam 5 to 7 minutes or until tender. Offer a dipping sauce or the basic sauce given on page 216. For stir-frying, cut into ½-inch rounds and stir-fry until just tender.

Plantain: Looks like a fat brown-pink banana, but the taste is not sweet. Ripe plantains are a deep brown color. In the Caribbean and Polynesian islands, plantain is baked or boiled and served as a bland starch to absorb the fiery heat of chili-flavored sauces. Also good mashed with curries. To bake, make an incision the length of the two side seams and bake at 350° for 30 to 45 minutes, or until very tender. To steam or boil, peel with a knife and cook until tender, 10 to 20 minutes. To stir-fry, slice into ½-inch rounds and cook 10 minutes in oil and butter.

Radicchio: Red-leafed chicory. Looks like a small red cabbage, and has a sharp flavor. Serve sliced into creamy white and brilliant purple-red shreds over green salads.

Taro: This root and its relatives such as dasheen, are the bland potato-like starch accompanying meals in the South Pacific. It grows in lengths from a few inches to over a foot. The flesh ranges from white to purplish and the flavor is faintly sweet. Boil until tender, like a potato, then peel and butter; or peel, cut into 1-inch-thick slices and steam until tender, 10 to 15 minutes. Serve as you serve potatoes, with hot Thai and Polynesian foods.

Tomatillos: Bunches of wrinkled green husks, with small green tomatoes inside that taste vaguely of sweet tomatoes or plums. From Mexico. Peel and wash before using. Serve sliced or halved in salads or on relish plates.

Turnip, Chinese: Use as a radish.

Winged beans: See BEANS, WINGED.

Winter melon: These vine-grown squashes look like oversize pale green pumpkins frosted with a white bloom. In China a soup made from the springy, bland white flesh is steamed and served in the shells as the last course of a banquet. Sold in our markets cut up by the pound. Seed and pare away the rind before cutting into bite-size chunks for soup. The recipe for Winter Melon Soup appears on page 72. Serve cooked until translucent in broth.

Stir-fried Asparagus and Water Chestnuts

Prep. Time 5 minutes • Serves 2 as a side dish
Cooking Time 4–5 minutes

Asparagus stir-fried with sweet rounds of fresh water chestnuts makes a delicious luncheon dish, or a wonderful side dish for meat and fish.

⅓–½ pound medium-thick fresh
   asparagus
2 tablespoons vegetable oil
1 green onion, trimmed to
   3 inches and minced
6 peeled fresh water chestnuts
   or drained canned water
   chestnuts, sliced into ⅛-inch-
   thick rounds

½ teaspoon sugar
¼ teaspoon salt
Salt and pepper to taste
Parsley sprigs

Sauce

½ cup beef broth
1 tablespoon soy sauce

1 teaspoon cornstarch

Snap off the bottoms of the asparagus stalks, bending from the bottom until the stalks break, keeping the break as close to the bottom as possible. Roll-cut the stalks into pieces 1 to 1¼ inches long. Combine the three sauce ingredients in a small bowl.

Place the measured ingredients beside the wok in the order in which they are to be placed in the wok.

Heat the wok to medium high (375°) and swirl in the oil. Add the onion and stir-fry 30 seconds. Add the asparagus and stir-fry 3 minutes, or until crispy-tender but still intense green. Push up onto the side of the wok. Add the water chestnuts and stir-fry 1 minute. Season with sugar and salt. Pour the sauce down the side of the wok and stir until it thickens and clears. Mix in the asparagus, season with salt and pepper to taste, and serve at once with parsley as garnish.

Stir-fried Broccoli and Button Mushrooms

Prep. Time 10 minutes • Serves 2 as a side dish
Cooking Time 5 minutes

This one-step stir-fry recipe is one of my favorites.

1 ¼-inch piece fresh ginger,
   peeled
1 green onion, trimmed to
   3 inches
1 medium clove garlic, peeled
1 tablespoon vegetable oil

1 cup button mushrooms or
   ¼ pound large mushrooms,
   wiped clean and quartered
1 cup broccoli florets about 1
   inch across (1 small head)

Sauce

½ cup chicken broth
1 tablespoon soy sauce
1 tablespoon rice wine or dry
   sherry

1 teaspoon sugar
¼ teaspoon salt
⅛ teaspoon pepper
1 teaspoon cornstarch

In a food processor or blender, or by hand, mince the ginger. Add the onion and garlic and chop coarsely. Combine the sauce ingredients in a small bowl.

Heat the wok to medium high (375°), swirl in the oil, then stir in the ginger mixture. Add the mushrooms and stir-fry 2 minutes. Add the broccoli and stir-fry 1½ minutes. Push the vegetables up the side of the wok and pour in the sauce. Stir until it thickens and clears, then combine the vegetables with the sauce and serve as soon as possible.

Sweet and Sour Broccoli

Prep. Time 5 minutes • Serves 4 as a side dish
Cooking Time 10 minutes

Here's a two-step stir-fry recipe for two vegetables in which the vegetables are first steamed and then stir-fried with ginger.

½ pound broccoli (a medium-large head)
1 large carrot, peeled
2 tablespoons vegetable oil

1 ½-inch piece fresh ginger, peeled
1 tablespoon rice wine or dry sherry

Sauce

2 tablespoons rice or cider vinegar
2 tablespoons light or dark brown sugar

1 tablespoon light soy sauce
1 teaspoon cornstarch
1 tablespoon water

With a potato peeler or a sharp knife, remove the coarse outer layer of the broccoli stem, then cut the head into florets 1½ × 1 inch and the stem into pieces the same size. Slice the carrot into rounds ¼ inch thick and cut the rounds into long diamond shapes. Combine the five sauce ingredients in a small bowl.

Spread the vegetables over the wok steamer rack and set into the wok. Fill the wok with hot water to within 1 inch of the rack, cover, bring the water to simmer (about 200°), and steam the vegetables 4 minutes. When the vegetables are ready, turn off the heat, unplug the wok if it is electric, remove the rack, empty the wok, and wipe it dry.

Heat the wok to medium high (350°). Measure the oil into the wok and mince the ginger into the oil. Add the carrots and sprinkle with wine, stirring once or twice. Add the broccoli and stir-fry 1 minute more. Pour the sauce mixture over the vegetables and stir-fry until the sauce thickens and clears—about 1 minute more. Serve at once.

Broccoli in Crab Sauce

Prep. Time 15 minutes • Serves 2
Cooking Time 10–12 minutes

Surimi crab in salad-style slices is perfect for making soy sauce-flavored Cantonese sauce. The Chinese use this crab sauce also on shredded and steamed cabbage, spinach, or roll-cut asparagus.

1 ½-inch piece fresh ginger, peeled and minced
2 tablespoons rice wine or dry sherry
4 ounces lump crabmeat or surimi crab salad-style, thawed

2 tablespoons vegetable oil
1 green onion, trimmed to 3 inches and minced
1 cup broccoli florets 1 inch across (a small head), steamed (see page 188)

Sauce

½ cup bottle clam juice or chicken broth
1 teaspoon soy sauce
1 tablespoon rice wine or dry sherry

½ teaspoon sugar
⅛ teaspoon pepper
1 teaspoon cornstarch

In a food processor or a blender, or by hand, mince the ginger with the rice wine. Add the crab and process just enough to shred. In a small bowl, combine the six sauce ingredients.

Place the measured ingredients beside the wok in the order in which they are to be placed in the wok.

Heat the wok to medium (350°) and swirl in the oil. Add the green onion and stir-fry 1 minute. Add the crab with its marinade and stir-fry 1 minute. Push the crab up onto the side of the wok. Stir in the sauce and cook until it thickens and clears. Mix the crab gently into the sauce, and then fold in the broccoli. Serve as soon as possible.

Sweet Peppers in Sweet and Sour Sauce

Prep. Time 10 minutes • Serves 4 as a side dish
Cooking Time 6–7 minutes

Late summer vegetables in a sweet and sour sauce are a delicious accompaniment for grilled meats and barbecues, and particularly good with chicken entrées.

1 large Bermuda onion
1 ¼-inch piece fresh ginger, peeled
1 large clove garlic, peeled
2 tablespoons vegetable oil
2 sweet red or yellow peppers, seeded and sliced into ½-inch strips

1 small garden-ripe tomato, chopped coarsely
1 6-inch summer squash or zucchini, stemmed and sliced into ½-inch-thick rounds
Parsley sprigs, optional

Sauce
1 cup chicken broth
2 packed tablespoons brown sugar
2 tablespoons rice vinegar or cider vinegar

1½ tablespoons soy sauce
1 tablespoon cornstarch

Cut off the top and bottom of the onion and divide it into six wedges; separate the onion leaves. In a blender or food processor, or by hand, mince the ginger and garlic together. Combine the five sauce ingredients in a small bowl.

Place the measured ingredients beside the wok in the order in which they are to be placed in the wok.

Heat the wok to medium high (375°) and swirl in the oil. Add the ginger-garlic mixture and stir-fry half a minute. Add the peppers and stir-fry 1½ minutes. Add the onion and stir-fry 1 minute. Stir in the tomato, then the squash, and stir-fry another minute. Push the vegetables up onto the side of the wok, pour in the sauce, and stir until it thickens and clears. Combine all the ingredients with the sauce and serve at once, with parsley garnish if you wish.

Winter Vegetables, Vietnam

Prep. Time 12–15 minutes • Serves 6 as a side dish
Cooking Time 6–7 minutes

A crunchy combination of winter vegetables, perfect as part of any multiple-entrée Chinese-style meal.

4 tablespoons vegetable oil
1 cup cauliflower florets, 1 inch wide
1 cup carrot shreds
1 cup turnip shreds
2 medium stalks celery, cut in ¼-inch slices
2 medium leeks, or 1 medium onion, shredded

2 tablespoons nuoc mam, fish sauce, or soy sauce
¼ teaspoon five spice powder, or a pinch each of ground anise, clove, and pepper
Salt to taste
Parsley sprigs, optional

Place the measured ingredients beside the wok in the order in which they are to be placed in the wok.

Heat the wok to medium high (375°) and swirl in the oil. Add the vegetables one at a time in the order given, stir-frying each about 1 minute before adding the next. Stir-fry a total of 5 minutes, then season with the nuoc mam, five spice powder, and salt to taste. Serve soon, while the vegetables are still crunchy, with a garnish of parsley if you wish.

Black-eyed Peas, Indian Style

Prep. Time 5 minutes • Serves 2; 4 as a side dish
Cooking Time 30 minutes

Black-eyed peas cook into a delicious, meaty mash that is substantial enough to serve as a main course. My family loves this recipe served with Spring Rolls (page 60), yellow or red tomato slices, and a fruit chutney.

2 tablespoons vegetable oil
1 large yellow onion, peeled and coarsely chopped
½ pound fresh shelled black-eyed peas (about 1 cup), rinsed and drained
½ cup tomato sauce
1 cup water
2 teaspoons ground coriander
2 teaspoons ground cumin
½ teaspoon turmeric

⅛ teaspoon black pepper
½–1 teaspoon salt
2 tablespoons tamarind liquid, or 1 tablespoon fresh lemon juice
2 tablespoons butter
Chutney
Raita (page 220)
Parsley sprigs

Place the measured ingredients beside the wok in the order in which they are to be placed in the wok.

Heat the wok to medium low (300°) and swirl in the oil. Turn the onion into the oil and stir-fry until it begins to brown a little. Add the peas and continue to stir-fry until the onions are browned. Reduce the heat to simmer and stir in the tomato sauce and water. Stir until the bubbling quiets and the bottom stops sticking. Cover and cook 15 minutes.

When the peas have cooked, measure the spices and seasonings into the peas, stirring after each addition. Start with half a teaspoon of salt, and add more to taste. Stir in the tamarind liquid and cover. Cook until the peas are tender-crispy and the sauce is reduced, about 15 minutes. If during the cooking the sauce is reduced to nothing, add more water. When done, the peas and sauce should make a fragrant mushy mass, like lumpy mashed potatoes, but with the peas standing out somewhat intact. Stir in the butter and serve hot with chutney, Raita, and parsley as garnish.

Eggplant in Spices and Tomato, India

Prep. Time 6–8 minutes • Serves 4 as a side dish
Cooking Time 12–15 minutes

This spicy eggplant dish is good with grilled meats, baked chicken, and lamb. Use Chinese eggplants if you can find them, or small eggplants, because they have smaller seeds.

1 ½-inch piece fresh ginger, peeled
1 small onion, peeled
2 large cloves garlic, peeled
1 teaspoon fennel seeds
1 tablespoon ground coriander
1 tablespoon ground cumin
½ teaspoon turmeric
1 cup tomato sauce

1½ teaspoons salt
3 tablespoons vegetable oil
1 Chinese eggplant or small eggplant, skin on, stemmed, and cut into ½-inch chunks (2 cups cut up)
1 tablespoon minced cilantro or Italian parsley

In a blender or food processor, or by hand, mince the ginger, then add and coarsely chop the onion and garlic. Combine the spices in a cup and the tomato sauce and salt in a small bowl.

Heat the wok to medium high (375°) and swirl in the oil. Add the ginger mixture and stir-fry 1 minute. Add the spices and stir-fry 1 minute. Add the tomato sauce and stir 1 minute. Add the eggplant, mix well, and reduce the heat to simmer (about 200°). Cover and cook 10 minutes, stirring once or twice to make sure the sauce doesn't burn. The eggplant will seem less opaque. Turn off the heat. Reheat when ready to serve. Garnish with chopped cilantro.

Potatoes with Spices, India

Prep. Time 10 minutes • Serves 6–8 as a side dish
Cooking Time 30 minutes

This is a wonderful potato salad to serve at room temperature on hot days, or hot on cold days. Marvelous with grilled meats, steamed fish, and Chinese dishes with lots of sauce.

3 pounds small new potatoes
Salt
1 tablespoon vegetable oil
4 tablespoons butter
2 teaspoons fennel seeds
2 teaspoons ground cumin
½ teaspoon mustard powder
½ teaspoon red pepper flakes

2 teaspoons turmeric
2 teaspoons salt (or more)
3 tablespoons tamarind liquid
 (page 36) or lemon juice
1 bunch green onions, trimmed
 to 4 inches and minced

Set the potatoes in a large cooking pot in cold water over high heat, cover, and cook until just tender—the stage *before* they fall apart when you stick a fork into the smallest one. Drain the water and sprinkle the potatoes lightly with salt. Let them dry out in the cooking pot while you heat the wok to medium high (375°) and measure the remaining ingredients. With two knives, cut the potatoes in the pot very coarsely, breaking them into halves and thirds.

Place the measured ingredients beside the wok in the order in which they are to be placed in the wok.

With the wok heated, swirl in the oil and melt the butter. Add the spices one at a time, stirring briefly after each addition, then add the potatoes, stir to combine with the spices, and reduce the heat to simmer (about 200°). Turn the potatoes continually but gently for about 3 minutes, then sprinkle with the salt, tamarind liquid, and minced green onions. Turn off the heat and toss the potatoes with the onion until the onion is evenly dispersed through the potatoes. Serve tepid.

Long Beans and Pork Shreds

Prep. Time 10 minutes • Serves 2; 4 as a side dish
Cooking Time 8–9 minutes

This tasty dish is a popular use of long beans in Thailand, and a good companion to any sweet and sour dish.

2 tablespoons vegetable oil
4 large garlic cloves, peeled
2–3 ounces pork loin, cut in
⅛- × ⅛- × 2-inch shreds
½ pound long beans or green
beans, cut in 2-inch lengths

8 fresh or drained and rinsed
canned water chestnuts, cut
in ¼-inch-thick rounds

*Sauce*_____

1 cup water
3 tablespoons fish sauce or soy
sauce

1 teaspoon brown or white sugar

*Thickener*_____

1 tablespoon cornstarch

2 tablespoons water

In separate small bowls, mix the sauce and the thickener. Heat the wok to medium high (375°), swirl in the oil, and slice the garlic into the wok. Stir-fry until it begins to brown. Add the pork and stir-fry until it browns, 2 to 3 minutes. Add the beans and stir-fry 1 minute. Add the water chestnuts and the sauce, mix together, cover, and cook 3 to 4 minutes, or until the beans are crispy-tender but still very green. Push the ingredients up onto the side of the wok and pour in the thickener. Stir until it thickens and clears. Push the ingredients down into the sauce, mix well, and serve as soon as possible.

Green Beans Fukien

Prep. Time 10 minutes • Serves 4
Cooking Time 15 minutes

This is a favorite for our family gatherings, wonderful with shrimp tempura and rice. Good for parties because it can be kept warm before it is served.

1 tablespoon cornstarch
¼ cup cold water
2 tablespoons vegetable oil
1 large clove garlic, peeled and minced
1 pound lean ground pork
2 tablespoons soy sauce

6 fresh or drained and rinsed canned water chestnuts, slivered, or ½ cup diced celery
3 cups green beans, in roll-cut diagonals (about 1 pound)
1½ cups hot water
Soy sauce

Combine the cornstarch and cold water in a cup. Heat the wok to medium high (375°), swirl in the oil, add the garlic, and stir-fry 1 minute. Mash the pork into the oil and stir-fry until it is crumbly and brown, 7–8 minutes. Season with the 2 tablespoons soy sauce, then stir in the water chestnuts and stir-fry 2 minutes more. Mix the beans into the pork mixture and stir-fry 3 minutes. Pour the water into the wok, scrape up the pan juices, cover the wok, and reduce the heat to simmer (about 200°). Uncover, push the ingredients up onto the side of the wok, and stir in the cornstarch and water. Stir until the sauce thickens and clears. Taste and season with more soy sauce, if desired. Keep warm until ready to serve.

Vegetarian Delight

Prep. Time 15 minutes • Serves 4
Cooking Time 8–10 minutes

These crunchy steamed vegetables, stir-fried in a savory sauce, are another popular Bell Wong dish.

2 dried tree fungus
1 small head broccoli (about ¼ pound), cut in 1-inch-wide florets
12 snow peas, strings removed
½ sweet red or green pepper, seeded and shredded
¼ cup canned bamboo shoots, drained and rinsed

12 pieces canned baby corn, drained and rinsed
¼ carrot, peeled and cut in ¼-inch diagonal slices
1½ tablespoons vegetable oil
1 green onion, trimmed to 3 inches and minced

Sauce
¼ cup chicken broth
1 tablespoon soy sauce
1 tablespoon mushroom soy sauce or soy sauce
½ tablespoon sugar

Grinding of pepper
1 teaspoon sesame oil
1 tablespoon rice wine or dry sherry

Thickener
2 teaspoons cornstarch

2 tablespoons cold water

Soak the fungus in hot water to cover until soft, 5 to 10 minutes. Drain, discard the hard parts, and shred. Set the steaming rack in the wok and fill the wok with hot water to within 1 inch of the rack. Arrange all the vegetables but the green onion in separate piles on the rack. Heat the wok to simmer (about 200), cover, and after steam starts escaping from under the lid, cook the vegetables 4 minutes. While the vegetables steam, combine the seven sauce ingredients in a small bowl. In another combine the two thickening ingredients.

When the vegetables are ready, turn off the heat, remove the steaming rack, drain the wok, and wipe it dry. Reheat to medium (350°). Swirl in the oil, stir in the green onion, and stir-fry 30 seconds. Pour in the sauce. As soon as it simmers, mix in the vegetables just long enough to reheat them, then push the vegetables up onto the side of the wok, and pour the thickener down the inside of the wok. Stir until the sauce thickens and clears. Combine with the vegetables, and serve as soon as possible.

Lentils with Garam Masala, India

Prep. Time 5 minutes • Serves 6–8
Cooking Time 40 minutes

Lentils are wonderful with curries and grilled meats, steak, or as a main course. They are part of the family of legumes, known as "dhals" in India, where they are eaten daily with some form of bread or rice.

2 cups red lentils
6 cups water
2 tablespoons garam masala
½ small lemon, sliced and
  seeded
1½ teaspoons salt

1 tablespoon vegetable oil
3 tablespoons butter
1 teaspoon whole cumin seeds
Salt and pepper

In a medium saucepan over high heat, bring the lentils and water to boiling with the garam masala. Cover, reduce to a simmer, and cook about 25 minutes. Stir the lemon into the lentils with the salt. Cook another few minutes, or until the lentils are tender. All the cooking liquid should have been absorbed. Turn off the heat.

When you are ready to serve the lentils, heat the wok to medium high (375°) and swirl in the oil. Add the butter and while it is still frothing, add the cumin seeds and stir until they begin to darken, half a minute. Pour over the lentils, mix well, and return the lentils to the wok long enough to heat them. Taste, and add salt and pepper if needed. Serve the lentils hot.

Eleven

Salads, Condiments, Sauces, and Garnishes

European tossed salads and creamy dressings are not traditional Eastern fare. In Chinese-style meals, the vegetable crunch is in the entrées, and in Indian-style meals, in the relishes and side dishes.

In spite of tradition, I've included salads in this book because many of us consider salads a healthful addition to our daily diet. The dressings for my salads are soy sauce and sesame oil-based, and go particularly well with soy sauce-flavored Chinese and Japanese type dishes. The two salads made with vegetables are excellent luncheon entrées. To add to the protein value of the salads, mix in ¼ to ½ cup of rinsed and diced tofu. Toss well so the tofu absorbs the flavor of the dressing.

It is the custom to serve several little side bowls of condiments with curries. Chutney is one of the most delicious. While I recommend you try my recipe for Chutney with Peaches, Mango, and Ginger, you can also purchase good commercial chutneys; Major Grey's is perhaps the most popular. Raita, which is chilled cucumber in yogurt, and Onion Samball, with its lemon-lime and mint-basil tastes, are offered in India with curry entrées. Chopped apples, peanuts with pepper, and coconut side dishes add crunch to an Indian meal.

Use the dipping sauces in this chapter with any of the appetizers in Chapter 3. They're also good with steamed meats, fish, and vegetables. All of the sauces can be made a day or two ahead and refrigerated until needed; they will keep in the refrigerator three or four days more.

Beautiful garnishes using vegetables, fruits, and herbs are an integral part of serving Oriental dishes. Many are simple, but can turn a meal into a special event. I'm sure that after you try any of the garnishes in this chapter, you'll find myriad ways to use them.

Salads and Dressings

Radish Slices with Sesame Oil

Prep. Time 5–7 minutes; Marinate 2–3 hours • Serves 4–6
Cooking Time 0

A chilled, tart accompaniment for any of the soy sauce-flavored entrées or for a Japanese dinner.

4 long white radishes or 1 big
  daikon or 1–2 small kohlrabi, peeled

Spinach leaves
2 tablespoons sesame oil

Marinade

2 tablespoons rice vinegar or
  cider vinegar
2 tablespoons soy sauce or
  shoyu

2 teaspoons sugar

Combine the marinade ingredients in a small bowl. Slice the radishes thinly on the blade of a food processor or with a sharp knife. Arrange the slices around a small round plate, with the spinach leaves as garnish. Sprinkle the marinade over the radish, cover, and chill 2 to 3 hours. Sprinkle with sesame oil before serving.

Golden Tomato Salad

Prep. Time 5 minutes • Serves 4
Cooking Time 0

Yellow tomatoes seem less acid than red tomatoes and have a distinctive flavor. They are great with curries and beautiful to look at!

2 large ripe yellow tomatoes
   stemmed and sliced into
   4–6 rounds each
1 tablespoon rice wine or dry
   sherry
1 teaspoon sesame oil
½ teaspoon soy sauce
⅛ teaspoon salt

2 teaspoons minced fresh basil,
   mint, or dill
4–6 fresh basil florets, pinks,
   squash, chives, mint blossoms, or other flower garnish
   (see page 236–237)

Arrange the tomato rounds on a serving plate and sprinkle with the rice wine, sesame oil, soy sauce, salt, and minced herb. Garnish with flowers and chill until ready to serve.

Bean Sprout Salad

Prep. Time 5 minutes • Serves 4
Cooking Time 0

A nice side dish with a crisp texture and a meaty flavor. Very good with savory entrées as a substitute for a vegetable dish.

2 cups fresh soybean sprouts

Dressing_____

½ clove garlic, peeled
4 tablespoons soy sauce
1 tablespoon cold water

½ teaspoon sugar
½ teaspoon rice vinegar or cider vinegar

Place the sprouts in a medium serving bowl. With a garlic press, crush the garlic into a small bowl and combine with it half of the soy sauce and the remaining ingredients. Toss the sprouts with the dressing, taste, and if desired sprinkle the remaining half of the soy sauce over the sprouts and toss well once more. Serve chilled.

Variation:

Two Sprout Salad—Prepare as above, but instead of 2 cups soybean sprouts, use 1¾ cups soybean sprouts and ¼ cup alfalfa sprouts. Combine the soybean sprouts with the dressing, then sprinkle the alfalfa sprouts over the bean sprouts as both flavoring and garnish.

Three Color Salad

Prep. Time 15 minutes • Serves 4
Cooking Time 0

Raw spinach, shredded radicchio, mandarin oranges, and walnut meats combine in this pretty salad flavored with Soy and Sesame Salad Dressing (page 216). An excellent choice with any combination of Chinese entrées.

2 cups 1-inch pieces spinach leaves (no ribs included)
1 cup shredded radicchio or red cabbage
2 mandarin oranges, segmented, skinned, and seeded

¼–⅓ cup shelled walnut halves
6 tablespoons Soy and Sesame Salad Dressing (page 216)
4 parsley sprigs

Spread the spinach pieces over four small salad plates. Sprinkle with radicchio shreds. Arrange the orange segments in a wheel in the center of each plate. Sprinkle with walnut halves, then with dressing. Put a sprig of parsley in the center of each orange segment wheel. Serve chilled.

Celery and Lettuce Salad

Prep. Time 10 minutes • Serves 2–3
Cooking Time 0

A good accompaniment for any of the chicken entrées, and can be served instead of rice or a vegetable dish.

½ cup celery slices ¼-inch thick
¼ cup shredded celery inner leaves
1¼ cups 1–2-inch pieces lettuce
¼ cup Soy and Sesame Salad Dressing (page 216)

2 tablespoons, shredded red pepper or carrot
1 teaspoon grated orange rind, optional

In a medium salad bowl, combine the celery and greens and pour the salad dressing over them, but do not toss. Garnish with red pepper or carrot shreds and sprinkle with orange rind, if you wish. Chill until ready to serve. Toss just before serving.

Mushroom and Alfalfa Sprout Salad

Prep. Time 10–12 minutes • Serves 4
Cooking Time 0

A tossed salad with fresh mushroom slices and greens, very good with any of the entrées in the book. Tear, don't slice, the greens.

6 medium large firm mushrooms, wiped clean, stemmed, and sliced into T-shapes
¼ cup Soy and Sesame Salad Dressing (page 216)
¼ cup celery slices ¼ inch thick
½ cup 1–2 inch pieces spinach
1 cup 1–2 inch pieces lettuce

¼ cup loosely packed alfalfa sprouts
¼ cup diamond-shaped slices carrot ⅛ inch thick, or peeled, seeded tangerine or orange slices

In a medium salad bowl, toss together the mushrooms and the salad dressing. Pile the remaining ingredients onto the mushrooms and chill the salad until ready to serve. Toss just before serving, making sure to bring the colorful carrot or fruit slices to the top.

Wilted Green Vegetable Salad

Prep. Time 10 minutes • Serves 4
Cooking Time 3 minutes

This vegetable mélange is Chinese in origin and a delightful addition to a large, rich meal. Should be chilled after stir-frying.

2 large leafless celery stalks
½ small cucumber
1 very small zucchini or summer squash
2 tablespoons vinegar
2 tablespoons soy sauce

1 teaspoon sugar (or more)
1 tablespoon vegetable oil
Sesame oil, optional
Squash blossoms, or 4 tip sprigs parsley

With a potato peeler, pare the celery stalks into long thin strips. Slice the cucumber, unpeeled, and the zucchini or squash, into very thin ovals. In a small bowl, blend the vinegar, soy sauce, and sugar, adding more sugar if desired.

Heat the wok to medium high (375°), swirl in the oil, and add the vegetables one at a time; stir-frying 20 seconds after each addition. Remove to a serving dish and mix lightly with the vinegar mixture. Chill, covered. Serve cold. Before serving, sprinkle with sesame oil if you wish. Garnish one end of the plate with a bouquet of squash blossoms or parsley sprigs.

Vegetable Salad with Shrimp Dressing

Prep. Time 30 minutes • Serves 4–6
Cooking Time 6 minutes

From Indonesia, a crunchy, steamed salad with a delicate shrimp dressing topped with grated coconut. Excellent as a side dish with broiled meats, breaded fish, curries, and Chinese entrées.

¼ head cabbage, shredded
1 large carrot, peeled and
 shredded
½ cup stringed green beans, or
 3 ounces thawed frozen
 Frenched green beans
1 cup fresh bean sprouts
½ cup fresh bamboo shoots, or
 canned shoots, drained and
 rinsed

1 tablespoon vegetable oil
2 green onions, trimmed to
 3 inches and minced
½ cup grated fresh coconut or
 dried coconut

Sauce

2 tablespoons lime juice, or rice
 vinegar, or cider vinegar
2 tablespoons cold water

2 tablespoons soy sauce
1½ teaspoons shrimp paste, or
 1 tablespoon dried shrimp

Fill the wok to within 1 inch of the steaming rack with hot water, set the rack in place, and arrange the vegetables, except for the green onions, on the rack. Cover and heat to simmer (about 200°). After the steam begins to escape from under the cover, cook 4 minutes. In a small bowl, combine the four ingredients in the sauce. When the vegetables are ready, remove the rack, drain the wok, and wipe with paper towel. Turn the vegetables into a salad bowl.

Heat the wok to medium high (375°), swirl in the oil, add the green onions, and stir-fry 30 seconds. Pour in the sauce and stir until it bubbles. Scrape the sauce over the vegetables, and toss together until well mixed. Sprinkle the coconut over the salad and serve at room temperature.

Soy and Sesame Salad Dressing

Prep. Time 5–8 minutes • Makes 1½+ cups
Cooking Time 0

An excellent oil and vinegar dressing for tossed salads served with Oriental foods. About ¼ cup of dressing covers 2 cups of salad greens. Store covered in the refrigerator and use as needed. The dressing will keep for months. Minced fresh parsley or cilantro are nice additions.

1 cup vegetable oil
1 tablespoon sesame oil
¼ cup rice vinegar or cider vinegar
¼ cup water
1 green onion, trimmed to 4 inches

2 large cloves garlic, peeled
1 teaspoon sugar
½ teaspoon Chinese prepared mustard
1–3 teaspoons soy sauce

Combine everything but the soy sauce in a blender or food processor, or mince the green onions and garlic and combine everything else by hand. Add the soy sauce 1 teaspoon at a time, tasting after each addition until the flavor is just right for you.

Sesame Sauce

Prep. Time 5 minutes • Makes 3 tablespoons
Cooking Time 0

An excellent sauce, rich in sesame flavor. Nice with raw vegetables or noodles.

1 tablespoon soy sauce
½ teaspoon sugar
1 teaspoon rice vinegar

1 tablespoon rice wine or dry sherry
1 tablespoon sesame oil

In a small bowl, combine all the ingredients and stir until the sugar grains dissolve. Cover and store in the refrigerator until ready to use. This recipe makes enough sauce to cover 1½ to 2 cups of vegetables or noodles.

Piña Colada Dressing

Prep. Time 5 minutes • Makes ⅓ cup
Cooking Time 0

This dressing has a very sharp sweet and sour taste that is wonderful with cold meats, fruits, and cold seafood.

3 tablespoons piña colada
   frozen concentrate
1 6-ounce can pineapple slices
   in their own juice, drained,
   juice reserved

1 teaspoon rice wine or cider
   vinegar
½ teaspoon Chinese prepared
   mustard

In a food processor or blender, or by hand, combine the piña colada frozen concentrate with 1 pineapple ring and 3 tablespoons of the reserved pineapple juice, the vinegar, and the mustard. Process, or mince, until well blended and smooth. Serve cold, in a small bowl.

Condiments and Curry Companions

Chutney with Peaches, Mango, and Ginger

Prep. Time 30–40 minutes • Makes about 2½ pints
Cooking Time 30 minutes

A delicious chutney that is a perfect accompaniment for curries. Look for firm-ripe, or even slightly overripe fruit: it's more flavorful. This chutney takes more time than most of my recipes, but it's so much richer in flavor than popular commercial chutneys that I think it's well worth the effort. Keeps well refrigerated to eight months.

¾ cup cider vinegar (or more)
⅞ cup granulated sugar
4 cups peeled, seeded, thinly sliced ripe peaches and mango (about 4 peaches and 1 big mango)
½ cup drained canned pineapple chunks, juice reserved
½ cup shredded sweet red pepper (1–1½ medium peppers)
1½ medium onions, chopped
2 big garlic cloves, peeled

½ cup seedless golden raisins
Peel of ¼ orange, slivered
Peel of ¼ lemon, slivered
3 tablespoons thinly sliced preserved or pickled ginger, minced fresh ginger, or chopped candied ginger
⅛–¼ teaspoon red pepper flakes (or more)
½ teaspoon salt

Place the measured ingredients beside the wok in the order in which they are to be placed in the wok.

Pour the vinegar into the wok, heat to medium low (300°), and bring the vinegar to a boil. Stir in the sugar as the vinegar is coming to a boil. Allow the mixture a full rolling boil about 2 minutes, then stir in the peach-mango mixture and the pineapple. When the mixture returns to a full boil, reduce the heat enough to keep the mixture simmering (about 200°) and cook 5 minutes. Stir in the peppers and onion. Mince the garlic into the wok, then add the raisins, orange and lemon peel, ginger, pepper flakes—double the pepper if you revel in hot food—and salt. Stir and cook long enough for the mixture to develop the thick consistency of a chutney or applesauce, about 30 minutes from the beginning. If the chutney cooks a bit dry, add a little vinegar or reserved pineapple juice and cook a moment longer. Turn off the heat and ladle the chutney into cleaned and dried half-pint jars. Cool several hours uncovered on a rack, then cap tightly and store in the refrigerator. Serve chilled.

Onion Samball

Prep. Time 7–10 minutes; Marinate 2 hours • Makes 2 cups +
Cooking Time 0

A tangy accompaniment for all curries. Allow 2 tablespoons per person.

**2 large onions, peeled and
  chopped coarsely**
½ teaspoon salt, or to taste
**4 tablespoons strained lemon
  juice or lime juice**

**Fresh mint or basil leaves or 1
  teaspoon spearmint flavoring**

Place the onions in a shallow bowl and salt to your taste. Toss with the lemon or lime juice and cover with the mint or basil leaves or toss with the spearmint flavoring. Cover and marinate 2 hours in the refrigerator before serving.

Raita

Prep. Time 10 minutes; Marinate 3–4 hours • Serves 6
Cooking Time 0

Another side dish almost indispensable for curries, especially hot curries. Best when made from very young cucumbers, or the new seedless varieties.

2 medium cucumbers	**1 teaspoon salt**
1 medium onion, peeled and	**1 teaspoon ground cumin**
minced	**½ pint plain yogurt**

With a fork, score about half the cucumber skin. If the cucumber looks big enough to have coarse seeds, halve it and scoop away the biggest seeds. In a food processor, or by hand, slice the cucumber. Drain off the cucumber liquid, place in a bowl, cover, and refrigerate for 2 to 3 hours.

Drain away the cucumber liquid once more and press the cucumber dry between paper towels. Put the cucumber in a serving bowl and mix it with the onion, salt, and cumin. Stir in the yogurt. Cover, and chill another hour before serving.

Chopped Apple Relish

Prep. Time 5–7 minutes • Makes about ¾ cup
Cooking Time 0

This is a simple accompaniment for curries and may be served instead of or with chutney, chopped onions, and other crispy relishes. Granny Smith apples are the best type to use. Apples discolor once chopped, so prepare this no more than one hour before serving.

1 large green apple	**Salt**
1 tablespoon strained lemon or	
lime juice	

Peel the apple, slice from the core, and chop into ¼-inch cubes. Or, peel and core the apple and chop as coarsely as possible in a food processor or blender. Toss with the lemon or lime juice and sprinkle with a few grains of salt. Cover tightly and store in the refrigerator until ready to serve.

Peanuts Crushed with Pepper

Prep. Time 5 minutes • Makes 1 cup
Cooking Time 0

This combination of salted peanuts combined with a little cayenne to zip up the taste is a simple crunchy accompaniment for curries.

1 cup shelled roasted salted   **Cayenne pepper**
  peanuts, chopped coarsely

Turn the nuts into a small serving bowl and sprinkle lightly with cayenne pepper. Toss with a spoon to combine, and serve.

Crisped Coconut Shreds

Prep. Time 5 minutes • Serves 4–6; Makes ⅓–¾ cup
Cooking Time 1–2 minutes

Crisped Coconut Shreds are delicious sprinkled over any curry. This recipe takes minutes when you have fresh chopped coconut or dried coconut on hand. To chop whole fresh coconut, see Thick Coconut Milk (page 34).

½–1 cup fresh or unsweetened   **2–3 cups vegetable oil**
  dried chopped or grated   **Salt**
  coconut

Heat the wok to high (400°), or until a day-old cube of bread browns in just under 1 minute. Heat 4 minutes more to stabilize, then turn the coconut into the oil. Fresh coconut spatters all over—so beware! Back away! When it simmers down, stir just long enough to see the coconut turning golden brown, then scoop it out with a slotted spoon onto paper towel. Spread the coconut over the paper towel to drain and cool. Salt the coconut very lightly. Change it to fresh paper towel. To keep it fairly crisp until you are ready to serve, place it between fresh sheets of paper towel and store it in a dry place, such as an oven. Before serving, transfer the coconut to a small serving bowl lined with a paper doily or napkin.

Tomato Relish with Cilantro

Prep. Time 5 minutes • Serves 4
Cooking Time 0

This is wonderful when the tomatoes are fresh from the garden. Excellent as a side dish to serve with curries.

2 large ripe tomatoes, coarsely chopped
2 green onions, trimmed and coarsely chopped
¼ teaspoon salt

2 tablespoons strained lemon juice
1 tablespoon minced cilantro
Grinding of black pepper

Turn the tomatoes and onions into a serving bowl. Sprinkle the remaining ingredients over the tomato-onion mixture and toss well. Cover and chill 15 minutes, or until ready to serve. Taste, and add more seasonings if desired.

Cold and Spicy Relish with Sesame Oil

Prep. Time 10 minutes; Marinate 2–3 hours • Serves 3–4
Cooking Time 2 minutes

This very good green vegetable relish is briefly stir-fried in a little vegetable oil, then seasoned with vinegar and chilled. A great accompaniment for Chinese meals.

4 celery stalks, strings removed, or 1 medium cucumber or zucchini

1 tablespoon vegetable oil
Sesame oil

Marinade

2 tablespoons rice or cider vinegar

2 tablespoons soy sauce
1 tablespoon sugar

With a food processor or by hand, shred the celery stalks; or cut unpeeled cucumber or zucchini into thin rounds. Blend the vinegar, soy sauce, and sugar in a bowl.

Heat the wok to medium high (375°), swirl in the oil, count to 30, add the vegetable, and stir-fry 1 minute only. Remove to a serving plate and toss with the vinegar mixture. Cover and chill 2 or 3 hours, or more. Just before serving, sprinkle with drops of sesame oil, as much as you enjoy, and toss lightly.

Tomato and Pepper Relish

Prep. Time 5 minutes • *Serves 4–6*
Cooking Time 0

A fresh, spicy relish to serve as an accompaniment for a curry or as a salad with a Thai meal.

2–3 sprigs cilantro, celery
  leaves, dill, or parsley
1 medium sweet green pepper,
  seeded
3 big green onions, trimmed to
  5–6 inches
2 medium garden-ripe tomatoes,
  seeded

½ teaspoon salt
Generous grinding of pepper
¼ teaspoon ground cumin
1½ tablespoons strained lime or
  lemon juice

In a food processor or blender, or by hand, mince the herb, then add and coarsely chop the pepper, then the onions, then the tomatoes. Turn into a serving bowl and mix in the salt, pepper, cumin, and juice. Taste, and add more seasoning if desired. Chill until ready to serve.

Dips and Sauces

Peanut Sauce

Prep. Time 4–5 minutes • Dip/sauce for about 36 pieces; or 1 cup
Cooking Time 5 minutes

A delicious sauce to serve with crunchy dim sum, or curried or grilled meats, poultry, fish, or vegetables. Some versions are made with bouillon instead of coconut milk. Do not use canned coconut cream, which has sugar added.

1 tablespoon vegetable oil
1 small garlic clove, peeled and minced
3 green onions, trimmed to 3 inches and minced
2 medium sweet red peppers, seeded and shredded
1 teaspoon sugar

2 tablespoons curry powder
1 cup coconut milk (page 34)
½ cup peanut butter
½ teaspoon (or more) chili paste, cayenne, or red pepper flakes
Sugar and salt to taste

Place the measured ingredients beside the wok in the order in which they are to be placed in the wok.

Heat the wok to medium (350°) and swirl in the oil. Add the garlic, then the onions, and stir-fry 1 minute. Add the peppers and stir-fry 1 minute more. Season with the sugar and curry powder, then stir in the coconut milk. Bring to a boil. Reduce the heat to simmer (about 200°) and mash in the peanut butter and chili paste. Stir-fry until the sauce is as thick as mayonnaise. If it becomes too thick, thin with coconut milk, cream, milk, or water. Taste, and add sugar and salt if desired. Serve warm.

Teriyaki Sauce

Prep. Time 5 minutes • Makes about ¾ cup
Cooking Time 0

This is my favorite dipping sauce, excellent with seafood and surimi, fish cakes, raw vegetables, or steamed dim sum.

1 1-inch piece fresh ginger, peeled
½ cup soy sauce, preferably Japanese soy sauce
⅓ cup sake, rice wine, or dry sherry

3 tablespoons loosely-packed brown sugar, or 2 tablespoons white sugar
1 large clove garlic, peeled
½ teaspoon Chinese prepared mustard

In a blender or food processor, or by hand, mince the ginger and process or stir with the other ingredients long enough to dissolve the sugar. Chill until ready to serve.

Thai Hot Dip

Prep. Time 15 minutes • Makes ⅓ cup
Cooking Time 0

This is a hot dip for raw vegetables, pakoras, fried or steamed won tons, or any appetizer. Use gloves when you seed the peppers!

4 tablespoons vegetable oil
2 thin slices medium onion
4 large cloves garlic, unpeeled
4 small red peppers, stemmed, seeded, membrane removed

1 tablespoon shrimp paste or dried shrimp
1 tablespoon brown sugar
2 tablespoons tamarind liquid (page 36) or lime juice

Heat the wok to medium (350°), swirl in the oil, and fry the onion and garlic, unpeeled, until they are browning. Add the peppers, stir around once or twice, and turn off the heat. Mix in the shrimp paste and sugar, then turn the contents of the wok into a blender or a food processor with the tamarind liquid and process until a thick paste forms. If it is too thick for dipping, add water by the teaspoonful and process until it is thin enough. Serve at room temperature.

Curry Dip

Prep. Time 5 minutes • Makes 1–1½ cups
Cooking Time 15 minutes

This is a very spicy golden sauce, rich in curry flavor. Serve with raw vegetables as an appetizer, cook meatballs or flounder fillets in it for an entrée, or pour it over hot, halved hard-boiled eggs as a first course.

1 1-inch piece fresh ginger, peeled
2 large garlic cloves, peeled
1 medium onion, peeled
2 medium-large yellow or red tomatoes, chopped, or canned tomatoes with liquid
2 tablespoons vegetable oil

1 tablespoon ground coriander
1 teaspoon ground cumin
½ teaspoon turmeric
½ tablespoon garam masala (page 36)
½ teaspoon salt (or more)

In a food processor or blender, or by hand, mince the ginger. Add and coarsely chop the garlic, then the onion. Turn into a small bowl. In the processor or blender, or by hand, coarsely chop the tomatoes (with liquid, if canned).

Heat the wok to medium low (300°), swirl in the oil, and add the ginger mixture. Stir-fry until the onion turns golden, about 4 minutes. Sprinkle with the coriander, cumin, and turmeric and stir-fry until a strong odor of spice arises, 2 to 4 minutes. Add the tomatoes and stir-fry until the liquid is almost gone and the sauce is thick, about 5 minutes. Turn off the heat and stir in the garam masala and salt. Taste, and add more salt if desired. Serve at room temperature or heated.

Mustard Dipping Sauce

Prep. Time 5 minutes • Makes about ⅓ cup
Cooking Time 0

This is hot! Delicious with deep-fried appetizers and steamed dim sum. Usually paired with a sweet and sour sauce.

¼ cup mustard powder
¼ cup cold water
1 teaspoon rice vinegar or cider
   vinegar

½ teaspoon salt
½ teaspoon brown sugar

Process in a blender, or mix by hand into a smooth paste. Let rest an hour before using.

Sweet and Sour Sauce

Prep. Time 5 minutes • Makes about ½ cup
Cooking Time 5 minutes

This is a dip for spring rolls and other deep-fried appetizers. It is bottled commercially, available at your local supermarket, but my version is simple and fast if none is on hand.

1 tablespoon cornstarch
3 tablespoons water
2 tablespoons soy sauce
1 tablespoon rice wine or dry
   sherry

3 tablespoons brown sugar
2 tablespoons rice or cider
   vinegar
1 tablespoon tomato ketchup

Combine the cornstarch and the water in a small bowl. In a small saucepan, combine the remaining ingredients and bring to a simmer. Stir in the cornstarch mixture and continue to stir as the sauce thickens and begins to clear. Serve at room temperature or slightly chilled.

Rich Sweet and Sour Sauce

Prep. Time 5 minutes • Makes about 1½ cups
Cooking Time 1–2 minutes

This is thicker and richer than the simple sauce above.

1 cup Chutney with Peaches,
  Mango, and Ginger (page
  218), or ½ cup other chutney
½ cup plum jam (only if using
  a commercial chutney)
¼ cup cold water

1 tablespoon rice wine or dry
  sherry
2 tablespoons rice or cider
  vinegar (or more)

In a small saucepan over medium heat, combine all the ingredients
and simmer for 2 minutes. Taste, and add more vinegar if desired.
Serve at room temperature or slightly chilled.

Black Bean Dip, China

Prep. Time 10 minutes • Makes ¾ cup
Cooking Time 0

An interesting sauce for raw vegetables, tofu, or fried shimp. Be
sure to soak the dried beans after rinsing them thoroughly. It makes
a distinct difference in the flavor of the sauce.

½ cup black beans, rinsed,
  drained
¾ cup hot water
3 teaspoons soy sauce
½ teaspoon sesame oil

2 teaspoons rice wine or dry
  sherry
Soaking liquid from the beans

Soak the well-rinsed beans 30 minutes or more in the hot water,
then drain, reserving the soaking liquid. Place the beans in a
blender or a food processor with the soy sauce, sesame oil, and
wine and process until the beans have disintegrated. As the sauce
thickens and sticks to the sides of the blender or processor container, add the bean-soaking liquid 1 tablespoon at a time until the
sauce becomes liquid enough to be a dip. This will take between 2
and 3 tablespoonsful. Serve at room temperature.

Hoisin Dipping Sauce

Prep. Time 3–5 minutes • Makes about ⅓ cup (dip/sauce for about 24 pieces)
Cooking Time 0

A rich, spicy dipping sauce flavored with sesame oil. Very good with hard-boiled eggs, raw vegetables, Won Ton Appetizers (page 58) and Spring Rolls (page 60).

½ cup hoisin sauce
2 tablespoons water

2 teaspoons soy sauce
4 teaspoons sesame oil

Measure the hoisin sauce into a small bowl, and stir in the other ingredients one at a time. Serve at room temperature.

Vietnamese Dipping Sauce

Prep. Time 5–7 minutes • Makes about 1¼ cups
Cooking Time 0

This is a light dipping sauce, particularly good with cold cooked crab, shrimp, or mussels, and steamed noodle cases stuffed with shrimp or crab. If you enjoy hot foods, increase the quantity of chili paste.

½ cup fish sauce
½ cup water
2 tablespoons plus 2 teaspoons
  strained lime juice

2 tablespoons sugar
⅛–¼ teaspoon chili paste
3 medium garlic cloves, peeled

Measure all the ingredients into a blender or food processor and process until the garlic has disintegrated. Serve chilled.

Kung Pao Sauce

Prep Time. 10 minutes • Makes ½ + cup
Cooking Time 2 minutes

A Bell Wong recipe for a hot and spicy sauce to serve with mild-tasting appetizers and dim sum.

6 tablespoons chicken broth
2 teaspoons sugar
2 teaspoons rice vinegar or cider vinegar
2 tablespoons thick soy sauce, mushroom soy sauce, or soy sauce .

2 teaspoons sesame oil
½–1 tablespoon Hunan or chili paste, or to taste
1 teaspoon cornstarch

In a small saucepan over medium heat, combine all the ingredients and stir until the sauce thickens, about 2 or 3 minutes. Serve hot or cold.

Sichuan Sauce

Prep. Time 20 minutes • Makes about ½–⅔ cup
Cooking Time 5 minutes

A creamy sauce with a spicy Sichuan flavor, this is delicious with raw vegetables, fried or steamed won tons, meatballs, fried shrimp, and other appetizers.

1 large garlic clove, peeled
1 1½-inch piece fresh ginger, peeled
1 small or ½ medium yellow onion, peeled
1 teaspoon ground coriander
½ teaspoon chili paste or red pepper flakes
3 tablespoons rice wine or dry sherry (or more)

1 tablespoon wine vinegar or cider vinegar
1½ teaspoons cornstarch
1½ teaspoons sugar
1 teaspoon sesame oil
1½ tablespoons dark or light soy sauce
1 tablespoon vegetable oil

In a blender or a food processor, mince together the garlic, ginger, and onion. Turn into a small bowl and stir in the coriander. In another bowl, combine the chili paste, wine, vinegar, and cornstarch. Then stir in the sugar, sesame oil, and soy sauce.

Heat the wok to medium (350°) and swirl in the oil. Add the onion mixture and stir-fry until the onion turns golden brown. Turn off the heat and pour in the cornstarch mixture. Stir-fry until the sauce thickens and clears. Turn back into the blender or processor and process until the sauce is smooth. If it seems too thick, thin a little with rice wine or sherry. Serve hot as a sauce, or chilled with cold appetizers.

Making Food Beautiful

An Oriental chef is concerned not only with making food delicious, but also with making it look beautiful. Fish covered with translucent "scales" of cucumber, seafood arranged in brilliant lobster carapaces, fruit in "fountains"—the effects can be breathtaking. It takes a moment to recognize familiar vegetables and fruits in their exotic new guises: White "roses" are carved daikons with a sliver of radish skin in the center; "jewels" on bowls of rice are diced zucchini, summer squash, and tomatoes; little white "packages" are bundles of vegetable shreds tied with a chive leaf for a string. Arrangements and garnishes are considered "high art" in Oriental cuisines. Beauty makes food taste better.

Below I offer two lists of ideas for exotic garnishes. One includes the more commonly used garnishes, such as parsley and cilantro, cucumber fans, rutabaga animals, pepper flowers, tomato roses. The other suggests some edible flowers to use as fancy and unusual garnishes. I hope these will provide ideas for many beautiful meals.

Fruit, Vegetable, and Herb Garnishes

Banana leaves: Long, flat silky leaves used for serving foods in Indonesia. Not edible, but make charming liners for trays of Oriental side dishes and appetizers.

Basil: Sprig tips are elegant, edible garnishes, specially suited to curry cooking. Gather 4 or 5 on the side of the plate.

Broccoli: Use florets 1 to 2 inches across on 1- to 2-inch peeled stems, steamed or deep-fried to bright green, as a garnish to brighten entrées. Nice with a few cherry tomatoes or carrot flowers for contrast. Or combine with a green onion brush.

Carambola stars: Slice carambola ⅛ inch thick and arrange slices in a small circle at the side of a circular dish. Nice with fish, sweet-flavored meat dishes, and fruit.

Carrot flowers: Peel a medium large carrot, remove the stem end and top. With a big knife, remove three to six shallow wedges from the length of the carrot. Now, slice the carrot into rounds ⅛–¼ inch thick. The missing wedges will create a daisy shape of the slices.

Cilantro: Also called Chinese parsley or fresh coriander. Gather two or three sprigs, remove the stems, and make mounds of green to garnish entrées. Or, arrange a few flat leaves on the side of a dinner plate and add carrot flowers or peeled mandarin orange segments for color. Float a leaf or two on clear soups. Mince over thick soups and any Chinese or Thai dish if you like the flavor. It's a cultivated taste.

Cucumber fans: Slice the end quarter of a small, meaty cucumber, seed it, and cut ⅛- to ¼-inch-thick ribbons in the length, but do not cut right through. The new seedless cucumbers work best for this. Scald the cucumber in boiling water 3 minutes, then curl each strip back on itself, and pin in place with a toothpick. This makes a fan shape. Chill until ready to serve. Remove the toothpicks before serving.

Daikon roses: Remove the leaves. Cut off the stem end. Cut into chunks, each suitable for carving into layers of spiky-round "leaves." Arrange each on a small spinach leaf and garnish with a fleck of red pimiento at the center.

Daikon shreds: Grate the daikon, gather into little heaps, and garnish with a cross made of slivers of red pimiento or red pepper. Or garnish with edible flowers (see pages 235–237). Or grate into long shreds with a food processor grater, and heap into elegant tangles spangled with edible florets or vegetable jewels.

Dill fern: With scissors, snip dill fern over fish, curries, salads, relishes.

Fennel fern: With scissors, snip fennel fern over soups, rice, pale vegetables.

Fruit garnishes: Arrange fruit wedges in decorative patterns on the side of meat and fish entrées, fu yungs, fried rice. Some suitable fruits are peeled papaya strips, seeded and skinned orange and mandarin orange segments, mangoes, and very ripe peaches.

Green onion brush: Trim a fat green onion to 4 to 6 inches. Remove the white end if it is bulbous. Cutting from the white into the green, slice the thinnest strands you can manage without severing them from the stalk (cut only halfway up the stalk). Arrange the strands in elegant swirls, curves, and tangles on the plate. Add carrot flowers, peeled mandarin orange segments, or other colorful accents.

Green onion bundles: Trim the onion and cut into 3-inch lengths. Cut into shreds, heap together, and tie around the middle with a wilted chive leaf or a long string of green onion.

Green onion shreds: Trim the onion and cut into thin 3- to 4-inch strips. Use the shreds to make Xs on the sides of steamed or deep-fried fish; stir a few shreds into soups and dipping sauces; sprinkle over salads, rice, entrées.

Kiwi daisies: Shape ½-inch-thick kiwi slices into daisies. Use with fruit plates, around meat dishes, or to center mounds of white rice.

Kohlrabi bundles: See DAIKON SHREDS.

Lemon rounds: Slice very thin, seed, and arrange around circular plates, especially with fish and seafood entrées. To make more elegant, snip off bits of rind in a pattern.

Lettuce greens: Make plate liners of frilly green lettuces, Boston lettuce, or Bibb lettuce. Break the spine of the leaf near the base to make it lie flat.

Lettuce, red: See LETTUCE GREENS. Golden curries, fruit desserts, and rice are very pretty on red lettuce.

Lime rounds: See LEMON ROUNDS.

Lime wedges: Cut into thin wedges and arrange around the outside of dishes of golden curry, especially seafood curries.

Mint: Leaves of every type of edible mint, such as spearmint, pineapple mint, and apple mint, are pretty added whole to Indian curries and relishes. Use very small whole leaves or shred larger mint leaves over fruit and cream desserts, especially with Indian meals.

Noodles, deep-fried: See the recipe on page 87 for deep-fried noodles. The tangle of white shreds makes an elegant crunchy garnish for almost any entrée.

Onion rounds and onion strings: Slice large red onions ⅛ inch thick, wilt in boiling water, and sprinkle as rounds or in strings (cut the rounds open) over curries, rice, salads, steamed fish.

Packages or bundles: Use a chive leaf to tie bundles of shredded fresh daikon, kohlrabi, zucchini, and water chestnuts, fresh or canned, into ornamental packages.

Parsley bunches: See CILANTRO. Very curly parsley makes elegant mounds of green; flat Italian parsley is better for use as leaves floating in soups or on sauces.

Pea jewels: Large round fresh peas, scalded in boiling water to a bright green—or frozen, thawed peas—are pretty scattered over rice, any sauced dish, fish entrées, salads.

Pepper flowers: Use hot peppers, which are small and thin. Wear gloves to seed them and remove the membranes, then slice into thin strips cutting toward the stem end and peel back the slices to make elegant flowers. Serve with spicy sauces, such as peanut sauce (page 224).

Peppers, sweet: Stem, seed, and slice into long thin shreds as a garnish for other garnishes, to make Oriental characters on top of fish, rice, entrées. Arrange short, thin shreds like daisy petals and give them a green onion stem. Dice to sprinkle over anything. Red peppers are most useful. Yellow, red, and green pepper shreds are pretty together.

Pimiento shreds: Cut pimiento shreds into long limp pieces and make elegant Xs and other figures to decorate rice, relishes, salads, entrées. Rounds of pimiento make petals for pimiento flowers.

Radish fans: Keep the prettiest leaves. Starting from the top and cutting only two thirds of the way into the radish, slice into pieces 1/16 inch thick, cutting toward the leaves. Spread the leaves of the fan as flat as you can. Restaurants remove the leaves and marinate their radish flowers in a mixture of 1 tablespoon sugar to 1 teaspoon salt for 6 or more hours. This leaves the radishes limp, and able to spread in a flat fan over the plate.

Rutabaga animals: For those talented and creative, peel one end of a small rutabaga, slice into rounds 1/8 to 1/4 inch thick, and carve leaping hares, fish shapes, and other small animals. Set around entrées served on flat dishes.

Sauce patterns: Many commercial dipping sauces are thick enough to mound—Chinese mustard and reddish sweet and sour sauce, for instance. Arrange sauces of contrasting colors in pairs in small shallow bowls, each occupying half the bowl and meeting the other in an S-curve.

Snow pea fans: Stem snow peas; steam till limp (3–4 minutes) and remove before the bright green fades. Arrange in a fan on one side of a flat serving dish or dinner plate. To make the peas glisten, brush lightly with sesame oil.

Tomato roses: Using a small, sharp knife and starting at the top of a very meaty tomato, peel the skin and 1/4 inch of flesh, working in a spiral toward the bottom. The strip must come away in one piece. Move the knife up and down in a sawing motion. Turn the tomato as you cut. Curl the bottom of the strip tightly around itself to make the center of the rose and spear it with a toothpick to keep it together. Arrange the rest of the strip in circles around the heart of the rose. (To use up the remaining flesh of the tomato, dice it to make a garnish of red "jewels" on whatever dish or salad the rose is to decorate.)

Tomato wedges: Slice small meaty tomatoes into long wedges and arrange, cut-side down, around curries and rice.

Vegetable jewels: Leaving the skin on, dice zucchini, summer squash, tomato and cucumber flesh, and carrots to make a garnish of multicolor "jewels." Pretty sprinkled on rice or any pale entrée.

Edible Flower Garnishes

These unusual and interesting garnishes are meant to be served and eaten as part of the meal. Many other flowers, not edible, can make pretty garnishes, too: sprigs of apple blossom, orange blossom, red salvia, daffodils. It's fun to experiment! Some other attractive plants, such as deadly nightshade and foxglove, are poisonous, and *should not be consumed. Please be sure to eat only flowers that you are sure are safe.*

Basil florets: Purplish on a rigid stem: use tips to center rosettes made of basil leaves.

Borage florets: Blue (white, purple) ¾-inch flowers on a plant whose woolly leaves taste of cucumber: set one floret at the base of a leaf and use to garnish a plate of relishes.

Cabbage flowers: Cabbage gone to seed in the garden or the crisper sometimes produces a big elegant golden flower which is a perfect garnish for any main dish.

Carrot leaves: Carrots left too long in the crisper will grow pretty golden leaves which make a suitable garnish or salad component.

Chive blossoms: Dry, purple-pink round flowers: arrange on small spinach or herb leaves to make a bouquet at the side of a plate. Particularly good with cucumber relishes.

Day lilies: These edible blossoms have a beanlike flavor, and make delightful decorations for curries and other entrées. Pick just before using.

Fennel flowers: Yellow and tasting of licorice, these are elegant scattered over curries, or grouped at the side of the plate.

Gardenia petals: Creamy white and tasting of perfume. Remove all the green part and sprinkle over desserts, fish, soups.

Geranium (*pelargonium*) petals: Choose brilliant colors and sprinkle over rice, soups, stir-fried dishes with sauce. Or heap beside little bunches of parsley or cilantro.

Mint flowers: Maturing mint plants send up fuzzy little spears of gray-purple blooms. These can be worked into garnishes for Indian curries and relishes, and added to platters of exotic finger fruits.

Nasturtiums: Bright and spicy, these blossoms are a great addition to salads for taste as well as color. Or arrange two or three at the side of a plate with nasturtium leaves beneath for a garnish. Nasturtium leaves also make a great garnish: they're very round, and have a peppery taste.

Onion flowers: Regular onions grow pretty round pink-purple flowers, like bigger chive blossoms. Set as a garnish on a large plate, with nasturtium petals or stemmed spinach leaves beneath.

Pinks (dianthus): Clove-flavored, these charming little flowers last well. Remove as much green as possible without destroying the flowers and set two or three beside mint leaves on fruit desserts.

Pumpkin blossoms: Orange and faintly nutty to taste, these are pretty as a garnish for stir-fried dishes. They're also nice as fritters. Handle as Pakoras, India (page 64).

Rocket flowers: Rocket (*Eruca sativa*)—also called rocket salad and tira—is an herb with the flavor of horseradish which is often used in salads, particularly in France. The white, yellow, or purple flowers are edible. Group several at the side of plate with rocket leaves underneath.

Rosemary flowers: This popular herb's light blue flowers make a pretty garnish. Gather into a small bouquet tied with a wilted chive strand.

Rose petals: These add more fragrance than taste, but are pretty sprinkled over desserts and salads. If any white-green shows at the base of the petals, cut this away with scissors.

Sage flowers: Garden sage (*Salvia officinalis*) has purple or white flowers and grayish hairy leaves used for flavoring. Arrange the flowers on a few sage leaves and set as a garnish on salad plates or with meat and chicken entrées. Especially nice with pork.

Squash blossoms: Big yellow flowers that make great garnishes, particularly backed with nasturtium leaves or big sprigs of flat Italian parsley or cilantro. They also make good fritters (handle as Pakoras, India, page 64).

Tomato blossoms: Pretty little yellow flowers from the tomato plant to scatter over delicately flavored stir-fried dishes and clear soups.

Violet: Fragrant and sweet, a beautiful color to sprinkle over salads or desserts. They wilt quickly so pick at the last minute.

Zucchini blossoms: See SQUASH BLOSSOMS.

Twelve

Sweets and Exotic Fruits

Eating a sweet dessert at the end of a meal is not the custom in the Orient as it is in the West. Sweet flavors are integrated into the meals, instead. Crispy Shrimp with Pineapple Sauce and Lamb in Honey Sauce, Peking Style, for example, are as sweet as desserts and better than many!

Still, like the Indians who serve spice seeds as mouth fresheners after dinner, I always hanker for something tangy and sweet after a meal, so I've gotten into the habit of ending Oriental meals with fresh fruit, preferably exotic fresh fruit. Indian Chilled Fruit Cream, glowing in the gold of saffron and sparked with bits of tangy fruit, has pleased our family and spread to our friends. When the peaches are ripe in Virginia, nothing tastes more like ambrosia than slightly overripe peaches, peeled and tossed in Honey-Lime Sauce. The exotic fresh finger fruits listed on pages 247–250 are delicious either by themselves or combined with Piña Colada Dressing or simply with thawed frozen piña colada concentrate. Those fruits that are tart are great with a spoonful of canned coconut cream.

What do you do for dessert when the entrée, or one of the entrées, is rich in fruit, like Duck with Pineapple and Cherries, for instance? Ginger Ice Cream or orange or lime sherbet are good choices. And, of course, fortune cookies, which are served in most American Chinese restaurants.

The fortune cookies and ice creams are the only desserts in this chapter that take any time at all to prepare. Fruit desserts are ready in a matter of minutes, which is just what you want after you've zipped your way through a stir-fried feast!

The most interesting desserts of all are made with exotic fresh finger fruits. Today's markets are rich in tropical fruits: kiwi, pineapple, coconut, dates, figs, mangos, papayas, custard apples, lychee nuts, pomegranates, and creamy-fleshed atemoyas. These are just some of the varieties of fruits now ready and waiting for you in most produce markets. Touch, explore, sniff—there's a whole world of new desserts out there!

Fortune Cookies

Prep. Time 45 minutes • Makes 30 cookies
Cooking Time 15 minutes

You can buy commercial fortune cookies, but here's a recipe that will allow you to make your own, with your own fortunes inside. Great fun for children or adults. They keep well sealed in a cookie jar.

3 eggs
½ cup packed brown sugar
½ cup all-purpose flour

½ teaspoon lemon extract
30–35 fortunes, each typed on a narrow strip of paper

In a large bowl, beat the eggs until frothy. Add the sugar, flour, and lemon extract, and beat until thick.

Heat a pancake griddle or a heavy skillet or your wok to medium high (375°), hot enough so a drop of water rolls on the

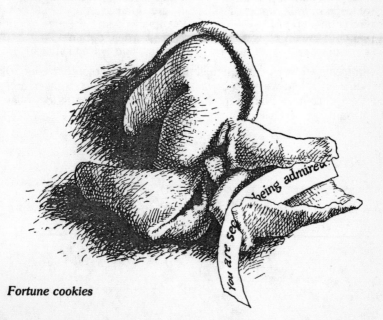

Fortune cookies

surface. With a soup spoon place three blobs of batter on the heated surface. With the back of the spoon, flatten the batter to make 3-inch rounds. Cook only until dry enough to flip with a pancake turner; turn, cook ½ minute, then lift onto a large platter. Immediately, lift a pancake onto the thumb and first two fingers of your hand, then gently push a fortune into the hollow formed. Press the edges of the pancake together firmly enough to seal. Keep trying till you get it right. The cookie looks like a folded pancake bent in half. If you have trouble sealing, moisten the edges of the pancake with uncooked batter. Continue to cook and seal pancakes until the batter is used up.

Chilled Fruit Cream, India

Prep. Time 15 minutes • Serves 6–8
Cooking Time 0

This has been a favorite dessert with my family and friends for a decade. It can be made with any fruit: crushed pineapple, mandarin orange segments, strawberries, dried red apples, or bananas. Leftovers are good the next day.

¼ teaspoon saffron, optional
1 tablespoon milk, optional
1 pint vanilla yogurt
1 pint sour cream
½ cup sugar

1 cup diced peeled mango or
  very ripe peach
¼ cup sliced strawberries or
  raspberries, optional
1 tablespoon almond slices

If using saffron, soak it in the milk until the milk is colored, about 10 minutes. In a large serving bowl, combine the yogurt, sour cream, sugar, and saffron. Fold in the fruit, and sprinkle almond slices over the cream. Serve chilled.

Ginger Ice Cream

Prep. Time 1½ hours • Serves 12–16
Cooking Time 0

This is a basic custard ice cream flavored with preserved ginger. Adding 1 cup of ginger preserve to the custard will result in a mild ginger ice cream; add more for a more intense flavor. Serve the ice cream topped with chopped candied ginger if you want to go all the way! You must use an ice cream maker for this recipe.

5 large eggs
⅛ teaspoon salt
2 cups milk, scalded

4 cups heavy cream, scalded
2 cups ginger preserve, at room temperature

In a large bowl with an electric beater, beat the eggs until thick, and, still beating, dribble in the sugar and add the salt. Fold in the milk and cream, then pour into a large, no-stick saucepan and stir over low heat until the custard thickens and coats the spoon. Set in the freezer and chill well, about 1 hour.

Combine 1 cup ginger preserve thoroughly with the custard. Taste, and add as much more preserve as you wish. Process in an ice cream maker, following the manufacturer's instructions. Store in the freezer in a large sealed tub.

Variation:

Piña Colada Ice Cream—Substitute 1 cup crushed pineapple and juice and 2 6-ounce cans of frozen piña colada concentrate for the ginger preserves. Stir in ½ cup sweetened shredded coconut, if you wish.

Peaches in Honey-Lime Sauce

Prep. Time 5 minutes • Serves 4
Cooking Time 0

A cool, tangy fruit dish to top off spicy meals. Tupelo honey*
—made by bees grazing on tupelo gum trees that grow along the
Chipola and Apalachicola rivers in Northwest Florida—has a unique
flavor and is the best for use in desserts, but any honey will be
good. For a variation, try strawberries instead of peaches.

4 large or 6 small ripe peaches,   **2 heaping teaspoons good honey**
** peeled**   **4 tip sprigs fresh mint, optional**
Juice of ½ lime

With a small, sharp knife, cut the peaches into wedges ½ to ¾ inch
thick. Arrange the slices in a circle in a round serving dish 8 to 9
inches across. Stir the lime juice with the honey until the honey is
dissolved, then pour the honey-lime mixture over the peaches.
Garnish with mint sprigs, if you wish. Cover, and chill 30 minutes or
until ready to serve.

*I get mine by mail order from L. L. Lanier, Wewahitchka, FL 32465.

Crushed Pineapple with Coconut Cream Topping

Prep. Time 5 minutes • Serves 2
Cooking Time 0

Pineapple and coconut were meant for each other. For variety add
bananas, strawberries, raspberries, chopped mangoes or chopped
ripe peaches, with a squeeze of lime.

1½ cups crushed fresh pineap-   **3 tablespoons canned coconut**
** ple or canned pineapple and**   ** cream (or more)**
** juice, chilled**

Divide the pineapple between two dessert cups and top with 1½
tablespoons of coconut cream, or more. Serve chilled.

Miniature Cantaloupe Stuffed with Mango

Prep. Time 10 minutes • Serves 2
Cooking Time 0

Miniature cantaloupe comes in many varieties. They taste like standard cantaloupe except for the small orangey smooth-skinned type called Israel or Jerusalem cantaloupe, which is perhaps the most exquisite. Stuffed with mangoes or peaches or crushed pineapple, they make an elegant dessert. Melon's flavor is best when served at room temperature.

½ small mango, peeled and diced
1 teaspoon lime juice
4 ounces vanilla yogurt
1 miniature cantaloupe, at room
  temperature, halved and
  seeded

½ tablespoon minced candied
  ginger, optional
2 pinks (page 236), optional
2 quarters of a regular
  cantaloupe

In a medium bowl, combine the mango with the lime juice and toss with the yogurt. Heap the mixture in the melon halves and top with candied ginger and a flower, if desired.

Fruit Platter with Yogurt Topping

Prep. Time 15 minutes • Serves 6–8
Cooking Time 0

Slices of orange, kiwi fruit, and pineapple, ovals of ripe banana, maraschino cherries, and pecans, served with a yogurt-sour cream topping . . . the perfect dessert for an Oriental dinner party. Easy on the hostess because it can be prepared hours ahead and easy to serve because guests can just pass the plate and pick and dip.

6 slices pineapple, or 1½ cups
    fresh pineapple chunks
¼ cup canned pineapple syrup,
    or pureed fresh pineapple
2 ripe bananas, peeled and
    sliced into ½-inch ovals
2 big navel oranges, peeled and
    sliced

2 kiwi fruit, sliced
¼ cup pecan halves
6 maraschino cherries
½ cup vanilla yogurt
½ cup sour cream

On a round serving plate, arrange rounds of pineapple so they touch but completely encircle the plate. Toss the banana slices in the pineapple syrup and arrange in the center of the plate. Fill the space between the pineapple rounds and the bananas with alternating rounds of sliced oranges and kiwi fruit. Sprinkle with pecan halves and garnish with cherries. Combine the yogurt and sour cream in a serving bowl. Cover and chill the fruit and the yogurt mixture until ready to serve.

Oriental Fruit Cup

Prep. Time 10 minutes • Serves 6–8
Cooking Time 0

This is a fun and exotic dinner party offering. To locate the canned Oriental fruits called for, you may have to find a local importer, though canned lychees are sold in some supermarkets. Palm seed fruit are silvery white, textured like lychee nuts, and canned in a sweet syrup.

1 20-ounce can palm seed fruit in syrup, drained, syrup reserved
1 20-ounce can lychee nuts in syrup, drained, syrup reserved
1 6-ounce can crushed pineapple in syrup

1 small ripe mango, peeled, sliced, and chopped
8 green or red maraschino cherries, halved
1 teaspoon grated fresh ginger, optional

Cut the palm seed fruit and lychees into bite-size pieces and combine in a serving bowl with the pineapple and its syrup. Mix in the mango and cherries. Add enough reserved palm seed fruit and lychee nut syrup to cover the fruit generously without drowning them, and stir in the crushed ginger if you wish. Serve chilled.

Platter of Exotic Finger Fruits

Prep. Time 15 minutes • Serves 16–20
Cooking Time 0

The mainstay of this dessert is fresh pineapple. It must be ripe, so check carefully before you buy: there should be a whiff of pineapple, and the color should be yellow around the base and up the sides. If it's soft and smells fermented, it's overripe. Any colorful fruit may be used with the pineapple, but the ones I've suggested here are easy to find in most seasons.

2 large ripe pineapples
1 pint strawberries, stems on
1 large mandarin orange, peeled,
   segmented, and seeded, or
   8 oz. can

2 kiwi fruit, cut into ¼-inch-thick
   slices

Slice off the tops of the pineapple and set the tops in the center of a large round platter. Slice off the bottom. Set the pineapple on its bottom, and slice away the skin, taking care to cut away as many eyes as possible. Use the tip of a potato peeler to gouge out remaining eyes. Halve, then quarter the pineapple. Cut away and discard the hard core. Lay the four pieces flat, halve them in their length, then cut each into four or five large chunks. Heap the chunks around the pineapple tops. Garnish with the whole berries, mandarin segments, and kiwi slices. Serve either at room temperature or just a bit chilled.

A Guide to Selecting, Preparing, and Serving Exotic Fresh Finger Fruits

Suddenly, the market shelves are full of fascinating fruit shapes and colors—nutlike lychees and longans, cactus pears and carambola (the star fruit), mangoes and papayas and passion fruit. An adventure in sweet eating, these fruits are no-work desserts to eat with your fingers, yet glamorous enough to serve with wok meals.

Atemoya: From Latin America, this knobbly, peach-sized fruit has dark seeds and a creamy flesh with a flavor between banana and pineapple.

Cactus pear: Also called prickly pear, this is sold with the prickles removed. Choose yellow-to-red fruit. Peel and slice into fruit salads.

Carambola: The ridged ovals of this Malaysian fruit slice into star shapes perfect for garnish. The flesh is citrus-like, sweet in the larger varieties. Serve chilled and sliced, with other sliced fruits.

Cherimoya: A variety of custard apple (see below) from Latin America, now grown in California, it has tough green "alligator" skin, is usually irregularly shaped or oval, and can reach as large as 15 pounds. The creamy white custard-like flesh, flecked with black seeds, is very delicate: a cross of strawberry, pineapple, and banana. Buy large fruit, firm-going-soft. Brown skins indicate overripeness. Eat as soon as possible. Serve at room temperature in halves or quarters, with a spoon or chill, seed, and serve as a sherbet.

Coconut: See page 34 for information on shelling. Serve chilled and sliced into 3- to 4-inch sticks, with sliced bananas and other fruit.

Custard apple: A relative of the sugar apple, this is a rounded fruit the size of an orange with a green, green-brown, or red-brown rind. The flesh is soft and sweet, with a delicate flavor and a custard texture. Remove the seeds inside with a knife or your teeth. Serve washed and peeled, with the fruit sliced away from seeds, and offer a knife and fork or spoon.

Dates: Big delicious dates are now sold in markets everywhere. Serve three or four on a plate with other fruits. Offer a fork, but encourage fingers.

Figs: Fresh green and red figs are offered in produce centers. The red figs are sweeter. Select firm-to-tender fruit; avoid fruit that is cracked or sticky. Serve two or three on a plate with a few pecans. Offer a knife and fork, but encourage fingers.

Guava: A small, oval fruit, 2 to 4 inches around, with a thin skin that may be yellow, red, or purple. You can tell they're ripe when they give a little under pressure from your fingers. Serve sliced in ½-inch-thick rounds on a plate with other sliced fruits—carambola, for instance. Offer a knife and fork.

Kiwi: Originally called the Chinese gooseberry, this small fruit was renamed by its New Zealand exporters for the hairy brown bird its skin resembles. The surprisingly beautiful green flesh patterned with dark edible seeds makes kiwi a good candidate for any fruit combination. Serve with the skin on, sliced, and offer a knife and fork. Or, peel and slice and combine with other sliced fruits.

Kumquat: A miniature golden orange native to Chin-Chu in China, with sweet skin and tart fruit. Usually sold with leaves and a bit of stem attached. It is eaten whole, skin and all, and makes a neat garnish for sweet entrées. Serve two or three on a plate with other sweet finger fruits.

Longan: A smaller relative of the lychee nut (see below), this should be peeled, seeded, and eaten like fruit. Serve several on a plate or in a bowl, with a knife and fork, but encourage fingers.

Loquat: Though it is sometimes sold as a Japanese plum, this walnut-sized fruit probably originated in the region of Canton. The skin is yellow to orange, and may be fuzzy. The best varieties have a single seed—others have four. Choose semi-soft fruit—the flavor is moderately sweet-sour. Serve on a plate with other finger fruits, or peel, remove seeds, and slice onto fruit platters and salads.

Lychee nut: A plum-sized fruit from China with a dry broken skin that earns it the title "nut." Lychees have a big central seed and crisp, delicious white to cream-colored flesh. Serve several on a plate or in a bowl with their skins on, with a knife and fork to help with peeling and eating, but encourage fingers. Or, peel, seed, and serve in a small sherbet glass with a sprig of mint for garnish.

Mango: A tropical fruit that tastes like a pineapple-flavored ripe peach, and makes the best chutney. The new hybridized varieties are 6 or more inches long. Yellow or purplish-red in the smooth skin indicates ripening. Choose semi-firm but not mushy fruit, and ripen to yielding at room temperature. Chill well before serving. Peel over the sink—it's juicy!—and with a sharp knife, slice the orange flesh away from the big, flat central seed. Serve two or three large slices on a plate with a knife and fork and a sprig of pineapple mint for garnish.

Papaya: A large, green-to-yellow oval fruit famous for its vitamin A and C content, and for its ability to tenderize meat (papaya cooked with a tough meat makes a tender stew). Usually available in 2– or 4–pound sizes, but papayas can grow to 20 pounds. Choose one with lots of yellow skin and ripen it at room temperature until it yields a little under pressure from your thumbs. The flesh is salmon to orange and the flavor sweet but a bit bland. Serve half a chilled papaya on a small plate: leave in the seeds, but offer a spoon so they can be scooped out. Or, seed the fruit, fill it with sliced berries, and serve with a spoon.

Passion fruit: The name originated from the flower the fruit grows from, which has a shape that brings to mind a crown of thorns. The fruit is egg-shaped and about 3 inches long, and when ripe is wrinkled and dark purple. It is full of dark, clinging edible seeds and deep yellow, pulpy flesh that is very sweet. Serve halved, seeds intact, with a dusting of ground coriander and lime wedges. Offer a spoon.

Persimmon: A bright orange tomato-sized Oriental fruit which is extremely astringent when unripe. Two hybrids are found on the American market: the larger, slightly pointed variety are called Hachiya, and must be really soft before they are eaten; the smaller, flatter type, Fuyu variety, may be eaten a little firmer and are more flavorful. Serve one on a plate. Offer a knife and fork, but encourage guests to get their fingers involved.

Pineapple: Choose fruit showing a golden yellow around the bottom and up the sides, or expect a very acid fruit. Sniff the base: if it smells of sweet pineapple, it's ripe; if it smells a bit fermented and is soft or mushy to touch, it is fermented and not good. Green pineapple will not sweeten with age. Peel as described on page 246 before serving. Very tart pineapple is best chopped in a food processor and sweetened with honey or sugar. Sweet pineapple is attractive quartered with the skin on, and the flesh sliced from the skin and cut into ½-inch-wide slices, then returned to the skin quarters as though intact. Serve crushed pineapple in a fruit cup; serve sliced quarters on dessert plates and offer a knife and fork.

Pomegranate: An exotic fruit the size of a large orange, that has purple to red-orange skin like thin leather, and is full of seeds encased in juicy red flesh. This flesh—the "meat," or edible portion of the fruit—has a distinctive sweet-sour taste. Choose large pomegranates, as their seeds are the meatiest. Serve quartered, with a spoon to scoop out the seeds. Remove the tough connecting membrane and discard it. Chew the seeds and spit the hard centers into your hand, then discreetly slip them back onto the dessert plate. The seeds also make a beautiful garnish for fruit salads.

Pomelo: A large greenish yellow to pinkish Asian ancestor of our grapefruit. The citrus segments, encased in a thick pith and rind, have no bitterness. Serve halved and invite guests to peel the fruit with their fingers.

Sapota: See CUSTARD APPLE.

Sugar apple: The "sweetsop" of Shakespeare's day. This relative of the custard apple is knobbly and peach-sized, with flavor between banana and pineapple. Serve on a small plate, with a knife and fork.

Appendix

You can order Oriental specialties not available locally from one of the many mail-order suppliers listed below. These businesses fill mail orders, have no mail-order minimum unless indicated, and carry all types of Far Eastern specialties unless otherwise stated. All are, in addition, retail shops. They are listed in alphabetical order by state.

Bezjian's Grocery Inc.
4725 Santa Monica Blvd.
Hollywood, CA 90029
Mail order minimum $15.
Catalog available.

Mee Wah Lung
608 H St. N.W.
Washington, DC 20001

Indian Gifts and Foods
1031–33 West Belmont Ave.
Chicago, IL 60657
Catalog available.
Indian specialties.

Star Market Inc.
3349 North Clark St.
Chicago, IL 60657

Central Grocery Co.
923 Decatur St.
New Orleans, LA 70116
Mail order minimum $20.

Bangkok Oriental Market Inc.
79 Harrison Ave.
Boston, MA 02111
Chinese, Japanese, Thai,
    Philippine specialties

Cardullo's Gourmet Shop
6 Brattle St.
Cambridge, MA 02138
Mail order minimum $10.

Aphrodisia Products Inc.
282 Bleecker St.
New York, NY 10014
Catalog available.

Indian Spice World, Inc.
126 Lexington Ave.
New York, NY 10016
Mail order minimum $22.

K. Kalustyan Orient Export
  Trading Co.
123 Lexington Ave.
New York, NY 10016
Mail order minimum $25.
Catalog available.
Also Canada, overseas.

Katagiri and Co., Inc.
224 East 59 St.
New York, NY 10022
Catalog available.
Japanese specialties.

Anzen Japanese Foods Importers
736 Northeast Union St.
Portland, OR 97232
Price list available.
Chinese, Japanese, Thai
  specialties

House of Spices (India), Inc.
4101 Walnut St.
Philadelphia, PA 19104
Mail order minimum $15.
Catalog available.

House of Rice
4112 University Way N.E.
Seattle, WA 98105
$2 charge for mail orders under
  $10.
Catalog available.

Uwajimaya, Inc.
519 6th Ave. South
Seattle, WA 98104
Catalog available.
Chinese, Japanese, Thai
  specialties

S. Enkin, Inc.
1203 St. Lawrence Blvd.
Montreal, Quebec
Canada H2X 256
Catalog available.

Index

Ⓟ   (0452)

GOOD FOOD & DRINK
WITH PLUME